Heidi Hartmann
Editor

Women, Work, and Poverty: Women Centered Research for Policy Change

Women, Work, and Poverty: Women Centered Research for Policy Change has been co-published simultaneously as *Journal of Women, Politics & Policy*, Volume 27, Numbers 3/4 2005.

Pre-publication REVIEWS, COMMENTARIES, EVALUATIONS . . .

"FRESH AND EXCITING. . . . MUST READING for policymakers, educators, and employment counselors. . . . The contributors mobilize the latest developments in social science and feminist theory to argue persuasively that the emphasis needs to be on improving the quality of jobs women hold while increasing women's access and ability to hold these jobs. This is a really important book."

Eileen Appelbaum, PhD
*Professor, School of Management
and Labor Relations
Director, Center for Women and Work
Rutgers University*

More pre-publication
REVIEWS, COMMENTARIES, EVALUATIONS . . .

"ESSENTIAL READING FOR STUDENTS OF PUBLIC POLICY, for policymakers, and for those who believe the United States must develop a truly humane and rational social policy. AN URGENTLY NEEDED ANALYSIS of the complexity of low-income women's lives. Avoiding the all-too-frequent focus on simplistic slogans and individual behavior, Heidi Hartmann and her contributors map out the reality of women's economic status and provide REALISTIC AND WORKABLE SOLUTIONS to the destructive trap of poverty and discrimination."

Ruth Sidel, PhD
Professor of Sociology
Hunter College; Author of Unsung Heroines: Single Mothers and the American Dream

"A NICE MIX of qualitative work, where women themselves describe their lives, and quantitative work, where the authors present a statistical picture of such issues as poverty, work, childcare, mental health, and hardship among low-income women. Overall, this book offers A USEFUL PICTURE OF WOMEN'S LIVES in the low wage labor workforce and the challenges that they face—from conflicting demands by employers versus children, to poorly organized public health systems and unstable employment."

Rebecca M. Blank, PhD
Dean, Gerald R. Ford School
of Public Policy
and Henry Carter Adams Professor
of Policy and Economics
University of Michigan

The Haworth Political Press
An Imprint of The Haworth Press, Inc.

Women, Work, and Poverty: Women Centered Research for Policy Change

Women, Work, and Poverty: Women Centered Research for Policy Change has been co-published simultaneously as *Journal of Women, Politics & Policy*, Volume 27, Numbers 3/4 2005.

Journal of Women, Politics & Policy™ is the successor title to *Women & Politics*™, which changed title after Vol. 26, No. 3/4, 2004. The *Journal of Women, Politics & Policy*™, under its new title, begins with Vol. 27, No. 1/2, 2005.

Women, Work, and Poverty: Women Centered Research for Policy Change, edited by Heidi Hartmann (Vol. 27, No. 3/4, 2005). *"Fresh and exciting. . . . must reading for policymakers, educators, and employment counselors. . . . The contributors mobilize the latest developments in social science and feminist theory to argue persuasively that the emphasis needs to be on improving the quality of jobs women hold while increasing women's access and ability to hold these jobs. This is a really important book." (Eileen Appelbaum, PhD, Professor, School of Management and Labor Relations and Director, Center for Women and Work, Rutgers University)*

Gendering Politics and Policy: Recent Developments in Europe, Latin America, and the United States, edited by Heidi Hartmann (Vol. 27, No. 1/2, 2005). *"A thoughtful and much-needed assessment of how women's efforts to access power and influence policy are faring after thirty years of feminist organizing and advocacy. Most of the contributions explore avenues for change that go beyond the earlier literature on women's ministries and state feminism." (Jane S. Jaquette, PhD, Bertha Orr Professor of Politics and Chair of Diplomacy and World Affairs, Occidental College, Los Angeles)*

Women and Congress: Running, Winning, and Ruling, * edited by Karen O'Connor (Vol. 23, No. 1/2, 2001). *"Bridges the past, present, and future wonderfully. Very well written . . . accessible for students and experts alike." (Joanne Connor Green, Associate Professor, Department of Political Science, Texas Christian University, Fort Worth)*

Politics and Feminist Standpoint Theories, * edited by Sally J. Kenney and Helen Kinsella (Vol. 18, No. 3, 1997). *"Illuminating . . . This collection will be useful to scholars and students interested in explor - ing how we should understand the explosion in knowledge generated by feminist projects." (Sandra Harding, Professor, Education and Women's Studies, UCLA)*

The Politics of Pregnancy: Policy Dilemmas in the Maternal-Fetal Relationship, * edited by Janna C. Merrick, and Robert H. Blank (Vol. 13, No. 3/4, 1994). *"A valuable resource for teachers or upper-level college students." (Science Books & Films)*

Women and Public Administration: International Perspectives, * edited by Jane H. Bayes (Vol. 11, No. 4, 1992). *"A long-awaited important six-nation comparative analysis of women's role in public administration." (Joyce Gelb, Professor, Department of Political Science, City College and Graduate Center, CUNY)*

Women, Politics and the Constitution, * edited by Naomi B. Lynn (Vol. 10, No. 2, 1990). *"Fresh, new, and challenging. Naomi Lynn has done well in assembling these diverse perspectives on women and the Constitution." (R. Darcy, Professor, Department of Political Science, Oklahoma State University)*

Feminism and Epistemology: Approaches to Research in Women and Politics, * edited by Maria J. Falco (Vol. 7, No. 3, 1988). *Here is a timely and informative introduction to a new phase of the ongoing feminist dialogue, reflecting the special dimension feminists have added to the debate over the positivist-behavioral paradigm.*

The Politics of Professionalism, Opportunity, Employment, and Gender, * edited by Sarah Slavin (Vol. 6, No. 3, 1987). *Presents a picture of the complex social processes we characterize as "political," and a better sense of the less obvious elements that determine the political process.*

Women as Elders: Images, Visions, and Issues, * edited by Marilyn J. Bell (Vol. 6, No. 2, 1987). *"Recommended for any woman who is interested in the issues of aging . . . and any woman who is attempting to create an empowered, positive identity for herself, at any age." (Common Ground)*

Gender and Socialization to Power and Politics, * edited by Rita Mae Kelly (Vol. 5, No. 4, 1986). *Illustrates how the interaction of childhood socialization and the reality of the adult woman's life produces variations in political attitudes and in perceptions of available options for political behavior.*

Criminal Justice Politics and Women: The Aftermath of Legally Mandated Change, * edited by Claudine Schweber and Clarice Feinman (Vol. 4, No. 3, 1985). *"A good introduction to the subject. . . . The book will enlighten readers who may believe that discrimination can be readily eliminated through legal changes alone." (Corrections Today)*

United Nations Decade for Women World Conference, * edited by Naomi B. Lynn (Vol. 4, No. 1, 1984). *Experts assess the progress that has been made, lament the failure of nations to take more steps to improve women's status, and analyze the divisive issues that have been at the forefront of concern and have limited the achievements of the two United Nations conferences on women.*

Biopolitics and Gender, * edited by Meredith W. Watts (Vol. 3, No. 2/3, 1984). *"Provocative. . . . Welcomed as a way to broaden discussion of gender beyond an exclusive focus on sex links to oppression and discrimination." (Political Science Quarterly)*

Women in Developing Countries: A Policy Focus, * edited by Kathleen Staudt and Jane Jacquette (Vol. 2, No. 4, 1983). *"Recommend[ed] . . . to any reader who would like to learn more about how it is possible, through mismanagement, ignorance, lack of powerful women staff members, and the deliberate ignoring of women's needs, to pour substantial amounts of money into development programs without helping women at all." (International Journal of Women's Studies)*

The Equal Rights Amendment: The Politics and Process of Ratification of the 27th Amendment to the U.S. Constitution, * edited by Sarah Slavin (Vol. 2, No. 1/2, 1982). *An exploration of the attempt to ratify the Equal Rights Amendment and efforts of organizations and individual states to either secure or defeat ratification.*

Women, Work, and Poverty:
Women Centered Research
for Policy Change

Heidi Hartmann
Editor

Women, Work, and Poverty: Women Centered Research for Policy Change has been co-published simultaneously as *Journal of Women, Politics & Policy*, Volume 27, Numbers 3/4 2005.

The Haworth Political Press
An Imprint of
The Haworth Press, Inc.

New York • London • Victoria (AU)
www.HaworthPress.com

Women, Work, and Poverty: Women Centered Research for Policy Change has been co-published simultaneously as *Journal of Women, Politics & Policy*, Volume 27, Numbers 3/4 2005.

The development, preparation, and publication of this work has been undertaken with great care. However, the publisher, employees, editors, and agents of The Haworth Press and all imprints of The Haworth Press, Inc., including The Haworth Medical Press® and Pharmaceutical Products Press®, are not responsible for any errors contained herein or for consequences that may ensue from use of materials or information contained in this work. With regard to case studies, identities and circumstances of individuals discussed herein have been changed to protect confidentiality. Any resemblance to actual persons, living or dead, is entirely coincidental.

The Haworth Press is committed to the dissemination of ideas and information according to the highest standards of intellectual freedom and the free exchange of ideas. Statements made and opinions expressed in this publication do not necessarily reflect the views of the Publisher, Directors, management, or staff of The Haworth Press, Inc., or an endorsement by them.

Cover design by Marylouise E. Doyle

Library of Congress Cataloging-in-Publication Data

Women, work, and poverty : women centered research for policy change / Heidi Hartmann. editor.
     p. cm.
     "Co-published simultaneously as Journal of women, politics & policy, volume 27, numbers 3/4 2005."
     Conference papers.
     Includes bibliographical references and index.
     ISBN-13: 978-0-7890-3245-4 (hard cover : alk. paper)
     ISBN-10: 0-7890-3245-7 (hard cover : alk. paper)
     ISBN-13: 978-0-7890-3246-1 (soft cover : alk. paper)
     ISBN-10: 0-7890-3246-5 (soft cover : alk. paper)
     1. Poor women–United States–Congresses. 2. Women heads of households–United States–Congresses. 3. Wages–Women–United States–Congresses. 4. Women–United States–Social conditions–Congresses. I. Hartmann, Heidi I. II. Journal of women, politics, & policy.
HV1445.W664 2005
331.40973–dc22

                                               2005031479

Indexing, Abstracting & Website/Internet Coverage

This section provides you with a list of major indexing & abstracting services and other tools for bibliographic access. That is to say, each service began covering this periodical during the year noted in the right column. Most Websites which are listed below have indicated that they will either post, disseminate, compile, archive, cite or alert their own Website users with research-based content from this work. (This list is as current as the copyright date of this publication.)

(continued)

(continued)

(continued)

- *Social Sciences PlusText. Contents of this publication are indexed and abstracted in the Social Sciences PlusText database (includes only abstracts . . . not full-text), available on ProQuest Information & Learning <http://www.proquest.com>* 1992
- *Social Scisearch <http://www.isinet.com>* 1999
- *Social Services Abstracts <http://www.csa.com>* 1990
- *Social Work Abstracts <http://www.silverplatter.com/catalog/swab.htm>*. 1992
- *Social Work Access Network (SWAN) <http://cosw.sc.edu/swan/media.html>* 2005
- *SocioAbs <http://www.csa.com>* 1990
- *Studies on Women and Gender Abstracts <http://www.tandf.co.uk/swa>* 1992
- *SwetsWise <http://www.swets.com>* 2002
- *Wilson OmniFile Full Text: Mega Edition (available only electronically) <http://www.hwwilson.com>* 1994
- *WilsonWeb <http://vnweb.hwwilsonweb.com/hww/Journals/>* 2005
- *Women Studies Abstracts <http://www.nisc.com>* 1992
- *Women's Resources International Abstracts* 1998

Special Bibliographic Notes related to special journal issues (separates) and indexing/abstracting:

- indexing/abstracting services in this list will also cover material in any "separate" that is co-published simultaneously with Haworth's special thematic journal issue or DocuSerial. Indexing/abstracting usually covers material at the article/chapter level.
- monographic co-editions are intended for either non-subscribers or libraries which intend to purchase a second copy for their circulating collections.
- monographic co-editions are reported to all jobbers/wholesalers/approval plans. The source journal is listed as the "series" to assist the prevention of duplicate purchasing in the same manner utilized for books-in-series.
- to facilitate user/access services all indexing/abstracting services are encouraged to utilize the co-indexing entry note indicated at the bottom of the first page of each article/chapter/contribution.
- this is intended to assist a library user of any reference tool (whether print, electronic, online, or CD-ROM) to locate the monographic version if the library has purchased this version but not a subscription to the source journal.
- individual articles/chapters in any Haworth publication are also available through the Haworth Document Delivery Service (HDDS).

Acknowledgments

The contributions of the following people to this volume are greatly appreciated:

MANAGING EDITOR

LARA HINZ
Institute for Women's Policy Research

EDITORIAL ASSISTANTS

ELIZABETH MANDEVILLE
United Nations

WHITNEY POTTER
Institute for Women's Policy Research

SONILA TURSHILLA
Tirana University

ABOUT THE EDITOR

Heidi Hartmann, PhD, is the President of the Washington-based Institute for Women's Policy Research, a scientific research organization that she founded in 1987 to meet the need for women-centered, policy-oriented research. She holds a PhD degree from Yale University in economics. Dr. Hartmann is also Research Professor at The George Washington University.

Dr. Hartmann is a co-author of *Unnecessary Losses: Costs to Americans of the Lack of Family and Medical Leave*; *Equal Pay for Working Families*; and *Survival at the Bottom: The Income Packages of Low-Income Families with Children*. She has published numerous articles in journals and books and her work has been translated into more than a dozen languages. She lectures widely on women, economics, and public policy, frequently testifies before the U.S. Congress, and is often cited as an authority in various media outlets.

Prior to founding IWPR, Dr. Hartmann was on the faculties of Rutgers University and the New School for Social Research and worked at the National Research Council/National Academy of Sciences and the U.S. Commission on Civil Rights. In 1994, Dr. Hartmann was the recipient of a MacArthur Fellowship Award for her work in the field of women and economics, and, in 1995, she received an honorary Doctor of Law degree from Swarthmore College, her alma mater. She is Vice-Chair of the National Council of Women's Organizations.

Women, Work, and Poverty: Women Centered Research for Policy Change

CONTENTS

Introduction

Heidi Hartmann, Institute for Women's Policy Research
and The George Washington University

The articles in this volume are motivated by the desire to understand the sources of women's poverty and low earnings and to recommend changes in public policy that can improve the incomes and well-being of women and their families. Not surprisingly, the articles point to labor market problems, such as the lack of comparable worth and living wage policies, and family care problems, such as the lack of affordable child care, as reasons for women's plight. They also address less commonly explored issues such as the lack of social capital in poor communities, the prevalence of disabilities among the poor, and the inflexible work schedules common to many low-wage jobs. The role income supports such as welfare and unemployment insurance play in alleviating hardship is examined. Several specific ways to transform opportunities for women of color are also explored: increasing access to higher education, to scientific careers, and to business ownership. *Women, Work, and Poverty: Women Centered Research for Policy Change* gathers together the insightful work of 21 economists, political scientists, sociologists, social workers, educators, and other policy experts to provide sound solutions based on evidence generated by both quantitative and qualitative research methods.

Nearly all the authors represented in this volume presented their work at the Seventh International Women's Policy Research Conference, "Women Working to Make a Difference," held in Washington,

[Haworth co-indexing entry note]: "Introduction." Hartmann, Heidi. Co-published simultaneously in *Journal of Women, Politics & Policy* (The Haworth Political Press, an imprint of The Haworth Press, Inc.) Vol. 27, No. 3/4, 2005, pp. 1-4; and: *Women, Work, and Poverty: Women Centered Research for Policy Change* (ed: Heidi Hartmann) The Haworth Political Press, an imprint of The Haworth Press, Inc., 2005, pp. 1-4. Single or multiple copies of this article are available for a fee from The Haworth Document Delivery Service [1-800-HAWORTH, 9:00 a.m. - 5:00 p.m. (EST). E-mail address: docdelivery@haworthpress.com].

DC, in 2003. The conference is convened every two years in June by the Institute for Women's Policy Research (IWPR) and co-sponsored by the Women's Studies and Public Policy programs at The George Washington University and the Washington Office of the Friederich Ebert Stiftung. Ten of the twelve papers published here were selected from the more than 100 papers presented after an exhaustive review process, in which many authors revised their papers in response to reviewers' comments. Two additional papers were included in this volume based on the relevance of their content and following the usual review process for submitted manuscripts.

This volume opens with an important re-examination of the feminization of poverty in the United States by economist Hilarie Lieb and sociologist Susan Thistle. Based on their analysis of the public use samples from the 1960 through 1990 censuses, Lieb and Thistle note that the extent and causes of women's poverty have changed, and argue that women have been shifting from marriage to employment as their main source of income. They suggest that forward looking strategies such as improving labor market conditions and outcomes rather than backward looking strategies like marriage promotion hold greater promise for improving women's incomes and reducing their poverty.

Using a large public employer in the northeastern United States as a case study, sociologists Pamela Stone and Arielle Kuperberg examine the relative merits of two kinds of labor market policies designed to raise wages, living wages and comparable worth (or equal pay for jobs of equal value), and find that both would reduce poverty dramatically, but that only comparable worth policies would significantly close the gap between women's and men's wages and contribute substantially to women's, especially minority women's, ability to achieve long-term economic independence.

Four articles illustrate the challenging interplay of family and health needs on the one hand, and employment demands on the other. Anthropologist Jo Anne Schneider synthesizes ethnographic research she has conducted in many settings in the East and Midwest to reveal the importance of social and cultural capital in helping low-income women succeed in employment. She also points out that in a labor market characterized by many low-wage jobs, supportive family oriented policies like paid parental leave and subsidized child care and health insurance must be provided by nonprofits and government programs to supplement inadequate wages and fringe benefits on the job. Analyzing the Philadelphia Survey of Child Care and Work, sociologists Julie Press and Janice Johnson-Dias and social work professor Jay Fagan highlight the importance of inadequate child care as an obstacle to full-time work by low-income mothers; with women receiving welfare affected equally with other low-income mothers, improving child care would help both groups. Sociologists Mary Kay Schleiter, Anne Statham, and Teresa Reinders, based on in-depth interviews with 178 women receiving welfare in Wisconsin, provide powerful testimony from the women themselves on how their own health conditions, inadequate access to health care, and inflexible work places exacerbate their efforts to maintain employment. Like the Philadelphia child care study, this study also finds that mental health problems present a significant barrier to maintaining employment. Political scientist Peggy Kahn studies single mothers who work at nursing homes in Michigan, noting the often complex arrangements these mothers must make to ensure they have reliable child care for jobs that require strict adherence to schedules in order to provide patient care. Kahn notes the need for legislation providing leave for sickness and "small necessities," which would allow parents to take time off to care for sick children, take children to the doctor or to attend meetings at their children's schools.

Several authors explore pathways to advancement for women of color, who are affected by both gender- and race-based discrimination. Political scientist Avis Jones-DeWeever, bringing to the fore the voices of low-income parents in California who are enrolled in or have graduated from college, finds that higher education has substantial payoffs for both parents and children, challenging the primacy of work-first welfare reform policies. Education professor Angela Johnson reports on an ethnographic study of high achieving students enrolled in a minority enrichment program at the University of Colorado. She finds that programs that help retain women of color in science majors not only raise graduation rates with benefits for the students involved but also have an added benefit for the public since many women of color have altruistic reasons for pursuing science careers and go on to work in careers that serve the public. Sociologist Mélanie Knight analyzes Canadian literature and training materials designed to encourage women to become entrepreneurs and argues that these materials tend to exclude women of color as active participants in this discourse.

The final group of papers in this volume examines several aspects of women's income. Economists Jonathan Fisher and Angela Lyons use the Panel Study on Income Dynamics to explore the high rates of bankruptcy for divorced women; they find that divorced women who receive welfare are less likely to default and note that the increase in default rates in the early 1990s can be partially accounted for by decreases in average welfare benefits. Using the Survey of Income and Program Participation, policy experts Vicky Lovell and Gi-Taik Oh explore the impact that periods of unemployment have on women's experiences of hardship. They find that unemployment is associated with such increased hardships as loss of telephone service or housing, food insufficiency, and loss of medical and dental care, hardships that make the case for improving the coverage and adequacy of unemployment benefits. More family supportive policies, such as paid leave and improved child care, would also enable women especially to maintain employment and minimize work disruptions. Finally, economists Tamara Ohler and Nancy Folbre, using the Current Population Survey, explore ways to improve the measurement of income to include child care expenses and income pooling and thus present a more accurate picture of the adequacy of women's income.

Together the articles in this volume make the case for a range of policies that can help low-income women achieve a higher quality of life for themselves and their families. Transformative policies like pay equity and higher education may take longer but clearly have larger outcomes. More accessible child care would also significantly increase the well-being of low-income mothers, because it would increase their ability to work consistently full-time. Other family-friendly measures like having paid leave for illness and family care and added flexibility on the job are also key to improving women's job tenure and thus their long-term earnings. Finally, improved access to health care, especially for mental health, is essential if low-income parents are to strengthen and lengthen their ties to the labor market and improve their chances for long-term economic independence.

MARRIAGE, WORK, POVERTY, AND CHILDREN

The Changing Impact of Marriage, Motherhood and Work on Women's Poverty

Hilarie Lieb, Northwestern University
Susan Thistle, Northwestern University

SUMMARY. This study evaluates historical changes in the relative importance of key factors influencing white, African American, and Hispanic women's poverty. Empirical results, based on reduced form logistic regressions, indicate that work has become, relative to marriage, a potentially better way to decrease women's poverty. The greater relative importance of work when compared to marriage is strongest for blacks and weakest for whites, although for all three groups of women this pattern holds. This trend is consistent with the move from women's main economic support being generated through marriage to instead being generated through work. At the same time, children continue to increase women's chances of being in poverty, though their impact has changed differently among the three groups. The findings suggest that resources directed towards alleviating poverty should ideally be

[Haworth co-indexing entry note]: "The Changing Impact of Marriage, Motherhood and Work on Women's Poverty." Lieb, Hilarie, and Susan Thistle. Co-published simultaneously in *Journal of Women, Politics & Policy* (The Haworth Political Press, an imprint of The Haworth Press, Inc.) Vol. 27, No. 3/4, 2005, pp. 5-22; and: *Women, Work, and Poverty: Women Centered Research for Policy Change* (ed: Heidi Hartmann) The Haworth Political Press, an imprint of The Haworth Press, Inc., 2005, pp. 5-22. Single or multiple copies of this article are available for a fee from The Haworth Document Delivery Service [1-800-HAWORTH, 9:00 a.m. - 5:00 p.m. (EST). E-mail address: docdelivery@haworthpress.com].

allocated towards efforts to create good job opportunities combined with support to reduce the costs associated with balancing market and family responsibilities. *[Article copies available for a fee from The Haworth Document Delivery Service: 1-800-HAWORTH. E-mail address: <docdelivery@ haworthpress.com> Website: <http://www.HaworthPress.com> © 2005 by The Haworth Press, Inc. All rights reserved.]*

KEYWORDS. Children, employment, poverty, marriage, African Americans, Hispanics, whites, single mothers

INTRODUCTION

Female-headed families and their presence among the poor began to increase in the 1960s and have been the subject of much debate for several decades. A multitude of studies has shown that the loss of marriage and the burdens of single parenthood have played a central role in this "feminization of poverty." Women's lives have changed dramatically over the last forty years, however, suggesting the causes of their poverty may also have altered. Emphasis upon the unchanging level of women's poverty since the late 1960s, joined with an assumption that the causes of such poverty have remained the same, has hampered a full understanding of women's poverty, while also encouraging a backward-looking focus in policies to resolve such hardship.[1]

In this article we set women's poverty in a new analytic framework, bringing a dynamic historical perspective to such hardship. We place women's rise among the poor in the context of other dramatic changes taking place in women's lives, most centrally their turn from marriage to the market for support, or the "employment revolution" noted by many analysts.[2] Examination of poverty from this perspective reveals that, beneath the surface, important changes have indeed taken place in women's poverty over the latter part of the 20th century, especially among women of color.

Analysis of white, Hispanic, and African American women using decennial census data from the Integrated Public Use Microdata Samples through a series of logistic regression analyses reveals significant shifts in the rate, causes and composition of women's poverty between 1960 and 1990. Secondly, the relative importance of the causes of poverty has also changed. Most centrally, work, rather than marriage or the avoidance of motherhood, has increasingly become the most important way for women, especially African American women, to avoid economic hardship. This process has not been uniform, however. Rather, while the majority of women have turned from marriage to paid employment for support, others have held to the domestic role despite the breakdown of support for their work in the home. This process has intersected with changes in the wage economy, impeding many women's efforts to provide for themselves and their families through their own earnings. The end result is that while the majority of women have adjusted to the changing location of their support, others have been left behind in deteriorating circumstances. In brief, we have seen the formation of a female underclass, based on women's own shifting relationships to work at home and for pay.[3]

These findings provide support for a more dynamic historical understanding of women's poverty, tied to women's shifting opportunities both at home and in the wage economy and differing responses to such changes. Secondly, these findings have important implications for how the economic hardship still afflicting many single mothers might best be addressed. In brief, they point toward the importance of improving conditions in the wage economy rather than limiting involvement in motherhood or turning women back toward marriage as their key means of support.

THEORETICAL PERSPECTIVES ON POVERTY AND PAST FINDINGS

In the largest sense, consideration of changes in women's poverty over time brings a dynamic historical or temporal dimension to analyses of women's poverty. Debates over poverty have emphasized the presence of a long-term group of poor due to either behavioral failings (Gilder 1981; Lewis 1961; Murray 1984) or the failure of a market economy to provide work for all (Edwards, Reich, and Weisskopf 1972). Neither approach could provide a satisfactory explanation of women's rising presence among the poor in the years after World War II.[4]

Instead, understanding of the "feminization of poverty" came from analysts who looked at changes in family structure. Many studies, both quantitative and qualitative in nature, have established that marital breakdown and the burdens of single parenthood were central to the poverty experienced by women of all backgrounds in the first decades after World War II (Bane and Ellwood 1989; Caspar, McLanahan, and

Garfinkel 1994; Garfinkel and McLanahan 1986; Kniesner, McElroy, and Wilcox 1988; Lichter, McLaughlin, and Ribar 1997; McLanahan, Sorensen, and Watson 1989; Ross and Sawhill 1975; Wojtkiewicz, McLanahan, and Garfinkel 1990). These analyses made a crucial contribution in recognizing the negative impact of changes in the traditional structure of marriage on women's economic well-being.

These explanations have dominated discussions of women's poverty for several decades, encouraging the assumption that the loss of men's support carries an insurmountable cost for women resolved only through a return to marriage. While the high incidence of poverty faced by single mothers is indeed a matter of great concern, such focus obscures the steps women may have taken to address the economic hardship they have faced, and ways in which changes in the world of work as well as the home may have affected such efforts. In sum, like explanations of poverty stressing limitations in people's behaviors or the market economy, these explanations also run the danger of suggesting an unchanging set of causes, implying as well that marriage is the sole means of resolving such poverty.

Here, we reintroduce a point made in the 1960s, that of the need "to see poverty in dynamic, or longitudinal terms" (Thernstrom 1968, 161). This approach recognizes poverty may stem not just from persistent shortcomings in the economy or a segment of individuals, but also from a larger move from an older form of work into the urban industrial labor force. The hardship faced by different groups of men as they were pushed off the land and into work for wages is a well-known story.

We argue the feminization of poverty is of a similar nature, tied not simply to a "time of transition" between husbands, but to the large-scale breakdown of marriage as women's primary means of support, and their turn instead to wages. Such breakdown has thrown many women into new or deeper poverty until they could gain access to jobs paying a decent wage, and new provisions for the domestic tasks still placed upon their shoulders.[5]

A number of studies point to the importance of considering changes in the causes of women's poverty over time and the role of the market economy and paid work as well as marital breakdown in contributing to economic hardship. A key analysis establishing the role played by marriage and single parenthood in women's poverty between 1950-1980 also stressed that, while the poverty gap between men and women widened over these decades, poverty rates actually decreased substantially for women as well as men (McLanahan, Sorensen, and Watson 1989). In the 1980s, however, such gains were offset by a rise in never-married mothers and a decrease in employment opportunities tied to the growth of poorly paying service occupations, heightening difficulties for black single mothers in particular (Spain and Bianchi 1996; Browne 1997, 2000). Other analyses have demonstrated the importance of considering women's own labor force experience as well as the burdens of single motherhood in assessing economic outcomes among unmarried women (Morgan 1991; Peterson 1989). Also, a recent analysis has found that marriage may be effective in reducing poverty among disadvantaged women, but only if the marriages are stable and long lasting; marriage that results in divorce or separation actually increases the incidence of poverty (Lichter, Graefe, and Brown 2003).[6]

These studies point to the importance of assessing possible alterations in women's poverty over time, and to considering the impact of work as well as marriage and children upon such poverty. Further, it is clear that greater attention should be focused on the potential similarities and differences in the experience of poverty among women of different racial and class backgrounds. Investigations of racial differences in women's poverty have found seemingly conflicting patterns, emphasizing first differences (Bane 1986), then "striking racial similarities" in female-headed family formation, movement into poverty and relationship to the labor force (Kniesner, McElroy, and Wilcox 1988, 88; Hao and Brinton 1997; McLanahan, Sorensen, and Watson 1989), and then once again differences in economic outcomes by race (Browne 1997; Corcoran 1999).

Thus, it is important to carry out an analysis of possible changes in the levels, causes and composition of women's poverty in the years after World War II, with careful attention to women's relationship to the labor force as well as to marriage and children.

THE PRESENT STUDY

In order to look more closely at possible changes in the nature of women's poverty we undertook an examination of factors affecting poverty among white, African American and Hispanic women from 1960 to 1990, asking a series of questions and employing a number of analytic strategies in order to assess changes in women's poverty. (Reliable data are not available for Hispanic women for 1960; thus we begin with data from 1970.) The first question we ask is whether factors associated with women's poverty have changed over time among these groups of women. We then look more closely at potential changes in the level and causes of poverty among unmarried women, and alterations in the composition of poor single mothers. We focus on single mothers, as this is the group experiencing the most intense poverty and making up the majority of poor women, and the group of greatest concern to policy-makers and the public.

Data from the Integrated Public Use Microdata Series (IPUMS), consisting of samples from the federal census for 1960, 1970, 1980 and 1990 (with inclusion of 2000 when available) was used to carry out this analysis.[7] These years span a key period of increased marital breakdown and the rise of female-headed families and women's presence among the poor.[8] Use of census data provides a sufficient number of cases to allow separate analyses of white, Hispanic, and African American women. It also allows for the analysis of differences by education and marital status in these respective groups' experiences of poverty.

Our overall study, of which this analysis is one part, examines possible changes in factors associated with poverty over time through a series of logistic regression analyses. We use simulation techniques to assess the importance of potential shifts, joined with more detailed analysis of changing levels of poverty and their causes over successive decades through decomposition of our results. We ask finally whether changes have taken place in the group of women facing poverty, using an index of dissimilarity. Changes are assessed decade by decade, in order to get a more precise sense of how these shifts unfolded and intersected with shifts in the wage economy.

In the study presented here, the first part of this analysis is given. As noted, logistic regression analysis is used to evaluate the determinants of poverty for white, Hispanic, and African American women. The dependent variable is a dichotomous indicator for poverty which equals 1 if the family's income is less than or equal to 125 percent of the official poverty threshold. This level is chosen to enable consideration of more than the very poor, as it is considered a more realistic estimate of poverty by many analysts (Fisher 1997). For the simulations, designed to evaluate the impact of certain factors holding everything else equal, a reduced form specification of the relationship between poverty and key explanatory variables is used. Included in the independent variables are standard human capital variables to measure investments in education; three categories of employment (full-time year-round work, part-time work, and no work in the previous year[9]); and occupational variables. Family circumstances are captured with independent variables for the number of children less than 18 and marital status. Age and regional variables are used to measure cohort and cost of living influences respectively.

In terms of the above theoretical approaches, if women's poverty is the result of the persistent costs of behavioral failings, the economy, or the loss of marriage and burdens of single parenthood, we would expect marital status, children, education, or paid employment to carry a constant heavy cost. We would also expect little change in the rate of poverty or characteristics of the poor. In sum, if any of the existing explanations of poverty are correct, we would expect to see some basic cause of poverty which did not change over time.

Alternatively, our analytic framework predicts changes in the causes and levels of women's poverty over time, most centrally the increased importance of paid employment in lessening poverty as women adjust to reliance upon wages for support. Secondly, our approach, stressing the unexpected breakdown of women's traditional livelihood, would also predict that initially a large number of women would be vulnerable to poverty, but that over time such poverty would be restricted to those who lack the resources or opportunities to succeed within the labor force. Finally, while such changes should be seen among both white women and women of color, we would also expect some differences in such changes by race and ethnicity, due to changing patterns of opportunity in the labor force.

In this article, we present the first part of our analysis, that of possible alterations in the relative importance of factors associated with poverty among white, African American, and Hispanic women between 1960/ 1970 and 1990.

Looking first at white women, we find that full-time year-round work helped white women a bit more in terms of avoiding poverty in 1960 than did marriage (Table 1). In 1960, the great majority of white women did not work at all in the preceding year, or were employed only part-time; thus few gained the benefits of full-time employment (Table 2). In 1990, both work and marriage lessen the probability of poverty for white women slightly more than in 1960, while the presence of children under eighteen continues to raise such probability. Secondly, full-time year-round work, especially in professional, managerial, or technical jobs, where almost as many white women are now employed as in sales or administrative support, is now clearly a more effective way of avoiding poverty than marriage. The greater importance of work becomes clearer when we look at the situation the other way around, starting with a white woman possessing both a husband and a job. In 1990, loss of employment raises the probability of poverty by over 50 percent more than the loss of marriage (Table 2). The gains from full-time employment are also now realized by a much larger segment of white women (Table 1).

The gains from work versus marriage are a bit stronger among women raising children. Again looking at white women, the impact of work compared to marriage has also increased in 1990. Marriage decreases poverty by almost 53 points; full-time year-round work by 63

TABLE 1. Effects of Marriage, Work, and Children on Probabilities of Poverty: White Women, 1960 and 1990

White Women			
	Probability of poverty	Absolute change	Proportional change
1960			
unmarried no work no children	0.454		
married no work no children	0.110	−0.344	−0.758
unmarried **work** no children	0.077	−0.377	−0.831
married work no children	0.012	−0.441	−0.973
unmarried no work **children**	0.664	0.210	0.464
married no work **children**	0.227	−0.437	−0.658
unmarried **work children**	0.165	−0.499	−0.751
1990			
unmarried no work no children	0.504		
married no work no children	0.087	−0.416	−0.826
unmarried **work** no children	0.046	−0.458	−0.908
married work no children	0.005	−0.499	−0.991
unmarried no work **children**	0.701	0.198	0.393
married no work **children**	0.181	−0.520	−0.741
unmarried **work children**	0.101	−0.601	−0.856

Source: Authors' own calculations based on unpublished 1960 and 1990 I-PUMS data
Note: Poverty = 125 percent of poverty threshold; children = presence of own child under 18; work = full-time year-round worker. Reference category in each year is unmarried women with no work, husband or children, except when assessing impact of marriage or work on women with children; reference then is women with children, but no husband or employment. Women assessed here are typical of their race/ethnicity in terms of age, education, number of children, region, and occupation. However, most white women were either not employed or employed only part-time in 1960, significantly reducing the effect of work on the probability of poverty.

TABLE 2. Descriptive Statistics

Means	White Women		Black Women		Hispanic Women	
	1960	1990	1960	1990	1970	1990
Age	37.8	36.6	36.9	35.8	35.8	35.5
Education (in years)	10.8	13.2	8.9	12.6	9.8	11.5
Married	0.831	0.671	0.622	0.350	0.720	0.534
Have own child under 18 in home	0.664	0.514	0.559	0.549	0.685	0.551
Occupation						
Professional/managerial	0.098	0.279	0.050	0.174	0.062	0.155
Technical, clerical, sales	0.315	0.362	0.067	0.313	0.245	0.290
Blue collar worker	0.138	0.098	0.125	0.144	0.256	0.155
Private domestic worker	0.013	0.005	0.234	0.012	0.015	0.030
Other service occupation	0.083	0.130	0.164	0.204	0.100	0.155
Farm, forest, fishery	0.010	0.007	0.053	0.003	0.006	0.005
No stated occupation	0.342	0.121	0.306	0.150	0.317	0.211
Employment						
Full-time year-round worker	0.190	0.414	0.201	0.412	0.213	0.343
Part-time worker	0.281	0.381	0.404	0.342	0.305	0.332
No work last year	0.529	0.205	0.394	0.246	0.482	0.325
Region						
Midwest	0.293	0.258	0.193	0.187	0.131	0.058
South	0.274	0.326	0.556	0.525	0.226	0.275
West	0.162	0.213	0.061	0.092	0.208	0.275
Northeast	0.271	0.203	0.190	0.196	0.409	0.392
Number of cases	332150	466608	38214	71153	8810	20014

Source: Authors' tabulations based on unpublished 1960 and 1990 I-PUMS data
Note: In 1990 white women and black women are non-Hispanic women only

points. The probability of poverty is almost twice as great among married mothers without jobs as unmarried mothers with full-time year-round work.

Among black and Hispanic women, a larger shift, that is most dramatic for blacks, occurred. In particular, among black women, the relative importance of marriage and work upon poverty has shifted. The impact of paid employment has increased much more strongly, replacing marriage as the most effective way of avoiding poverty. In contrast to popular belief, a husband was once much more important in reducing the chances of poverty than work, even on a full-time year-round basis, for the typical black woman. This is in part due to the fact that the most common area of employment for black women in 1960 was still that of private domestic work, paying wages too low to keep most black women out of poverty, especially if they were caring for children.

By 1990, this situation has reversed. Work has become much more effective in reducing the probability of poverty than marriage. While marriage reduced poverty by 45 points, full-time employment throughout the year dropped poverty by 61 points (Table 3). For Hispanics, work also grew in importance relative to marriage from 1970-1990, but less so than observed for black women. In particular, by 1990 marriage reduced the probability of poverty for Hispanic women who were unemployed with no children by approximately 42 points; whereas employment for single Hispanic women with no children dropped it by 52 points (Table 4). Like blacks, improvement in the median occupation from blue collar to technical and sales jobs helps to explain part of this drop (Table 2).

DISCUSSION

This analysis reveals important and heretofore unseen changes in women's poverty. Most centrally, paid employment has become a more effective way of avoiding poverty than marriage, especially for black and Hispanic women, who realized major gains primarily due to movement into better occupations. The decreasing role played by marriage in reducing poverty among black women is most likely due partly to the increased employment difficulties faced by black and Latino men. For white, non-Hispanic women, though a husband continues to have a strong impact, the effectiveness of work relative to marriage in reducing the probability of poverty has grown.

As our simulations illustrate, both white and black employed women realized some increased gains from work relative to those without jobs, for reasons beyond an increase in hours or movement into better occupations (or, as our more detailed analysis shows, greater returns to work experience). Other research suggests women's demands have lessened discrimination in wages, and that a rise in benefits also helped. Secondly, non-wage income has decreased. By 1990, welfare payments were less than half those of 1970 and support from parents and other

TABLE 3. Effects of Marriage, Work, and Children on Probabilities of Poverty: Black Women, 1960 and 1990

Black women			
	Probability of poverty	Absolute change	Proportional change
1960			
unmarried no work no children	**0.862**		
married no work no children	0.536	−0.326	−0.378
unmarried **work** no children	0.703	−0.159	−0.184
married work no children	0.305	−0.557	−0.646
unmarried no work **children**	0.957	0.095	0.110
married no work **children**	0.806	−0.173	−0.177
unmarried **work children**	0.895	−0.084	−0.086
1990			
unmarried no work no children	**0.708**		
married no work no children	0.257	−0.451	−0.637
unmarried **work** no children	0.075	−0.633	−0.894
married work no children	0.011	−0.696	−0.984
unmarried no work **children**	0.879	0.172	0.243
married no work children	0.509	0.579	0.659
unmarried **work children**	0.196	−0.683	−0.777

Source: Authors' own calculations based on unpublished 1960 and 1990 I-PUMS data
Note: Poverty = 125 percent of poverty threshold; children = presence of own child under 18; work = full-time year-round worker. Reference category in each year is unmarried women with no work, husband or children, except when assessing impact of marriage or work on women with children; reference then is women with children, but no husband or employment. Women assessed here are typical of their race/ethnicity in terms of age, education, number of children, region, and occupation. However, most black women were either not employed or employed only part-time in 1960, further reducing the effect of work on the probability of poverty.

family members, as well as husbands, also dropped, as single parents moved out on their own.[10]

The central change in women's poverty, especially for white women, came from women's own turn toward paid employment, increasingly on a full-time year-round basis. Thus, a key way that work has grown more important in alleviating poverty is that, by 1990, it is the main way

TABLE 4. Effects of Marriage, Work, and Children on Probabilities of Poverty: Hispanic Women, 1970 and 1990

Hispanic women			
	Probability of poverty	Absolute change	Proportional change
1970			
unmarried no work no children	**0.552**		
married no work no children	0.124	−0.428	−0.775
unmarried **work** no children	0.091	−0.461	−0.835
married work no children	0.011	−0.541	−0.980
unmarried no work **children**	0.782	0.230	0.417
married no work **children**	0.293	−0.489	−0.625
unmarried **work children**	0.227	−0.555	−0.710
1990			
unmarried no work no children	**0.627**		
married no work no children	0.160	−0.467	−0.745
unmarried **work** no children	0.069	−0.558	−0.890
married work no children	0.008	−0.619	−0.987
unmarried no work **children**	0.823	0.196	0.313
married no work **children**	0.345	0.419	0.509
unmarried **work children**	0.169	−0.654	−0.795

Source: Authors' own calculations based on unpublished 1970 and 1990 I-PUMS data
Note: Poverty = 125 percent of poverty threshold; children = 1 or more own children under 18 in household; work = full-time year-round worker. Reference category in each year is unmarried women with no work, husband or children, except when assessing impact of marriage or work on women with children; reference then is women with children, but no husband or employment. Women assessed here are typical of their race/ethnicity in terms of age, education, number of children, region, and occupation. However, most Hispanic women in 1970 were not employed or employed only part-time, further reducing the effect of work on the probability of poverty.

the majority of women avoid economic hardship when on their own.[11] By 1990, 80 percent of white women are working full- or part-time (43 percent and 38 percent respectively [part-time/full-time .89]); whereas in 1960, only 47 percent were employed, most only part-time (part-time/full-time 1960 = 1.71). For black women in 1990, close to 76 percent of all women are working compared to 60 percent in 1960; the shift here is from part- to full-time employment (part-time/full-time 1960 = 2.44, 1990 = .80). Among Hispanic women, only 51 percent working in 1970 compared with 67 percent in 1990 (part-time/full-time 1970 = 1.98, 1990 = .1.10) (see also Table 2).

Overall, in contrast to explanations that stress failures of the economy, individual behavior, or marital breakdown as the central cause of poverty, these findings (and those of our more detailed analyses) support a more dynamic theoretical approach. In the mid-20th century, regaining a husband played a key role in lessening poverty stemming initially from the loss of marriage. By 1990, however, we see women coping with the decreasing security of marriage by increasing their own involvement in paid work and making gains in the wage economy.

These findings make clear that marriage is not the most effective way to reduce poverty among women. Paid employment now has a greater impact. African American and Hispanic women, for whom marriage is clearly less effective than paid employment in addressing poverty, now make up half of poor women, based on Current Population Survey data.[12] When we consider the group of greatest concern, that of single mothers, the importance of paid work increases even further.

In other words, marriage as the solution for women's poverty is an outdated approach, a story for the 1950s rather than today. Secondly, it is an approach that is not race neutral, since statistically it is less likely to be advantageous to women of color. Good jobs, both for women and the men they might marry, are clearly a more effective way of lessening poverty among women.

These findings might, as in the past, be used to argue women could, if they simply applied themselves, follow earlier groups up the economic ladder. As the situation of black women in 1960 and Hispanic women in 1970 illustrates, however, work in and of itself does not end poverty. Rather, such work must provide decent wages and benefits.

Secondly, women raising children face the highest poverty, in part due to the difficulties of combining work at home and for pay. Thus, we emphasize instead the implications of this analysis for improving the conditions of women's paid work and for policies that aid the integration of work at home and for pay.

CONCLUSION

In summary, in contrast to more static explanations of poverty, emphasizing failures of the economy, individual behavior, or marital breakdown, a dynamic historical perspective reveals important changes in women's poverty over time, tied to women's shifting opportunities both at home and in the wage economy and differing responses to these events. Analysis of the impact of marriage, children, and work on poverty among white, African American, and Hispanic women between 1960/1970 and 1990 shows employment is now the most effective means of avoiding poverty, especially for women of color and those with children. Such analysis exposes a focus upon marriage as a backward-looking response to the hardship faced by women on their own, and one that is not race neutral. Although there are implied benefits from marriage, those associated with good jobs are greater. Thus, policy that improves the conditions of paid work, providing adequate wages and new provisions for the domestic tasks still essential to human life, is a more efficient way to spend public funds designed to reduce poverty.

AUTHOR NOTE

The authors of this paper are listed in alphabetical order.

NOTES

1. Female-headed families and women on their own grew from 26 percent of the poverty population in 1959 to 50 percent by 1973. U.S. Department of Commerce, Bureau of the Census 1975: Figure 1; 1970:1. The term "feminization of poverty" was first coined by Diana Pearce (1978). See also Pearce 1989.

2. The phrase is from Mott 1988. See also Bianchi and Spain 1986, 1996; Goldin 1990, Smith and Ward 1984.

3. Exogenous events and related public policy helped shaped women's educational choices, improving market outcomes for some, but at the same time widening the gap between women with and without advanced education (Lieb 2000).

4. Longitudinal analyses widened our concept of the poor, presenting a picture of a more general population moving in and out of poverty, joined with a small group of persistent poor (Duncan, Corcoran, and Hill 1986; Duncan 1984).

5. Quote is from Ross and Sawhill (1975). For explanation of why and how support for women's domestic role broke down, see Hartmann 1987, Kessler-Harris and Sacks 1987, Thistle 2000. Evidence of the extent to which the majority of both African American and white women relied upon the performance of domestic tasks within marriage as their central source of support is based on the authors' own calculations of IPUMS data (Thistle, forthcoming). See also United States Department of Commerce, Bureau of the Census 1971, and Cancian, Danziger, and Gottschalk 1992.

6. A rich literature analyzing factors affecting women's labor force participation and earnings has not yet been fully utilized in analyses of women's poverty (see, for example, England et al. 1994, Rosenfeld and Kalleberg 1990, and Waldfogel 1997). Bane (1986) found the majority of black women were poor prior to losing their husbands while for most white women poverty began with divorce. Kniesner, McElroy, and

Wilcox (1988), finding marital breakdown and parenthood played a similar role in poverty among women of both races, discuss flaws in her methodology.

7. These are precise samples drawn from census data collected by the United States government and standardized by a team led by Steve Ruggles in the History Department at the University of Minnesota. See *http://www.ipums.umn.edu.*

8. It is also a period of conflicting federal action, prohibiting discrimination by race or sex in the labor force while providing and then withdrawing support for single mothers in a form that hampered waged work. Other studies of shifting patterns of stratification between 1972 and 1987 point to the importance of further examination of this period (DiPrete and Grusky 1990).

9. The Census Bureau calculates poverty thresholds for each family size each year. See *http://www.census.gov/hhes/poverty/histpov/hstpov1.html* (site last visited 3/22/03). In 1960 and 1970, we had to estimate (impute) full-time year-round employment, as hours of work were given only for the preceding week. Those employed 50 or more weeks in the previous year and full-time in the preceding week were coded full-time year-round workers. Those working all or part of the past year, but less than full-time in the preceding week, were considered part-time workers, based on the assumption they worked part-time during the preceding year as well. Those with no history of work in the past year were coded as not employed last year. Comparison of full-time year-round work in 1990, when "usual hours of work" can be used to determine hours of employment in the preceding year, with our method shows it provides a close estimate of actual work patterns. We use the same method for estimating work in 1980 and 1990 as in 1960 and 1970. We used categorical variables for work due to distribution of women into these three groups rather than continuously across number of hours.

10. Ellwood 2000, esp. 16, 27.

11. Decomposition of logistic regressions using a more detailed set of variables shows work increased in importance due to women's increased turn to paid work, as well as their increased gains from paid employment. These decompositions make up the second and major segment of our study.

12. In 1973, the earliest year for which Current Population Survey data are available for both Hispanic and white non-Hispanic women, black and Hispanic women made up 42.1 percent of women in poverty. In 2000, they made up 49.8 percent of poor women, an increase of almost 20 percent (18.3). U.S. Census Bureau, Historical Poverty Tables, Table 14, *http://www.census.gov/hhes/poverty/histpov/hstpov14.html* (site visited 5/10/2003).

REFERENCES

Bane, Mary Jo. 1986. "Household Composition and Poverty." In *Fighting Poverty: What Works and What Doesn't*, ed. Sheldon Danziger and Daniel Weinberg. Cambridge, MA: Harvard University Press, 206-231.

_____, and David Ellwood. 1989. "One Fifth of the Nation's Children: Why Are They Poor?" *Science* 245(4922)(September): 1047-1053.

Bianchi, Suzanne and Daphne Spain. 1986. *American Women in Transition*. New York: Russell Sage Foundation.

Browne, Irene. 1997. "Explaining the Black-White Gap in Labor Force Participation Among Women Heading Households." *American Sociological Review* 62(April): 236-252.

Browne, Irene. 2000. "Opportunities Lost? Race, Industrial Restructuring, and Employment Among Young Women Heading Households." *Social Forces* 78:3 (March): 907-929.

Cancian, Maria, Sheldon Danziger, and Peter Gottschalk. 1992. "Working Wives and Family Income Inequality Among Married Couples." In *Uneven Tides: Rising Inequality in America*, eds. Sheldon Danziger and Peter Gottschalk. New York: Russell Sage Foundation, 195-221.

Casper, Lynne M., Sara McLanahan, and Irwin Garfinkel. 1994. "The Gender Poverty Gap: What We Can Learn from Other Countries." *American Sociological Review* 59: 594-605.

Corcoran, Mary. 1999. "The Economic Progress of African American Women." In *Latinas and African American Women at Work: Race, Gender, and Economic Inequality*, ed. Irene Browne. New York: Russell Sage Foundation.

DiPrete, Thomas A. and David B. Grusky. 1990. "Structure and Trend in the Process of Stratification for American Men and Women." *American Journal of Sociology* 96:1(July): 107-43.

Duncan, Greg. 1984. *Years of Poverty, Years of Plenty*. Ann Arbor: Institute for Social Research.

_____ , Mary Corcoran, and Martha S. Hill. 1986. "The Economic Fortunes of Women." In *Women and Poverty*, ed. Barbara C. Gelpi, Nancy C.M. Hartsock, Clare C. Novak, and Myra H. Strober. Chicago: University of Chicago Press, 7-23.

Edwards, Richard C., Michael Reich, and Thomas E. Weisskopf, eds. 1972. *The Capitalist System; A Radical Analysis of American Society*. Englewood Cliffs, NJ: Prentice Hall.

Ellwood, David. 2000. "Winners and Losers in America: Taking the Measure of the New Economic Realities." In *A Working Nation: Workers, Work, and Government in the New Economy*, eds. David T. Ellwood, Rebecca M. Blank, Joseph Blasi, Douglas Kruse, William A. Niskanen, and Karen Lynn-Dyson. New York: Russell Sage Foundation, 1-41.

England, Paula, Barbara S. Kilbourne, George Farkas, Kurt Beron, and Dorothea Weir. 1994. "Returns to Skill, Compensating Differentials, and Gender Bias: Effects of Occupational Characteristics on the Wages of White Men and Women." *American Journal of Sociology* 100:3(November): 689-719.

Fisher, Gordon M. 1997. "Poverty Lines and Measures of Income Inadequacy in the United States Since 1870: Collecting and Using a Little-Known Body of Historical Material." Presented at the Social Science History Association Conference.

Garfinkel, Irvin and Sara McLanahan. 1986. *Single-Mother Families and Public Policy: A New American Dilemma*. Washington, DC: Urban Institute.

Gilder, George. 1981 *Wealth and Poverty*. New York: Basic Books.

Goldin, Claudia. 1990. *Understanding the Gender Gap: An Economic History of American Women*. New York: Oxford University Press.

Hao, Linxin and Mary C. Brinton. 1997. "Productive Activities and Support Systems of Single Mothers." *American Journal of Sociology* 102(5)(March): 1305-44.

Hartmann, Heidi. 1987. "Changes in Women's Economic and Family Roles in Post-World War II United States." In *Women, Households and the Economy*, ed. Catherine R. Stimpson and Lourdes Beneria. New Brunswick, NJ: Rutgers University Press, 33-64.

Kessler-Harris, Alice and Karen Brodkin Sacks. 1987. "The Demise of Domesticity in America." In *Women, Households and the Economy*, eds. Catherine R. Stimpson and Lourdes Beneria. New Brunswick, NJ: Rutgers University Press, 65-84.

Kniesner, Thomas, Marjorie McElroy, and Steven Wilcox. 1988. "Getting into Poverty Without a Husband and Getting Out, With or Without." *American Economic Review* 78: 86-90.

Lewis, Oscar. 1961. *The Children of Sánchez: Autobiography of a Mexican Family*. New York: Modern Library.

Lichter, Daniel T., Diane K. McLaughlin, and David C. Ribar. 1997. "Welfare and the Rise in Female-Headed Families." *American Journal of Sociology* 103(1)(July): 112-43.

_____ , Deborah Roempke Graefe, and J. Brian Brown. 2003. "Is Marriage a Panacea? Union Formation Among Economically Disadvantaged Unwed Mothers. *Social Problems* 50(1): 60-86.

Lieb, Hilarie. 2001. "Federal Policy and the Gender Gap: The Baby-Boom Generation," PhD diss. Northwestern University.

McLanahan, Sara, Annemette Sorensen, and Dorothy Watson. 1989. "Sex Differences in Poverty, 1950-1980." *Signs* 15(1): 102-122.

Morgan, Leslie A. 1991. *After Marriage Ends: Economic Consequences for Midlife Women*. Thousand Oaks, CA: Sage Publications.

Mott, Frank, ed. 1982. *The Employment Revolution: Young American Women in the 1970s*. Cambridge, MA: MIT Press.

Murray, Charles. 1984. *Losing Ground: American Social Policy, 1950-1980*. New York: Basic Books.

Pearce, Diana M. 1978. "The Feminization of Poverty: Women, Work and Welfare." *Urban and Social Change Review* 11(February): 28-36.

_____. 1989. "The Feminization of Poverty: A Second Look." Washington DC: Institute for Women's Policy Research.

Peterson, Richard. 1989. *Women, Work, and Divorce*. Albany: State University of New York Press.

Rosenfeld, Rachel A. and Arne L. Kalleberg. 1990. "A Cross-National Comparison of the Gender Gap in Income." *American Journal of Sociology* 96:1(July): 69-106.

Ross, Heather and Isabel Sawhill. 1975. *Time of Transition: Growth of Families Headed by Women*. Washington, DC: The Urban Institute.

Ruggles, Steven, Matthew Sobek, Trent Alexander, Catherine A. Fitch, Ronald Goeken, Patricia Kelly Hall, Miriam King, and Chad Ronnander, eds. 2004. *Integrated Public Use Microdata Series: Version 3.0* [Machine-readable database]. Minneapolis, MN: Minnesota Population Center [producer and distributor]. http://www.ipums.org (last accessed January 9, 2005).

Smith, James, and Michael Ward, 1984. *Women's Wages and Work in the Twentieth Century*. Santa Monica, CA: Rand Corporation.

Spain, Daphne and Suzanne Bianchi. 1996. *Balancing Act: Motherhood, Marriage and Employment Among American Women.* New York: Russell Sage Foundation.

Thernstrom, Stephan. 1968. "Poverty in Historical Perspective." In *On Understanding Poverty: Perspectives from the Social Sciences,* ed. Daniel P. Moynihan. New York: Basic Books, 160-186.

Thistle, Susan. 2000. "The Trouble with Modernity: Gender and the Remaking of Social Theory." *Sociological Theory* 18:2(July): 275-289.

_____. N.d. *From Marriage to the Market: The Transformation of Women's Lives and Work in the Late 20th Century United States.* Berkeley: University of California Press, forthcoming.

U.S. Department of Commerce. Bureau of the Census. 1971. "Differences Between Incomes of White and Negro Families by Work Experience of Wife and Region: 1970, 1969 and 1959." Current Population Reports, Special Studies, no. 39. Washington, DC: Government Printing Office.

U. S. Department of Commerce, Bureau of the Census. 1970. *Characteristics of the Poverty Population, Current Population Reports*, Series P-60, No. 92. Washington, DC: United States Government Printing Office.

_____. 1975. *Characteristics of the Poverty Population*, Current Population Reports, Series P-60, No. 98. Washington, DC: United States Government Printing Office.

Waldfogel, Jane. 1997. "The Effect of Children on Women's Wages." *American Sociological Review* 62(April): 209-217.

Wojtkiewicz, Roger A., Sara S. McLanahan, and Irwin Garfinkel. 1990. "The Growth of Families Headed by Women: 1950-1980." *Demography* 27(1)(February): 19-30.

Anti-Discrimination vs. Anti-Poverty? A Comparison of Pay Equity and Living Wage Reforms

Pamela Stone, Hunter College, CUNY
Arielle Kuperberg, Hunter College, CUNY

SUMMARY. Welfare reform focuses attention on the potential of pay equity and living wage strategies to move women out of the ranks of the working poor. In this study, we use data from a large municipality in the Northeast to simulate implementation of the two policies and compare their relative effectiveness in raising the earnings of female- and minority-dominated jobs, narrowing gender- and race-based earnings differentials, and lifting workers out of poverty. Results show that pay equity raises salaries across-the-board, but especially among low-skilled and minority-dominated jobs, and closes the wage gap. Both pay equity and living wage dramatically reduce the incidence of poverty; living wage, however, leaves virtually untouched the type of discrimination targeted by pay equity and has little impact on the wage gap. The implications of these results for addressing the needs of women transitioning off public assistance and wage justice are discussed. We conclude that both policies should be an integral part of welfare reform efforts, as well as key planks in an overall wage justice strategy. *[Article copies available for a fee from The Haworth Document Delivery Service: 1-800-HAWORTH. E-mail address:*

[Haworth co-indexing entry note]: "Anti-Discrimination vs. Anti-Poverty? A Comparison of Pay Equity and Living Wage Reforms." Stone, Pamela, and Arielle Kuperberg. Co-published simultaneously in *Journal of Women, Politics & Policy* (The Haworth Political Press, an imprint of The Haworth Press, Inc.) Vol. 27, No. 3/4, 2005, pp. 23-39; and: *Women, Work, and Poverty: Women Centered Research for Policy Change* (ed: Heidi Hartmann) The Haworth Political Press, an imprint of The Haworth Press, Inc., 2005, pp. 23-39. Single or multiple copies of this article are available for a fee from The Haworth Document Delivery Service [1-800-HAWORTH, 9:00 a.m. - 5:00 p.m. (EST). E-mail address: docdelivery@haworthpress.com].

Available online at http://www.haworthpress.com/web/JWPP
doi:10.1300/J501v27n03_03

KEYWORDS. Job segregation, wage gap, race discrimination, sex discrimination, low-wage jobs, pay equity, comparable worth, living wages, poverty, welfare reform

INTRODUCTION

Welfare reform has brought new attention to employment-based strategies to move people, especially women and women of color, out of poverty to economic self-sufficiency. The challenges facing TANF recipients who seek to transition from welfare to work are increasingly well documented. One of the major obstacles to their success is the sex- and race-segregated nature of the labor market, which channels women, especially women of color, into low-paying, devalued, and dead-end jobs. There is considerable evidence that the earnings of female-dominated jobs are depressed by the concentration of women in them; evidence is mixed with regard to the effect of minority concentration in jobs, but there, too, the preponderance of evidence points to underpayment linked to the race of workers. To the extent that earnings in predominately female and/or minority jobs *are* depressed, this plays a role in understanding the seemingly greater difficulty of women of color to leave welfare rolls.

In the current political climate, where employment-based solutions are at the heart of welfare reform, these patterns suggest that employment per se (even in the relatively red-hot labor market that characterized the early days of welfare reform) is not enough to move women, particularly women of color, out of poverty. Two major policies–pay equity (formerly comparable worth) and living wage–seek to move beyond the employment status quo by redressing the low and/or discriminatory pay that is a feature of the jobs held by women transitioning off welfare.

Pay equity directly identifies and eliminates any underpayment of jobs that is due to the concentration of female and minority workers in them through a process that evaluates jobs according to their skill, effort, responsibility, and working conditions. Living wage reform focuses on jobs at the bottom of the earnings hierarchy, and raises the pay of jobs to a level that is adequate to raise a family of four above the federal poverty level of $18,100 per year, equivalent to an hourly wage of about $8.70 (Roston, Baughn, and Berestein 2002). In practice, living wage laws typically stipulate an annual salary of up to 130 percent of the federal poverty level (Economic Policy Institute 2001). Unlike pay equity, which focuses on rectifying discrimination on the basis of sex or race throughout the earnings hierarchy, living wage reform takes as its starting point the notion of a family-sustaining wage, challenging the notion that people who are working full-time should be forced to live at or below the poverty line (Murray 2001). Thus, the philosophy of living wage is *anti-poverty* while that of pay equity is *anti-discrimination*, with living wage seeking to address the needs of the so-called "working poor," and pay equity, the needs of workers who have been discriminated against on the basis of sex and/or race. Living wage advocates seek a *just and humane* wage for the most low-paid workers; pay equity advocates a *fair and sex- and race-blind* wage for women and minority workers. In this paper, we simulate pay equity and living wage adjustments and compare their effectiveness in (1) erasing sex- and race-based pay discrimination; (2) narrowing gender- and race-based earnings differentials; and (3) lifting workers out of poverty.

DATA AND METHODS

Data are taken from a study conducted during the mid-1980s preparatory to the negotiation of a new contract between a large municipality in the Northeast and the union (a local of a large national union) representing the majority of city workers in that municipality. The analysis is restricted to the 639 jobs having 5 or more incumbents[1] employed in agencies directly under mayoral control. The jobs in our analysis employ 154,270 workers, or 95 percent of the workforce covered by the contract, and reflect a heterogeneous mix of occupations. Although certain sectors, e.g., manufacturing, are missing entirely, in other respects the job composition of this dataset reflects trends in the larger national economy in its mix of managerial, administrative/clerical, health, and other service occupations. It differs primarily in that, countering national trends, it is entirely unionized. Moreover, in a prior contract negotiation, the union had taken steps to remedy underpayment of clerical titles that employed large numbers of women. Thus, for the purposes of simulating pay equity and living wage policy implementations, it can be seen to represent the best-case scenario.

The workforce of this municipality is very diverse. Minorities and women make up sizeable segments of the total employee base: 47.7 percent are minority and 39.3 percent are women. Women and, to a lesser extent, minorities are concentrated in a relatively small number of segregated jobs with large numbers of employees and low salaries relative to the jobs in which men and whites predominate.

Variable Measurement

The city provided written job specifications for each job that were used as the basis for the creation of an evaluation scheme that bears close resemblance to those typically used in pay equity implementations. The information provided by the city was supplemented with measures taken from the *Dictionary of Occupational Titles* (U.S. Department of Labor 1977). Annual starting salary (for full-time, year-round employment) was provided for each job by the city in 1986 dollars, which were adjusted to 2002 dollars for purposes of this analysis. Starting salary has the advantage of being unconfounded with worker characteristics and differences thereof that may be correlated with the sex or race of workers performing the job, such as time-in-grade (see, for example, Baron and Newman 1989). In this study, use of starting salary was also indicated because the available job specifications, on which assignment of ratings on compensable factors was based, clearly pertained to entry-level responsibilities and requirements. The other variables used in the analysis, along with variable means and standard deviations, are given in Appendix 1.

RESULTS

Assessing Discrimination

Our pay-setting model, results for which are shown in Appendix 2, explains a substantial 76 percent of the variation in starting salaries in this municipality's pay plan, providing a reliable basis on which to make pay equity adjustments. We find significant underpayment by race and, to a lesser extent, by sex. The relatively smaller impact of sex probably reflects the union's aforementioned attention to raising salaries in clerical and other female-dominated titles. In other respects, our findings are similar to other studies that have examined both sex and race effects in more heterogeneous workforces (e.g., Lapidus and Figart

1998a). Annual starting salaries were debited $20.72 for each per-centage-point increase in female representation and $119.42 for each per-centage-point increase in minority representation. In results not pre-sented here but available from the authors, we also found that these effects were distinct and additive, not interactive; that is, the penalty to sex is the same whether or not the job is minority-dominated and vice versa. These estimates were used as the basis of simulating pay equity adjustments as described below.

Method of Pay Equity Adjustment

Following guidelines developed by the National Committee on Pay Equity (NCPE)[2] and adapted to this municipality's situation, fe-male-dominated titles are defined as those having 55 percent or more women; minority titles as those having 67 percent or more minorities. Minority designation encompassed both African-American and Latino ancestry, but not Asian. Pay equity salary adjustments were applied only to jobs that were sex-, race-, or sex- and race-dominated, in line with prevailing practice (Michael, Hartmann, and O'Farrell 1989). This was done by adding to such jobs' starting salaries an amount equal to fe-male (or minority) representation in the job multiplied by the amount of discriminatory underpayment ($20.72 and $119.42, respectively). Do-ing so effectively "purges" salaries of discrimination linked to the sex- or race-composition of workers in them and brings starting salaries of sex- and race-dominated jobs up to a non-discriminatory standard. Be-cause this is an analysis of jobs, and again in line with prevailing pay eq-uity practice, all incumbents in an underpaid job, regardless of their own gender or race, receive the pay equity increment.

Method of Living Wage Adjustment

In order to simulate implementation of a living wage policy, we used the Economic Policy Institute's (Economic Policy Institute 2001) defi-nition of a living wage as 130 percent of the federal poverty level of $18,100 for a family of four, which sets the national living wage stan-dard at $23,530 (2002 dollars). Following this municipality's policy of setting its poverty level at 125 percent of the federal level because of its high cost of living (Dunlea 2002), we set our living wage salary at 125 percent of the Economic Policy Institute's living wage standard, which comes to an annual salary of $29,412. All jobs with starting salaries below this amount received a living wage adjustment by which their starting salaries were increased to $29,412.

Characteristics of Jobs Before and After Policy Implementation

Table 1 presents results in which jobs are the unit of analysis. Because our focus in this table is on describing the characteristics of the jobs themselves, the results are not weighted by the number of employees in the job. Jobs employ 241 workers on average, but there is especially great variability across titles, with the median number of employees in a job title being only 31. About 20 percent of jobs are female-dominated by our criterion, and a roughly equal proportion (21 percent) is minority-dominated, with jobs overall averaging 27 percent female employ-

TABLE 1. A Comparison of Selected Characteristics of All Jobs and Those Eligible for Salary Adjustments

Job Characteristic	All Jobs Before Adjustment (N = 639)		Jobs at Poverty Level (N = 78)		Jobs Receiving Pay Equity Adjustment (N = 200)		Jobs Receiving Living Wage Adjustment (N = 84)	
	MEAN	MEDIAN	MEAN	MEDIAN	MEAN	MEDIAN	MEAN	MEDIAN
EDUCATION	11.91	12.00	7.97	6.00	11.63	12.00	7.95	6.00
EXPERIENCE	2.67	2.00	0.27	0.00	1.28	1.00	0.35	0.00
SUPERVISION	3.17	3.00	1.60	1.00	2.57	2.00	1.61	1.00
NUMBER IN TITLE	241.42	31.00	424.42	42.50	398.26	49.50	401.30	45.50
ENTRY SALARY	$45,983	$43,749	$25,968	$26,246	$35,403	$33,097	$26,189	$26,718
SALARY AFTER PAY EQUITY ONLY	$48,423	$45,748	$35,507	$35,478	$43,197	$42,117	$33,545	$35,478
SALARY AFTER LIVING WAGE ONLY	$46,407	$43,749	$29,412	$29,412	$36,480	$33,097	$29,412	$29,412
PERCENTAGE FEMALE	27.22	16.67	47.97	40.83	59.23	62.50	45.11	39.06
PERCENTAGE MINORITY	37.12	28.57	73.55	78.94	70.40	77.18	73.12	77.99
FEMALE-DOMINATED	19.72%		43.59%		63.00%		40.50%	
MINORITY-DOMINATED	21.13%		66.67%		67.50%		65.50%	

Note: Results are not weighted by number of employees; the job is the unit of analysis. Sixty-four jobs received both Pay Equity and Living Wage adjustments; 136 jobs received Pay Equity, but no Living Wage adjustment; 20 jobs received Living Wage, but no Pay Equity adjustment; 419 jobs received neither Pay Equity nor Living Wage adjustments.

ees and 37 percent minority employees. Median starting salary is $43,749, reflecting the effects of unionization and the high cost-of-living in this municipality, as well as the large number of managerial titles in the city's pay plan. A pay equity policy would increase median starting salaries by $1,999 to $45,748, or 4.6 percent; under a living wage policy, median salaries would remain unchanged because only salaries at the very bottom of the salary schedule are affected. Looking at mean outcomes instead, we find that living wage adjustments result in a $424 improvement overall.

Even in a unionized setting, 78 jobs pay below the poverty level. Following Lapidus and Figart (1998b), we measure poverty using the more generous Basic Needs Budget formulation (Renwick and Bergmann 1993), adjusting the national level by 125 percent for the cost-of-living in this municipality, rather than the federal poverty level because we are working with the relatively higher pay scale of a unionized municipal employer. Poverty-level jobs are much more likely to be low-skill and female- (44 percent) and minority- (67 percent) dominated. Median starting salary is $26,246, which is raised to $35,478 under pay equity and $29,412 under living wage adjustments, increases of 35 percent and 12 percent, respectively.

Jobs receiving pay equity adjustments, of which there are 200 in this pay plan, are, as would be expected, even more female-dominated (63 percent). In common with poverty-level jobs, about two-thirds of these jobs are also minority-dominated. Relative to all jobs, pay-equity jobs have about the same educational requirements, but require less experience and entail less supervisory responsibility. They also employ large numbers of workers. Their median salary is a relatively low $33,097, which is raised to $42,117 under pay equity and virtually unchanged under living wage.

Finally, jobs receiving living wage adjustments, of which there are 84 in this pay plan, are low-skill and, like the jobs at the poverty level and those receiving pay equity adjustments, disproportionately female (41 percent) and minority (66 percent). Median salary is $26,718, which is raised to $35,478 under pay equity and $29,412 under living wage.

These results indicate the existence of considerable sex- and race-segregation in this municipality's pay plan and considerable pay discrimination in starting salaries based on the sex and race of the job incumbents. At the job level, 200, or 31 percent of all jobs, are eligible to receive a pay equity adjustment; 84, or 13 percent, are eligible to receive a living wage adjustment. Pay equity adjustments are implemented for jobs throughout the pay scale, including jobs with salaries below poverty or below a living wage. The magnitude of discrimination in this pay plan means that pay equity adjustments are typically large, averaging 35 percent across all jobs, versus only 12 percent for living wage.

Salary Adjustments Under Pay Equity and Living Wage

Table 2 presents starting salaries for different sex and race groups, comparing outcomes simulated under each policy to actual, that is, unadjusted, salaries. Results for this and all subsequent tables are weighted to reflect the number of employees in each job and hence are analogous to the distribution of starting salaries across employees. In making these adjustments to starting salaries, we effectively impose a constant,

TABLE 2. Starting Salaries Under Pay Equity and Living Wage Adjustments

Race/Sex Composition	Before Adjustment	Pay Equity		Living Wage	
	MEAN	MEAN	MEAN CHANGE	MEAN	MEAN CHANGE
ALL JOBS	$39,396	$43,792	14.81%	$40,099	2.96%
FEMALE-DOMINATED	31,860	40,108	28.18	33,157	5.64
MALE-DOMINATED	44,812	46,431	5.09	45,053	0.91
SEX-INTEGRATED	41,442	44,828	11.72	42,162	2.90
MINORITY-DOMINATED	30,594	41,198	35.94	31,915	5.09
Female	29,489	40,668	38.55	30,757	4.88
Male	34,137	43,291	28.78	35,325	4.47
Sex-Integrated	30,026	39,894	34.16	32,112	8.40
WHITE-DOMINATED	48,460	48,467	0.01	48,463	0.01
Female	49,114	50,619	3.25	49,247	0.54
Male	47,936	47,936	0.00	47,937	0.003
Sex-Integrated	54,640	54,640	0.00	54,653	0.05
RACE-INTEGRATED	38,481	39,510	3.06	39,378	4.70
Female	36,954	38,686	5.15	38,335	7.43
Male	49,640	40,640	0.00	40,967	1.21
Sex-Integrated	40,820	40,820	0.00	40,822	0.01

Note: Results are weighted by the number of employees in each job. Minorities include African-American and Latino/a employees, but not Asians.

across-the-board adjustment to the salaries of all employees in a given job. As noted earlier, this simulation probably represents a best-case scenario for each policy, but unionization arguably has a greater effect on raising salaries above poverty than it does on eradicating longstanding discriminatory pay practices. As a result, our simulation may overstate differences between the two policies, underestimating the effect of living wage were it to be implemented nationally or in less highly unionized localities. With this caveat, we turn to an evaluation of the policies' ability to meet their stated objectives–anti-discrimination for pay equity versus anti-poverty for living wage.

We find that under both policies, workers in minority-dominated and, to a lesser extent, female-dominated jobs are big winners, with the magnitude of pay equity gains for all affected groups being four- to five-fold those of living wage. Female-dominated jobs received an average increase of 28.18 percent under pay equity compared to a 5.64 percent increase under living wage. Given the prevailing pattern of discrimination in this pay plan, however, the big winners are minority-dominated jobs, which receive an average increase of 35.94 percent under pay equity versus an average increase of only 5.09 percent under living wage policy.

Narrowing Discriminatory Gender- and Race-Based Earnings Differentials

In Table 3, we present the earnings ratios that result under each policy. For this municipal employer, given the large number of minority women employees, the ratio of women to men's earnings stands at 69.4 percent, as does the ratio of minority to white earnings. Looking within particular race-typed jobs, we find that white females have achieved parity with white males, a reflection of earlier union efforts to eradicate gender-based discrimination and the fact that we are analyzing starting salaries.[3] For minority-dominated jobs, however, whether female or male in their sex composition, we find that workers earn only about two-thirds the salaries of those working in jobs held predominately by white men. Under pay equity, these ratios are raised almost to parity, the gender ratio narrowing to 93.9 percent and the race-based ratio to 93.8 percent. In contrast, living wage adjustments make no dent in either gender- or race-based earnings ratios, leaving them virtually unchanged.

To assess whether or not a living wage policy would impact discrimination, we regressed starting salaries *after* living wage adjustments had

TABLE 3. Earnings Ratios of Median Starting Salaries

Ratio	Before Adjustment	Pay Equity	Living Wage
All JOBS			
Female: Male	.694	.939	.694
Sex-Integrated: Male	.963	.963	.963
Minority: White	.694	.939	.694
Race-Integrated: White	.946	.946	.946
MINORITY-DOMINATED			
Female: White Male	.694	.939	.694
Male: White Male	.687	.904	.690
Sex-Integrated: White Male	.658	.882	.690
WHITE-DOMINATED			
Female: White Male	1.118	1.166	1.118
Sex-Integrated: White Male	.904	.939	.904
RACE-INTEGRATED			
Female: White Male	1.272	1.272	1.272
Male: White Male	.863	.863	.863

Note: Following standard practice in the computation of earnings ratios, ratios are based on median earnings; results are weighted by the number of employees in each job.

been made on the same set of job characteristics that we used to estimate the actual starting salary model for pay equity (see Appendix 2). Results (not presented, but available from the authors) were nearly identical to those for actual salaries, with the model having similar overall explanatory power (R-squared of .74) and a similar pattern of predictors. Notably, the coefficients for percentage female and percentage minority were equivalent in magnitude, indicating that under a living wage scenario, race and, to a lesser extent, sex discrimination in starting salaries is left unremedied. Living wage salaries were penalized $120.56 (cf. $119.42 for actual salaries) for each percentage-point increase in minority representation and $21.43 (cf. $20.72 for actual salaries) for a one-point increase in female representation.

Lifting Workers Out of Poverty

Elimination of poverty-level wages is the stated goal of the living wage movement. It is also consistent with the goals of pay equity advocates insofar as discrimination results in poverty-level salaries for female- and minority-dominated jobs. We assessed poverty in two ways. The first pegged poverty at 125 percent of the federal poverty level of

$18,100 for a family of four. Adjusted for this municipality's higher cost-of-living, this came out to a poverty income in 2002 dollars of $22,625 per year. Following Lapidus and Figart (1998b), we adopt a second poverty index, the basic needs budget (BNB), which is based on a methodology developed by Renwick and Bergmann (1993) that addresses many of the shortcomings of the federal measure. The BNB assumes a family of three, a mother and two children, and thus more closely approximates the female-headed household structure typical of women transitioning off welfare. Using 125 percent of their U.S. estimate to take account of this municipality's higher cost-of-living, the BNB poverty level equates to an annual income of $28,814 in 2002 dollars. Results are presented in Table 4, for different sex-race groups.

Employees of this municipality receive relatively generous remuneration, and thus few (1.28 percent) are working in jobs that pay below the federal poverty level. Using the more liberal, and many would argue, more realistic BNB index, however, a different picture emerges. By this yardstick, one-fifth of all city workers (21.46 percent) are in jobs whose wages are inadequate to support a family of three, and almost all of these jobs are minority-dominated. Thus, just under half of workers employed in minority-dominated jobs are working for poverty-level salaries: 44.79 percent of those in minority female-dominated jobs and 49.19 percent of those in minority male-dominated jobs. Considering only female-dominated jobs, regardless of race of jobholders, one-third are so-called "working poor." As we have seen before, workers in white female-dominated jobs fare well, with only 2.52 percent working for poverty-level salaries.

Realizing the policy's intent, living wage adjustments reduce poverty across-the-board, raising the salaries of all affected workers to $29,412, which is just above the BNB level of $28,814. Pay equity also reduces poverty among all groups except white women, indicating that the salaries of these jobs, while low, are non-discriminatory and in line with prevailing practices in this municipality's pay plan. The clearest advantage of living wage over pay equity is for workers in race-integrated jobs, whose low starting salaries are untouched by pay equity but lifted out of poverty by a living wage policy.

DISCUSSION

The results from these simulations show that both pay equity and living wage adjustments achieve their policy goals: Pay equity raises the salaries of jobs held by women and minorities and closes the earnings

TABLE 4. Percentage of Workers in Jobs Paying Poverty-Level Starting Salaries

	Before Adjustment	Pay Equity	Living Wage
ALL JOBS			
Federal[1]	1.28	1.26	0.00
BNB[2]	21.46	2.69	0.00
WOMEN'S JOBS			
Federal	3.27	3.22	0.00
BNB	35.84	4.42	0.00
WHITE-DOMINATED			
Federal	0.00	0.00	0.00
BNB	2.52	2.52	0.00
MINORITY-DOMINATED			
Federal	0.07	0.00	0.00
BNB	44.79	0.00	0.00
RACE-INTEGRATED			
Federal	10.54	10.54	0.00
BNB	16.14	14.43	0.00
MEN'S JOBS			
Federal	0.00	0.00	0.00
BNB	10.56	1.85	0.00
WHITE-DOMINATED			
Federal	0.00	0.00	0.00
BNB	0.02	0.02	0.00
MINORITY-DOMINATED			
Federal	0.00	0.00	0.00
BNB	49.19	0.00	0.00
RACE-INTEGRATED			
Federal	0.00	0.00	0.00
BNB	19.62	19.62	0.00

Note: Results are weighted by the number of employees in each job.
[1] $22,625 per year for a family of 4; Adjusted for this municipality's cost of living at 125 percent of federal poverty level of $18,100 for a family of 4.
[2] $28,814 per year for a family of 3; Basic Needs Budget adjusted for this municipality's cost of living at 125 percent of national level of $23,051.

gap; living wage results in a decrease in the number of workers below the poverty line. While implementation of a living wage policy has virtually no impact on discrimination or the wage gap, a pay equity policy results in a dramatic decline in poverty, albeit not the complete eradication seen under living wage.

Our results suggest that, for this workforce, in which minorities are concentrated in low-paying jobs whose starting salaries are depressed by sex and race discrimination, poverty is primarily the result of discrimination, especially on the basis of race, and to the extent that one remedies discrimination, one remedies poverty. Pay equity is thus a more comprehensive policy in that it achieves both anti-discrimination and anti-poverty goals–fairness and "justness" while living wage meets only the "justness" criterion. The choice between them, however, is based on more than potential outcomes.

Pay equity is more far-reaching in its scope and hence far more costly to implement. In implementation, it is also potentially more divisive than living wage because it threatens established wage hierarchies. Because sex and race segregation of occupations and jobs is pervasive, pay equity also has the potential to pit workers in one occupation against others, a tension that can manifest itself along racial and gender lines, e.g., white male workers against female and minority workers. Living wage brings up the bottom, but essentially maintains existing hierarchies. Its advocates have often managed to build successful coalitions among low-income workers that cross gender and race lines by focusing on economic disadvantage and sidestepping questions of workers' gender and/or race-ethnicity, questions that are harder to ignore with pay equity. Living wage reform addresses the needs of the "deserving poor"–working poor who are trying to achieve economic self-sufficiency–while respecting the basic wage-setting processes of tradition and the market, processes that are challenged as discriminatory by pay equity. Pay equity is predicated on a relatively subtle form of discrimination (equal pay for *comparable* rather than *equal* work) that remains contested in the courts and by employers. Moreover, despite mounting evidence to the contrary (and evidence presented in our analyses), pay equity is often associated with white, middle-class feminism and other groups, especially black women, remain wary of it (Holleran and Schwartz 1988). Because it is implemented only on jobs that are extremely segregated, it also fails to address the salaries of low-paying jobs that are sex- and race-integrated, while living wage, which is essentially sex- and color-blind in the mechanics of its implementation, brings up the salaries of jobs at the very bottom irrespective of the composition of their workforce.

Against the broader context of welfare reform during a period of conservative ascendancy, for the reasons cited above, the minimalist, triage-like approach of living wage policy would appear to be more politically viable than the more comprehensive approach of pay equity.

Living wage's potential to move women, particularly women of color, out of poverty is demonstrated clearly by our analysis. Our results make clear, however, that a *living* wage should not be confused with a *fair, non-discriminatory* wage. For the most disadvantaged workers it is clearly a *better* wage and hence a worthy and sufficient first step, and one that, even with its more limited aim and reach, will be difficult to realize in the current economic and political climate. In this climate, for reasons having more to do with politics than policy design *per se*, in the spirit of putting poor women and children first, and creating the circumstances in which they can gain economic independence, living wage would seem to hold greater immediate promise than pay equity. In order to move women transitioning off welfare beyond mere self-sufficiency, however, and to achieve larger equity goals, our results indicate that a multi-pronged approach is required. Pay equity should be part of any such approach. By eradicating pay discrimination in the types of jobs women coming off welfare are likely to enter, pay equity can help these women and their families move beyond minimal and precarious self-sufficiency to sustained self-reliance. In their efforts to achieve economic independence, women of color face the dual obstacles of gender and race discrimination; pay equity appears to be an important mechanism by which such obstacles can be removed or reduced. We conclude that both pay equity and living wage should be an integral part of welfare reform efforts, as well as key planks in an overall wage justice strategy.

NOTES

1. This restriction follows now-standard practice in comparable worth studies, in an effort to avoid the rather arbitrary definition of jobs as female- or minority-dominated, which would result if low-incumbency jobs were included in the analysis. For further discussion, see Steinberg (1987) and Baron and Newman (1989).

2. NCPE (1993) recommends that 1.4 times each group's participation in the U.S. labor force be used to establish cut-off points for jobs in which women or minority workers are overrepresented. Because our data pertain exclusively to a particular municipality's workforce, we used each group's participation in this workforce as the basis for our definition of female- and minority-dominated titles.

3. This is also a reflection of the relative "cleanness" of our analysis: many of the differences in employment, e.g., sector or industry, that are correlated with sex but often uncontrolled result in an exaggeration of the earnings differences between men and women. In addition, our analysis pertains only to starting salaries, and there is considerable evidence to suggest that it is at later points in individual career trajectories that sex differences are greatest.

REFERENCES

Baron, James N. and Andrew E. Newman. 1989. "Pay the Man: Effects of Demographic Composition on Prescribed Wage Rates in the California Civil Service." In *Pay Equity: Empirical Inquiries*, eds. Robert T. Michael, Heidi I. Hartmann, and Brigid O'Farrell. Washington, DC: National Academy Press.

Dunlea, Mark. 2002. Testimony of the Hunger Action Network of New York State to the joint hearing of the Senate Finance Committee and Assembly Ways and Means Committee on the Proposed 2000-2001 NYS State Budget. February 4. http://www.hungeractionnys.org/leg-budg.htm

Economic Policy Institute. 2001. "Living Wage: Frequently Asked Questions." *www.epinet.org*

Holleran, Philip M. and Margaret Schwarz. 1988. "Another Look at Comparable Worth's Impact on Black Women." *Review of Black Political Economy* 16: 19-102.

Lapidus, June and Deborah M. Figart. 1998a. "Remedying 'Unfair Acts': U.S. Pay Equity by Race and Gender." *Feminist Economics* 4(3): 7-28.

Lapidus, June and Deborah M. Figart. 1998b. "Erasing Discrimination: Toward Family-Sustaining Wages for Poor Workers." Presented at the Fifth Annual Institute for Women's Policy Research Conference, Washington, DC.

Michael, Robert T., Heidi I. Hartmann, and Brigid O'Farrell, eds. 1989. *Pay Equity: Empirical Inquiries*. Washington, DC: National Academy Press.

Murray, Bobbi. 2001. "An Increasingly Sophisticated Movement Has Put Opponents on the Defensive: Living Wage Comes of Age." *The Nation.* July 23/30, 25-28.

National Committee on Pay Equity (NCPE). 1993. *Erase the Bias: A Pay Equity Guide to Eliminating Race and Sex Bias from Wage-Setting Systems.* Washington, DC: NCPE.

Renwick, Trudi J. and Barbara R. Bergmann. 1993. "A Budget-Based Definition of Poverty, with an Application to Single-Parent Families." *Journal of Human Resources* 28(1): 1-24.

Roston, Eric, Akuce Jackson Baughn, and Leslie Berestein. 2002. "How Much Is a Living Wage?" *Time* 159(14): 52-55.

Steinberg, Ronnie. 1987. "Radical Challenges in a Liberal World: The Mixed Success of Comparable Worth." *Gender and Society* 1(December): 466-475.

U.S. Department of Labor. 1977. *Dictionary of Occupational Titles.* 4th Edition. Washington, DC: Government Printing Office.

APPENDIX 1. Pay Equity Model: Variable Definitions and Descriptive Statistics (N = 634)

Variable	Definition	Mean	SD
ENTRY SALARY	Annual entry-level salary in 2002 dollars	$45,983.17	$15,275.01
PERCENTAGE FEMALE	Percentage of workers who are women	27.22	30.81
PERCENTAGE MINORITY	Percentage of workers who are African-American or Latino/a	37.12	29.86
EDUCATION	Years of schooling required for job entry	11.91	4.34
EDUCATION SQD	Education squared	160.62	100.60
EXPERIENCE	Years of experience required for job entry	2.67	2.33
EXPERIENCE SQD	Experience squared	12.55	17.32
EXTREMES	1 if job entails extreme temperatures; 0 otherwise*	.14	.34
HAZARDS	1 if job entails special hazards; 0 otherwise*	.03	.17
LICENSE	1 if job requires special license; 0 otherwise	.18	.38
SUPERVISION	Level of supervisory responsibility 1 to 8	3.17	1.77
LABOR MARKET INDEX	1 if salary indexed to local labor market; 0 otherwise	.05	.22
INFLUENCE	1 if job requires influencing or persuading people; 0 otherwise*	.13	.33
MANAGER	1 if job is managerial; 0 otherwise	.07	.26
PROTECTIVE SERVICE	1 if job is uniformed protective service; 0 otherwise	.07	.25

*Measures adapted from *Dictionary of Occupational Titles* (U.S. Department of Labor, 1977)

APPENDIX 2. OLS Regression Coefficients for Starting Salary Model Used as Basis of Pay Equity Adjustments (Standard Errors in Parentheses)

Independent Variable	Coefficient
PERCENTAGE FEMALE	−20.72# (12.13)
PERCENTAGE MINORITY	−119.42**** (35.29)
EDUCATION	−3680.61**** (503.20)
EDUCATION SQD	188.42**** (22.49)
EXPERIENCE	3325.83**** (373.33)
EXPERIENCE SQD	−191.57**** (44.62)
EXTREMES	1113.62 (909.95)
HAZARDS	2961.30 (1873.15)
LICENSE	3715.68**** (787.88)
SUPERVISION	1636.01**** (220.38)
LABOR MARKET INDEX	9582.36**** (1476.46)
INFLUENCE	2372.24* (1006.70)
MANAGER	14644.00**** (1240.07)
PROTECTIVE SERVICE	6857.58**** (1227.22)
INTERCEPT	49472.00**** (2581.31)
R SQD (ADJUSTED)	.76
N	634

Statistically significant at:
# $p < .05$ (1-tailed test) * $p < .05$ ** $p < .01$ *** $p < .001$ **** $p < .0001$ (two-tailed test)

Getting Beyond
the Training vs. Work Experience Debate:
The Role of Labor Markets,
Social Capital, Cultural Capital,
and Community Resources
in Long-Term Poverty

Jo Anne Schneider, Catholic University of America

SUMMARY. Policy makers and advocates often see either training or work experience as the way out of poverty. Research in Wisconsin and Pennsylvania suggests that family-supporting jobs continue to elude many low-income women for more complicated reasons: (1) a bifurcated labor market where over half of the jobs pay below-poverty wages with limited benefits, (2) a lack of bridging social capital, (3) limited bi-cultural workplace habits, (4) problems juggling kin obligations and work, and (5) inappropriate or limited training. The study suggests that policy makers should take a two-pronged approach to combating poverty. Training, combined with network development and appropriate cultural capital development, will help some women. Given the growing percentage of low-paying jobs, however, policy should also seek to raise wages, supplement wages, and provide universal benefits. *[Article copies available for a fee from The Haworth Document Delivery Service:*

[Haworth co-indexing entry note]: "Getting Beyond the Training vs. Work Experience Debate: The Role of Labor Markets, Social Capital, Cultural Capital, and Community Resources in Long-Term Poverty." Schneider, Jo Anne. Co-published simultaneously in *Journal of Women, Politics & Policy* (The Haworth Political Press, an imprint of The Haworth Press, Inc.) Vol. 27, No. 3/4, 2005, pp. 41-53; and: *Women, Work, and Poverty: Women Centered Research for Policy Change* (ed: Heidi Hartmann) The Haworth Political Press, an imprint of The Haworth Press, Inc., 2005, pp. 41-53. Single or multiple copies of this article are available for a fee from The Haworth Document Delivery Service [1-800-HAWORTH, 9:00 a.m. - 5:00 p.m. (EST). E-mail address: docdelivery@haworthpress.com].

1-800-HAWORTH. E-mail address: <docdelivery@haworthpress.com> Website: <http://www.HaworthPress.com> © 2005 by The Haworth Press, Inc. All rights reserved.]

KEYWORDS. Welfare reform, poverty, employment, Wisconsin, Pennsylvania, social capital, job training, wages

INTRODUCTION

Anti-poverty legislation focuses on single solutions to complex workforce development problems. While both of the welfare reform laws passed since the mid-1980s addressed work experience and training, each bill emphasized one of these strategies as the primary solution to poverty. The 1988 Family Support Act saw education and training as the way out of poverty, while the Personal Responsibility and Work Opportunity Act of 1996 relied primarily on work experience to end welfare use. Despite significant drops in the welfare rolls, policy has failed to reduce long-term poverty. Instead, most poor women continue work in unstable service-sector jobs, following patterns established long before legislative intervention (Bane and Ellwood 1994).

These policies fail because neither education nor work experience, in and of themselves, address the complexities of labor market conditions and family needs in the 21st century. Crafting appropriate policies involves looking toward multiple solutions focused simultaneously on macro-level economic factors and individual family circumstances. This presentation provides a policy summary of a series of studies of Philadelphia, Milwaukee, and Kenosha, Wisconsin, conducted between 1992 and 2000 (see Schneider 2006). I concentrate particularly on labor market conditions and family economic strategies. A companion study (Schneider 2000) looks at education and training programs in detail. While numerous factors contribute to individual outcomes, here I concentrate on five factors: (1) a bifurcated labor market, where more than half of the jobs pay below poverty wages with limited benefits, (2) a lack of bridging social capital, (3) limited bi-cultural workplace habits, (4) problems juggling kin obligations and work, and (5) inappropriate or limited training.

DATA AND METHODS

This presentation relies on holistic, ethnographic studies of three communities that combine quantitative surveys, ethnography, life history interviews, and analysis of Department of Labor and Department of Public Welfare statistics (see the Appendix for a list of studies). I use labor market data provided by Wisconsin and Pennsylvania to analyze economic opportunities. In order to understand requirements for different kinds of jobs, I examined functional attributes that are part of Federal Department of Labor codes, combining this information with descriptions of various positions from a wide range of sources. Data on family strategies come from a combination of life histories and observations of behavior in various settings.

LABOR MARKET CONDITIONS

Most anti-poverty policies focus on changing attributes of individuals, failing to see the overwhelming role that the labor market plays in structuring opportunities. Recent studies suggest a bifurcated labor market divided between high-wage jobs concentrated in education intensive high technology sectors, and low-wage support work primarily in services (Sassen 1998). Research in these three cities shows the same patterns as national data.

Table 1 shows the average number of employees and average wages by industry for 1995, 1997, and 2000 in the three communities. Service sector employment provides the largest share of jobs, but employment is spread across various industries. Proportions are similar in the two large metropolitan areas, with Kenosha showing an even greater mix of employment. Wages are relatively higher in Philadelphia than for the two Wisconsin cities.[1]

Wage levels for various industries raise great concern because many new retail and service-sector jobs offer lower wages, fewer benefits, and part time hours. Notice that the two largest categories–retail trade and service–pay far below family-supporting wages. Retail wages, in particular, provide less than half the median average wage in each community. The percentage of jobs in these low paying sectors increased over time in both large cities, but gradually fell in Kenosha to 42 percent. Over half of the available jobs in the Milwaukee (51 percent) and Philadelphia (52 percent) regions were in these two categories in 2000. The growth in these two lower paying categories also suggests greater competition for better paying jobs in the other sectors.

Table 2 examines available jobs by type of employment rather than industry.[2] Job types cross industrial sectors, revealing a finer grained picture of available opportunities. The nine categories outlined in Table 2

TABLE 1

Employees and Wages by Industry

Kenosha County	1995			1997			2000		
Industry	Avg. Employees	% Employees	Avg. Salary	Avg. Employees	% Employees	Avg. Salary	Avg. Employees	% Employees	Avg. Salary
All Industries	47,249	100%	$23,018	47,746	100%	$25,163	50,443	100%	$28,951
All Government	6,516	14%	$27,157	6,981	15%	$28,040	7,825	16%	$30,452
Private Coverage	40,732	86%	$22,350	40,765	85%	$24,669	42,618	84%	$28,682
Agriculture/Forestry/Fishing	414	1%	$14,443	438	1%	$14,672	500	1%	$17,470
Mining	7	0%	$0	0	0%	$0	0	0%	$0
Construction	2,152	5%	$29,907	2,134	4%	$34,352	2,182	4%	$38,131
Manufacturing	10,761	23%	$35,588	11,231	24%	$38,287	12,619	25%	$43,186
Transportation/Public Utilities	1,668	4%	$25,574	1,812	4%	$27,357	1,944	4%	$33,426
Wholesale Trade	2,050	4%	$26,981	2,196	5%	$32,029	2,810	6%	$36,181
Retail Trade	11,803	25%	$10,706	10,165	21%	$11,775	10,414	21%	$12,936
Finance/Insurance/Real Estate	1,587	3%	$24,049	1,622	3%	$25,009	1,394	3%	$30,057
Services	10,184	22%	$18,603	11,157	23%	$19,251	10,741	21%	$23,011

Milwaukee County	1995			1997			2000		
Industry	Avg. Employees	% Employees	Avg. Salary	Avg. Employees	% Employees	Avg. Salary	Avg. Employees	% Employees	Avg. Salary
All Industries	517,840	100%	$25,923	523,553	100%	$28,550	523,381	100%	$32,067
All Government	58,464	11%	$30,749	57,981	11%	$32,766	60,388	12%	$36,172
Private Coverage	459,375	89%	$25,296	465,572	89%	$28,014	462,993	88%	$31,554
Agriculture/Forestry/Fishing	1,442	0%	$17,448	1,538	0%	$1,846	1,575	0%	$20,945
Mining	37	0%	$0	0	0%	$0	0	0%	$0
Construction	12,129	2%	$31,566	12,887	2%	$35,076	12,757	2%	$38,975
Manufacturing	99,386	19%	$34,748	62,444	12%	$38,405	88,924	17%	$43,095
Transportation/Public Utilities	27,690	5%	$28,272	27,837	5%	$31,084	29,201	6%	$35,196
Wholesale Trade	25,815	5%	$31,839	26,256	5%	$34,846	24,834	5%	$39,801
Retail Trade	85,457	17%	$12,621	84,984	16%	$13,671	78,407	15%	$15,199
Finance/Insurance/Real Estate	41,687	8%	$32,742	42,573	8%	$39,225	39,432	8%	$44,249
Services	165,727	32%	$22,310	173,211	33%	$24,541	187,811	36%	$28,315

Philadelphia MSA (PA only)	1995			1997			2000		
Industry	Avg. Employees	% Employees	Avg. Salary	Avg. Employees	% Employees	Avg. Salary	Avg. Employees	% Employees	Avg. Salary
All Industries	1,664,022	100%	$32,196	1,728,100	100%	$34,999	1,822,983	100%	$44,0182
All Government	217,323	13%	N/A	208,053	12%	N/A	195,552	11%	N/A
Private Coverage	1,445,792	87%	N/A	1,519,021	88%	N/A	1,607,974	88%	N/A
Agriculture/Forestry/Fishing	13,358	1%	$19,994	14,567	1%	$21,571	17,558	1%	$25,184
Mining	N/A	0%	N/A	N/A	0%	N/A	986	0%	$54,492
Construction	55,391	3%	$36,052	62,794	4%	$39,701	74,232	4%	$44,325
Manufacturing	248,050	15%	$41,635	247,636	14%	$46,166	239,261	13%	$53,599
Transportation/Public Utilities	75,143	5%	$37,596	77,258	4%	$40,352	81,869	4%	$46,592
Wholesale Trade	87,655	5%	$40,429	85,892	5%	$44,332	88,665	5%	$51,034
Retail Trade	271,956	16%	$16,354	282,999	16%	$17,476	300,050	16%	$19,863
Finance/Insurance/Real Estate	129,615	8%	$41,940	134,311	8%	$48,035	140,305	8%	$59,118
Services	564,624	34%	$30,166	613,564	36%	$32,636	665,048	36%	$37,870

From *Social Capital and Welfare Reform: Organizations, Churches, and Communities*, by Jo Anne Schneider. Copyright © 2006 Columbia University Press. Reprinted with permission of the publisher.

TABLE 2

Types of Employment									
	Philadelphia		**Milwaukee**				**Kenosha**		
	Average Hourly Wage		*Percentage Employment*		*Average Hourly Wage*		*Percentage Employment*		*Average Hourly Wage*
Occupational Title	*1997*	*2000*	*1997*	*2000*	*1997*	*2000*	*1997*	*2000*	*1997*	*2000*
Professional entry level	$15.67	$17.07	4%	3%	$13.56	$15.91	3%	2%	$12.91	$15.57
Human services, front line	$9.43	$9.99	4%	4%	$9.86	$9.16	3%	4%	$7.82	$8.39
Human services, education, professionals	$18.87	$19.44	5%	7%	$14.99	$18.61	7%	6%	$15.17	$12.15
Other professional, managerial	$22.69	$27.64	17%	17%	$19.71	$25.17	15%	12%	$20.12	$24.04
Sales and service, unskilled	$8.27	$9.36	17%	12%	$7.51	$8.78	28%	20%	$7.51	$8.36
Sales and service, skilled	$17.20	$18.51	6%	4%	$15.62	$17.70	6%	7%	$15.32	$17.95
Clerical, entry level	$9.95	$10.27	3%	9%	$9.00	$11.03	3%	8%	$7.84	$9.51
Clerical, skilled	$12.36	$14.47	14%	16%	$11.56	$15.36	14%	14%	$11.11	$12.87
Blue collar, skilled	$16.00	$18.63	17%	13%	$14.85	$17.87	10%	13%	$15.15	$18.93
Blue collar, unskilled	$11.36	$12.41	15%	15%	$12.84	$12.84	13%	13%	$9.48	$11.71

rearrange U.S. Department of Labor job categories to group positions that require similar skills and pay similar wages. *Professional entry level* includes jobs like emergency medical technician, drafter, or paralegal that require significant technical training at an Associates or Bachelor's degree level. *Human services front line workers* include child care aides, nursing assistants, and similar occupations. The *human services and education professional* category includes jobs like nurse, teacher, and social worker that require at least a Bachelor's degree and usually graduate education.

Para-professional and human service positions are growing occupations as needs for child care, elder care, and similar services increase. In both Milwaukee and Kenosha, however, these jobs accounted for less than 15 percent of the labor force. Human services front line workers were only 4 percent of the labor market in both cities. While front line human service jobs pay better than retail, they still offer below poverty wages. Clearly, preparing a large proportion of the labor force for these jobs will not solve long-term poverty.

The *other professional* category includes the greatest range of jobs, and has the widest wage range. It includes well-paid medical professionals, writers, artists, researchers, and a number of other professional positions that require college education and extensive experience. The *sales and service: unskilled* positions include the fast growing positions like retail clerks, restaurant personnel, guards, and housekeeping. The *sales and service: skilled* occupations include hairdressers, real estate sales agents, and service sector managers that need some experience or training. All of the clerical positions require some skill, but the *clerical: skilled* positions require more education or experience. The *clerical: entry level* positions include file clerks, data entry, tellers, and similar positions which can be learned through on-the-job experience combined with quality high school education or a short training program. Blue-collar jobs divide roughly equally between unskilled and skilled occupations. *Blue-collar: skilled* positions required an apprenticeship or significant on-the-job experience while *blue-collar: unskilled* positions required very few skills and almost no training.

Taken together, these labor market statistics show a wide gap between jobs offering family supporting wages and the growing low-wage sectors of the economy. The current picture is worse because these statistics represent local economies before the high technology bubble burst–fewer good paying jobs exist today than in 2000. Contrary to stereotypes of welfare recipients, Table 3 shows that most participants in the studies used for this report held multiple jobs over their lifetime. If anything, their work history shows continued attempts to find jobs paying stable, living wages. Table 4 shows the jobs most frequently held by individuals in the three Philadelphia studies, patterns echoed in the Wisconsin data. The majority worked in the low wage sectors of the economy; only between 9 and 11 percent held jobs that could lead to more lucrative employment. Many of the professional entry-level jobs represent front line social service workers, jobs that pay little, despite increasingly requiring college degrees. The previous work experience patterns suggest individuals have the skills needed in the new economy; in fact, the ease with which low-skilled workers found jobs in recent years highlights that availability of work is not the problem. The shrinking employment sectors offering family-supporting wages and benefits, however, indicate the need for different strategies to move families out of poverty.

TABLE 3

	Social Network	CWEP	Rapid Attachment
Employment and Welfare Use			
Never worked	13%	4%	N/A
1 or 2 Jobs (1-4 CWEP)	42%	60%	55%
3 or more jobs (CWEP > 4)	45%	35%	45%
Ever on welfare	95%	76%	92% [*]
On welfare LT 1 yr.	22%	35%	N/A
On welfare 1-2 yrs.	28%	15%	N/A
On welfare 3-5 yrs.	22%	15%	N/A
On welfare over 5 years	27%	35%	N/A

[*]current figure

Sources: *Social Network, CWEP,* and *Rapid Attachment* studies

From *Social Capital and Welfare Reform: Organizations, Churches, and Communities,* by Jo Anne Schneider. Copyright © 2006 Columbia University Press. Reprinted with permission of the publisher.

Unquestionably, the more lucrative jobs require college, often graduate-level, education. Examining who actually gets jobs, however, shows that education alone does not lead to job stability. Instead, education combines with social and cultural capital to influence outcomes.

BRIDGING-SOCIAL CAPITAL

"Social capital" refers to trust-based networks that people use to find resources like jobs or education (Portes 1998). Bridging-social capital also depends on reciprocal, enforceable trust, but crosses boundaries of race, class, and community. Why is bridging-social capital an important ingredient in successful anti-poverty policy? Primarily because the people who get and keep good jobs have appropriate networks to achieve their goals. A plethora of studies show that poor families have strong

TABLE 4

Most Frequently Held Jobs	Social Network	CWEP	Rapid Attachment
Cashier	36%	27%	15%
Clerical	27%	44%	23%
Health/nursing assistant	17%	19%	14%
Sales	13%	22%	13%
Factory work	10%	20%	15%
Restaurant work/ food prep	19%	19%	15%
Security guard	10%	N/A	N/A
Maintenance/blue collar	10%	N/A	10%
Professional or professional entry level	9%	N/A	11%
Housekeeping	N/A	N/A	15%

Sources: *Social Network, CWEP,* and *Rapid Attachment* studies

networks that help them to survive (Stack 1974; Edin and Lein 1997; Newman 2001). People who move into professional employment equally depend on new connections that help them to make the right education and employment decisions. These people also help them to develop strong networks in new environments, providing the security to maintain professional employment in tough economic times.

A comparison of several individuals shows the importance of bridging-social capital. Tania, profiled elsewhere (Schneider 2001: 13), moved from a nursing assistant position into employment as an RN due to sustained support from the professionals in the hospitals where she worked. These trust-based relationships offered resources and all-important encouragement to widen her opportunities. In contrast, Alvin only found one job that used his graphic design degree through a small business associated with his ethnic community. Lacking appropriate bridging-social capital, further jobs failed to materialize when this company closed and Alvin returned to restaurant work. Mark had many years of work experience in a high technology field, but did not develop bridging-social capital due to workplace racism. As a result, he was unable to find comparable work when his company closed its local plant.

Developing bridging-social capital takes time and trust. Strategies that work include fostering internship programs, as well as various mentoring relationships that offer long-term trust across groups. Bridging-social capital is often an important element in teaching bi-cultural workplace habits, the next often overlooked attribute of workforce development.

BI-CULTURAL WORKPLACE HABITS

Most employment development programs provide some form of education on appropriate behaviors and dress in the workplace. Bi-cultural habits go beyond this surface advice. They involve a range of subtle behaviors that not only allow someone to fit into the work environment, but to know when it is appropriate to use elements of home culture in interacting with others. These behaviors are often learned through socialization, and bridging-social capital relationships can go a long way in helping a newcomer become comfortable in the workplace.

While much discussion of culture focuses on language, dress, and other behaviors, I often find that learned power dynamics become most problematic for low-skilled workers in any job. Previous experiences that cause trouble for low-skilled workers include lack of practice negotiating with supervisors or co-workers in conflicts, which can lead to quickly quitting jobs or hostile reactions toward other employees. Applying home community understandings of disrespect can lead to confrontations with customers as well as co-workers. While these learned behaviors often reflect true inequalities in the workplace, inappropriate responses only worsen job instability. Fostering different approaches to workplace culture among both employees and employers is the best approach to solving these problems. Solutions emphasize developing trust and, potentially, social capital.

PROBLEMS JUGGLING KIN OBLIGATIONS AND WORK

Analysis of labor market opportunities suggests that most jobs require flexibility from employees, expectations particularly difficult for women responsible for caring for various family members. The ongoing tension between work and family obligations is likely to worsen as states cut a variety of social programs given current budget deficits. The only possible solution here is to increase the web of elder care, after school programs, and other supports needed by working families. Given the trust issues associated with family care, encouraging development of community-based systems is the most appropriate strategy.

TRAINING

While most employers require a high school diploma, the appropriate kind of training beyond basic credentials remains the subject of much debate. Given limited space here, let me reiterate arguments made elsewhere (Schneider 2000, 2002), that education and training are most effective when combined with appropriate social capital, cultural capital, and work experience. Only when individuals understand the goals of education as related to other experiences can they adequately evaluate programs, apply classroom learning, and use skills toward more lucrative employment. In my experience, lack of *appropriate* education and critical thinking skills are a more important issue than general lack of credentials.

POLICY SOLUTIONS

Studies in three communities suggest a two-pronged approach to ending poverty. First, universal work supports such as health care, sick leave, family care programs, and income supports for low-wage jobs become crucial given the direction of current labor markets. Since many employers are small businesses, traditional employer targeted solutions will not work in the new economy. Instead, government and non-profit sector supplements are necessary to end poverty. These include encouraging the development of a web of child care, sick child care, after school, elder care, and other social support programs through local communities available for free or at low cost.

At the same time, facilitating workforce development requires programs that combine development of social capital, cultural capital, work experience, and training. These programs should be placed in the context of offering appropriate family supports to ease the tension between work and family obligations.

Given the increasing need for quality workers in low-paid caregiving professions, ending poverty will require even more creative solutions than in previous generations. How can we provide adequate incomes to people in these kinds of jobs given the growing cost containment concerns? I suggest that the debate needs to expand beyond the current focus on individual career paths to wider issues regarding health and welfare provision. The various services in the expanding sectors of the economy represent jobs as well as needed benefits. Placing workforce development within the context of societal needs may change the debate from fixing perceived individual deficits to providing appropriate supports for people fulfilling needed jobs.

NOTES

1. Pennsylvania and Wisconsin Department of Labor industry by employment figures.
2. These data come from Department of Labor annual wage surveys in each community. The figures are a subset of the total employment picture and do not add up to the employment figures on Table 1.

REFERENCES

Bane, Mary Jo and David Ellwood. 1994. *Welfare Realities: From Rhetoric to Reform.* Cambridge, MA: Harvard University Press.

Edin, Kathryn and Laura Lein. 1997. *Making Ends Meet: How Single Mothers Survive Welfare and Low Wage Work.* New York: Russell Sage Foundation.

Newman, Katherine. 2001. "Hard Times on 125th Street." *American Anthropologist,* 103(3): 762-778.

Portes, Alejandro. 1998. "Social Capital: Its Origins and Applications in Modern Sociology." *Annual Review of Sociology,* 1-24.

Sassen, Saskia. 1998. *Globalization and Its Discontents.* New York: The New Press.

Schneider, Jo Anne. 2000. "Pathways to Opportunity: The Role of Race, Social Networks, Institutions and Neighborhood in Career and Educational Paths for People on Welfare." *Human Organization* 59(1): 72-85.

_____. 2001. *Kenosha Social Capital Study,* available at. *http://www.nonprofitresearch. org/newsletter1531/newsletter_show.htm?doc_id=17368*

_____. 2002. "Social Capital and Community Supports for Low Income Families: Examples from Pennsylvania and Wisconsin." *Social Policy Journal* 1(1): 35-56.

_____. 2006. *Social Capital and Welfare Reform: Government, Non-profits, Congregations and Community in Pennsylvania and Wisconsin.* New York: Columbia University Press.

Stack, Carol. 1974. *All Our Kin: Strategies for Survival in a Black Community.* New York: Harper and Row.

APPENDIX
Research Studies

Pennsylvania Projects

1. *Social Networks, Career and Training Paths for Participants in Education and Training Programs for the Disadvantaged* (Social Network Study) is a statistical study of 338 people enrolled in nine training programs or community college in Philadelphia conducted in late 1995 through 1996. Study participants came from a stratified sample of people in training programs that served the range of low-income individuals in the Philadelphia area.

2. *Life Experience of Welfare Recipients*, the qualitative companion project to the Social Network Study, includes life history interviews of 20 individuals and participant observation of more than 100 public assistance recipients in education and training programs offered by the Institute for the Study of Civic Values. These data were supplemented with data from case files from the Alternative Work Experience Program from 1992 through 1997.

3. *Community Women's Education Project (CWEP) Anonymous Survey Analysis* is a statistical study of 373 people enrolled in the CWEP WorkStart program over 5 years. The sample included everyone who participated in CWEP programs during this time. CWEP is an innovative adult basic education and career preparation program for women. At the time of the study, 69 percent of the study population was on welfare and 76 percent had been on welfare at some point in their lives.

4. *The Alternative Work Experience Program Evaluation* is an evaluation of a model service learning workfare program for two-parent families on welfare, based on program statistics for 154 individuals and ethnographic observations of that program from 1993 through 1995.

5. *Economic, Racial, and Educational Census Mapping Project* analyzes 1990 census maps of Philadelphia and the Philadelphia region. The project consisted of creating a series of maps each for the city of Philadelphia and the SMSA that included data on race, Hispanic origin, income, poverty, education levels, employment, unemployment, types of employment, housing, welfare use, and travel to work.

6. *Survey of Training Providers in Philadelphia* is a questionnaire study of 29 training programs in Philadelphia conducted in 1992-93.

7. *The Education and Training System in Philadelphia* is the companion anthropological study to the Survey of Training Providers examining Philadelphia Private Industry Council and Commonwealth and federal documents on training and welfare reform, as well as my notes on working with training programs. Research was conducted between 1992 and 1997.

8. *The Rapid Attachment Study* is a statistical study of an administrative database for a short-term job readiness and job placement program in Philadelphia. The database includes demographic information; government program utilization; information on substance abuse and criminal history; work and

training history, interviewer assessments of presentation, attitude, dress, and interviewing techniques; Test of Adult Basic Education (TABE) math and reading scores; and job placement information for 718 people who participated in this program from February 1996 to February 1997.

Wisconsin Projects

1. *Kenosha Conversation Project* was a community needs assessment project on welfare reform in Kenosha, a small city in southeastern Wisconsin. Research consisted of focus groups with stakeholders involved in welfare reform [program participants; Kenosha County Job Center (KCJC) and Department of Human Services administrators, program managers, and line staff; social service agency staff; employers; government officials; church representatives; concerned advocacy organizations], combined with interviews with key people involved in welfare reform and participant observation in KCJC and one advocacy organization.

2. *Neighborhood Settlement House Evaluation Study* was an evaluation study of the effects of changing welfare and child welfare policy on a Milwaukee community-based organization, its neighborhood, and its participants. This project was a multi-method team study consisting of four components: (1) ethnography of the Neighborhood Settlement House and the agencies associated with the facility; (2) in-depth interview study of Neighborhood Settlement House participants (48 families); (3) community resource analysis through statistical mapping of the neighborhood, windshield survey of community organizations (tabulating available organizations and gathering basic information), and interviews with selected organizations and churches; and (4) analysis of Neighborhood Settlement House administrative databases and correlation of those data with available demographic resources on the community.

3. *Kenosha Social Capital Study* was a study of the Latino and African American sub-communities of Kenosha focusing on the dynamic between Latino and African American focused community-based organizations and churches, community residents, employers, and the city-wide community organization and church context. This multi-method team study consisted of four components: (1) ethnography in key organizations and churches serving these communities; (2) life history interviews with 26 families (15 Latino, 11 African American) regarding social resources, work, education, and involvement in organizations and churches; (3) interviews with key actors in Kenosha and the African American and Latino communities; and (4) a survey of employment practices of Kenosha employers.

4. *Milwaukee Interfaith Welfare Projects*. Research with Milwaukee Interfaith included three activities. First, participant observation of the agency and its advocacy programs were conducted by myself and a student for approximately a year and a half. Second, ethnographic research collected written material from the agency on these efforts, and, third, interviews were conducted with key staff in addition to the recording of participant observation notes.

Welfare Status and Child Care as Obstacles to Full-Time Work for Low-Income Mothers

Julie Press, Temple University
Janice Johnson-Dias, Temple University
Jay Fagan, Temple University

SUMMARY. In this study, we use new data from the Philadelphia Survey of Child Care and Work to expand on previous analyses: we include child care problems as a work obstacle, and we analyze both current welfare recipients and non-welfare "working poor" mothers. Results show that two main obstacles have a large impact on full-time work: poor mental health and child care problems. Net of other factors, mothers with severe child care problems are 22 percent less likely to work full time. Dividing the sample by welfare status, we find a child care problems effect for both groups. Among welfare recipients, the gap in full-time work between those with severe child care problems and those without is 30 percent. Among the working poor, child care problems reduce the chance of full-time work by about 18 percent. Our findings show that improving mothers' child care situation can significantly improve their ability to support their families. *[Article copies available for a fee from The Haworth Document Delivery Service: 1-800-HAWORTH. E-mail address: <docdelivery@haworthpress.com> Website: <http://www.HaworthPress.com> © 2005 by The Haworth Press, Inc. All rights reserved.]*

[Haworth co-indexing entry note]: "Welfare Status and Child Care as Obstacles to Full-Time Work for Low-Income Mothers." Press, Julie, Janice Johnson-Dias, and Jay Fagan. Co-published simultaneously in *Journal of Women, Politics & Policy* (The Haworth Political Press, an imprint of The Haworth Press, Inc.) Vol. 27, No. 3/4, 2005, pp. 55-79; and: *Women, Work, and Poverty: Women Centered Research for Policy Change* (ed: Heidi Hartmann) The Haworth Political Press, an imprint of The Haworth Press, Inc., 2005, pp. 55-79. Single or multiple copies of this article are available for a fee from The Haworth Document Delivery Service [1-800-HAWORTH, 9:00 a.m. - 5:00 p.m. (EST). E-mail address: docdelivery@haworthpress.com].

Available online at http://www.haworthpress.com/web/JWPP
doi:10.1300/J501v27n03_05

KEYWORDS. Children, employment, working poor, Philadelphia, mental health, TANF

INTRODUCTION

Over the past six years the dramatic decline in welfare caseloads has led to a plethora of research on the employability of recipients. Generally, these studies have found that welfare recipients' individual obstacles, either singly or in combination, interfere with getting jobs, keeping jobs and increasing wages. While the findings from these studies contribute significantly to our knowledge about recipients' employment barriers, typically they overlook and/or underestimate the role of child care problems, transportation to work, and structural problems, such as neighborhood poverty, in recipients' employment. Further, these studies typically exclude non-welfare "working-poor" families in their analyses–those who work, but who nonetheless remain poor. In this study, we investigate obstacles to full-time work for low-income urban mothers. We address both of these missing pieces of the literature by including the role of child care problems and neighborhood poverty effects, and by including welfare and non-welfare mothers in our sample to explore whether and how these two populations differ in access to full-time work. How women's individual, occupational, family, and neighborhood factors obstruct their access to employment is not only a question of theoretical interest that informs our understanding of the mechanisms of social inequality but it is also a question with significant policy importance. Obstacles like child care problems that prevent parents from working enough hours to support their families can be alleviated through a public policy response. In this analysis we shed light on the magnitude of the problem.

Building on the research of Danziger et al. (2000), we explore how a variety of individual, work, family, and structural factors influence both Temporary Assistance to Needy Families (TANF) and non-TANF mothers' employment outcomes. Danziger and colleagues provide a solid foundation on which to understand these issues. They expand on the traditional definition of barriers to employment by including mental and physical health issues, an approach that highlights the obstructive effects of co-occurring work problems on welfare recipients' employment chances. While a majority of their findings support previous research in this area, the findings also point to the need to pay closer attention to the influence of transportation, job skills, and women's mental and physical health on recipients' employment outcomes.

But like their predecessors, Danziger et al. (2000) underestimate the link between and structural factors and employment outcomes. As such, they do not examine how other crucially important structural issues such as neighborhood poverty may also influence women's employment chances. Further, they do not examine the influence of child care problems on work outcomes. Finally, because the sample used in their research is limited to welfare mothers, they cannot analyze how obstructive these work barriers are for low-income mothers who are not welfare-reliant. In this study, we theorize obstacles[1] facing the worker as operating at four distinct levels of analysis: individual, familial, occupational, and social structural. We attempt to fill in these gaps in the previous literature using data for low-income working mothers from the Philadelphia Survey of Child Care and Work (Press and Fagan 2003).

A strong argument could be made that many or perhaps most of the factors conceptualized in this study as work obstacles are more structural than they are individual, including child care, transportation, and even the more traditional individual human capital measures like educational attainment. A city like Philadelphia invokes this critique with its very low quality public education system that disadvantages those who cannot afford private school much more than similar individuals living in other U.S. cities. Personal illness seems like an individual obstacle, but we know that asthma, for example, is found in higher rates in poor neighborhoods, making it more structural than individual. Our child care system is privatized rather than publicly provided (with the exception of child care subsidies). Yet, the fact that child care provision is unequal as a social system, with more affluent families spending a lower share of their budget on higher quality child care, means that the structure of the child care system is not individual level or family level. Thus, without calling all of our measures "structural," we divided them into categories that align with the units of analysis.

Individual Level Obstacles

The role of individual level obstacles on poor women's employment is well documented in scholarly research, the media, and everyday chatter. Indeed, they have been posited as the most important reasons for why some women are able to gain employment while others are not. Both welfare and non-welfare studies have demonstrated that low educational attainment, few employment skills, poor work experience, and inadequate English language skills can either constrain or prevent mothers from obtaining viable employment (Bane and Ellwood 1994; O'Neil, Bassi, and Wolf 1987). The long-term effects of these individual failings are such that some women may secure employment, only to lose it again, while others simply are unable to get jobs (Stratton 1996).

Beyond educational attainment and job experience, health problems also adversely impact women's employment chances. Findings from welfare studies show that a significant number of recipients face a collection of co-occurring health obstacles that limit employment, or the kind and amount of work they can do (Loprest and Acs 1995). These include mental and physical health issues, addictions, and domestic violence (Olson and Pavetti 1996; Jayakody, Danziger, and Pollack 2000; Tolman and Raphael 2000).

Family Level Obstacles

Child care problems such as high cost, poor quality, and unreliability can have an adverse affect on low-income women's work outcomes. Turner (1998) found a high percentage (74 percent) of low-income respondents indicated they quit or were terminated from their jobs or training programs because they did not earn enough to pay for child care. Studies reveal that low-income mothers pay a disproportionately higher percentage of their income on child care than do higher income mothers (Anderson and Levine 2000). Households with incomes below $14,400 spent 25 percent of their yearly income on child care (U.S. Department of Health and Human Services 1999).

Poor child care quality also may have a negative effect on mothers' employment. Mothers on AFDC reported being more likely to drop out of job training programs when their child was in poor quality care, measured as staffing ratios and parental perceptions of safety (Meyers 1993). The issue of quality may be particularly relevant to families in the United States because of wide variation in the quality of available care. In the 1994 Nationwide Review of Health and Safety Standards at Child Care Facilities, a total of 1,000 violations were found in 169 child care facilities located in five states (U.S. Department of Health and Human Services 1999).

The reliability of a child care arrangement is a significant issue for many mothers. Myers (1993) found that 59 percent of low-income mothers missed school or work due to child care problems. Further, reliability is a significant predictor of mothers' dropping out of a training program (Myers 1993). Press (2000) found that child care problems significantly reduce mothers' chances of employment and work hours. In the present study, we hypothesize that the number of child care problems has a negative effect on the odds that low-income women work full time in the labor market.

Children's health problems and family responsibilities also negatively impact women's employment chances (Wolfe and Hill 1995). Brandon and Hogan (2001) found that disabled children generally reduced the number of hours that mothers work. Research from welfare-to-work demonstration studies also finds that child health problems among some recipients contribute to job loss (Hershey and Pavetti 1997). Even when mothers themselves are healthy and able to work, chronically ill children can make it difficult for them to obtain and keep employment.

An extension of family obstacles is transportation to work. Time spent commuting between home and work is a demand on parents' time and energy. Although riding the bus is cheaper than car ownership, busses have limited schedules and make it more difficult to change work hours and child pickups and drop-offs with short notice. We hypothesize that riding the bus to work is associated with the likelihood that low-income women do not work full time.

Occupation Level Obstacles

The hours that low-skilled women work are also affected by the characteristics of the occupation or job itself. Feminized occupations that employ at least 70 percent female workers are more likely to be part time, and very low-wage jobs are also associated with part-time work. This finding is further complicated by race and ethnicity, since women of color are disproportionately likely to serve in these less desirable jobs. Not only do Blacks have a lower probability than Whites of being employed full time, but Latinas and African American women face dual constraints on their opportunities: they are segregated into the lower paying female dominated positions, and they are further drawn into occupations that are heavily represented by coethnics (Reskin 1993; Browne, Tigges, and Press 2001). Hispanics, the fastest growing minority group, face similar challenges to Blacks; however, their immigrant status and language may also mean more employment obstacles and more barriers.

Structural Obstacles

Sociological perspectives on work obstacles for low-income mothers have focused on the role that structure plays in their employment outcomes. Factors such as neighborhood poverty (Wilson 1987), racial residential segregation (Massey and Denton 1993; Jargowsky 1997), and gender relations in families and the labor market (Pearce 1978) have all been found to obstruct employment chances and quality. While current discussions around these issues have also focused on welfare-reliant mothers, other compelling evidence suggests that low-income non-welfare working mothers experience similar challenges. In fact, welfare mothers and non-welfare working families who live side by side in the same impoverished neighborhoods and even households tend to cycle on and off welfare use and be each other's relatives and social ties, as opposed to being distinct groups (Newman 1999).

Low-wage, non-TANF mothers pay more than TANF moms for transportation because of commuting cost and travel to and from their day care provider (Edin and Lein 1997), but because the working poor often are not targeted for government subsidy programs, their employment challenges are sometimes ignored and/or overlooked.

Structural factors such as the neighborhood context and social resources can also impose additional obstacles for low-income mothers' employment. Neighborhoods, in particular, have both a direct and an indirect influence on the creation and perpetuation of unemployment and continued welfare use (Edin and Lein 1997; Harris 1996). Directly, place of residence can provide or restrict access to essential resources and thus influences employment outcomes. Impoverished neighborhoods often lack accessible or affordable child care and transportation (Bullard, Johnson, and Torres 2000); likewise, these neighborhood poverty rates may also constrain the number and types of available jobs (Wilson 1987). Typically, these communities do not have a sufficient number or adequate health care institutions, the result of which are higher rates of health problems among the poor (Shiono, Rauh, and Park 1997). Research has found that children living in poverty are at a higher risk of exposure to conditions that produce adverse health effects (Parker, Greer, and Zuckerman 1988). In addition, the daily stress of living in a poor neighborhood where, typically, social order has broken down is associated with depression (Ross and Jang 2000).

Indirectly, neighborhoods impact one's social networks, which are a major source of finding jobs (Montgomery 1992). The spatial isolation of low-income neighborhoods can lead to social isolation, and social isolation accompanied by labor market insulation can create an increased reliance upon neighbors and personal contacts for securing formal employment (Elliot 1999). Green, Tigges, and Diaz (1999) found that this kind of reliance on informal network members often leads to lower paying jobs. In sum, the personal factors that directly and nega-tively affect recipients' employment chances are linked to their place of residence, illustrating the ongoing role of the social environment on em-ployment. The combination of these individual and structural issues may dramatically reduce some recipients' likelihood of finding and keeping employment.

Philadelphia is an ideal place to study the impact of structural condi-tions on low-income women's employment outcomes. Philadelphia has suffered economically in ways common to many northern cities: this slow growth region continues to decentralize, separating inner-city resi-dents from jobs and economic activity. At the same time, its residents have fairly low educational attainment and low rates of labor market ac-tivity. In 2000, only 56 percent of working age adults in Philadelphia participated in the labor force. Socially, the population is also diversify-ing away from White, native-born residents toward non-White and im-migrant residents as well as toward an aging populace (Brookings Institution 2003). This diversification has been accompanied by a shrinking middle class and rising poverty for individuals and families. The poverty rate in 2000 was 23 percent in the city overall (a 2.6 percent increase from 1990) while the child poverty rate was nearly one-third. If we look at families in poverty or near poverty, recent findings from The Brookings Institution show that among the nearly 200,000 families with children in Philadelphia, 38 percent are living below 150 percent of the poverty line (Brookings Institution 2003).

With so many poor families, the city has both a substantial welfare population, as well as a substantial non-welfare, working-poor popula-tion. The welfare caseload fell 29 percent from the 1996 reform to 1999, and by 2001 the average monthly caseload in the city was about 40,000 (Michalopoulos et al. 2003). We estimate that roughly 44 percent of the 90,000 poor or near-poor families (< 185 percent of poverty) in Phila-delphia were receiving TANF in 2000.

DATA AND METHODS

Data Collection Procedures

To investigate the effect of child care issues on mothers' work out-comes, we collected new quantitative data, the *Philadelphia Survey of Child Care and Work* (PSCCW) (Press and Fagan 2003). The PSCCW is designed to broaden our knowledge and understanding of the relationship between child care problems and work outcomes. The PSCCW is a one-hour, door-to-door, face-to-face survey administered to a stratified random cluster sample of 1,070 Philadelphia, Pennsylvania, mothers. The U.S. Census tracts sampled were stratified three ways: by poverty concentration rate (high poverty: greater than 40 percent, medium poverty: 20-40 percent, low poverty: less than 20 percent); by racial residential segregation rate (highly segregated: 2/3 or more of one race/ethnicity dominates, and mixed race: no race has a majority); and by respondent race/ethnicity (Black/African American, White, or Hispanic/Latina). Participants had to have at least one child under age 13 in the household and had to have worked at least 6 months out of the last 12 months, for at least 10 hours a week to qualify. Given our work requirement for study participation, the hardest to employ are likely not included in the sample (e.g., serious substance abusers, seriously mentally ill, etc.).[2]

The response rate for the number of completed interviews divided by the number of eligible households is 53 percent. While this is an ample rate to conduct analysis, concerns about potential non-response bias led us to examine possible explanations. We found that the rate of census tract poverty or racial residential segregation had no significant impact on the likelihood of an eligible respondent completing a survey. Instead, we found that certain interviewers were less likely to follow through and complete surveys with eligible respondents. Therefore, we are confident that our findings do not differ drastically from the true population because our source of non-response is primarily the result of interviewer effects.

For this analysis we compare current welfare recipients with non-welfare working-poor mothers in poor neighborhoods. We therefore use a sub-sample of employed adult mothers (age 18 or older) selected only from the high and medium poverty neighborhoods. We include only respondents with household income below two times the federal poverty line for their given household size (n = 412). The sample with missing data excluded contains 395 respondents.

Analytic Strategy

Our research strategy is to examine the effects of obstacles facing working mothers to determine whether and to what degree these obstacles affect the probability of full-time work hours, defined as at least 35 per week. We also determine whether these effects differ for welfare mothers compared with similar non-welfare "working-poor" mothers.

First, we examine the welfare and working-poor populations at the univariate level to explore possible differences in the samples. Next, we conduct a bivariate analysis of those who work full time compared with those who work part time to test which work obstacles are different for full- and part-timers. Third, we use logistic regression analysis to model the effects of obstacles on full-time employment. We first estimate the effects for the full sample and then we model the TANF and non-TANF populations separately. Finally, we use the full model to simulate policy outcomes for different combinations of obstacles and make policy recommendations.

Variables and Measurement

Dependent Variable: Full-Time Work

The dependent variable in this study is full-time work hours. Respondents were asked about up to three current jobs. The survey question asked, "How many hours a week do you usually work at this job?" The dependent variable uses the total number of hours reported on all of these jobs. Mothers who spent 35 hours or more per week on all jobs are coded as 1 for full-time workers. Those working 1 through 34 hours are coded as 0 for part-time work. Seventy percent of the sample works full time by this definition. The first column of Table 1 shows the distribution of the variables used in the study as a percentage of 395 observations.

Independent Variables: Work Obstacles and Welfare

The independent variables included in the analysis are welfare status and a set of 11 dummy variables that represent hypothesized obstacles to full-time work. Welfare status is measured as a dummy variable with current TANF recipients coded as 1 (74 observations, 19 percent) and non-TANF, working-poor mothers coded as 0 (321 observations, 81 percent).

We theorize work obstacles as operating at the individual (mother) level, family level, and structural level. Mothers' individual level factors that obstruct her work hours comprise health (physical, mental), human capital (education, experience, English language skill), and job characteristics (low wage, feminized). Respondents who reported that a health condition limits the type of work they can do were defined as having a physical health problem (15.7 percent). Respondents who reported that they feel anxious or depressed "most of the time" or "usu-

TABLE 1. Description of Sample

	Total	TANF	Non-TANF
Dependent Variable: Work Hours			
Full time, 35 hours or more	69.9%	45.9%***	75.4%
Part time, < 35 hours	30.1	54.1	24.6
Individual-Level Obstacles			
Health			
Mother has physical health problem	15.7	25.7**	13.4
Mother has low mental health score (depressed, anxious)	14.4	18.9	13.4
Human Capital			
Education			
Less than high school	29.1	52.7***	23.7
High school graduate	62.3	44.6***	66.4
More than high school	8.6	2.7*	10.0
Low work experience (worked < 20% of time since age 16)	15.7	35.7***	11.5
Difficulty with English	8.9	13.5	7.8
Occupation-Level Obstacles			
Feminized occupation ($\geq$ 70% female)	60.0	59.5	60.1
Poverty wage job	18.5	39.2***	13.7
Family-Level Obstacles			
Child care problems (3 or more)	13.4	27.0***	10.3
Does not own car	57.7	73.0**	54.2
Child with health/behavior problem	20.3	23.0	19.6
Structural-Level Obstacles			
High poverty neighborhood	48.1	55.4	46.4
Controls			
Married/Cohabiting	32.2	18.9**	35.2
Race/Ethnicity			
Black	42.0	36.5	43.3
Hispanic/Latina	38.5	56.8***	34.3
White	19.5	6.8**	22.4
Age (mean, std. dev., range 18-66)	32.6 (8.5)	31.3 (8.4)	33.0 (8.5)
Number of children age 0-2 (mean, std. dev., range 0-2)	0.347 (.56)	0.540 (.67)***	0.302 (.53)
Number of children age 3-5 (mean, std. dev., range 0-2)	0.408 (.56)	0.405 (.57)	0.408 (.56)
N	395	74	321
	(100%)	(19%)	(81%)

ANOVA by Welfare Status

$* p < .05; ** p < .01; *** p < .001$

ally" were coded as having a general mental health problem (14.4 percent). A respondent is considered to have an education obstacle if she neither graduated from high school nor received a GED. To measure low work experience we first calculated work experience. We divided the number of years a respondent worked at least six months since age 16 by the difference between her age and years of education. We then coded a dummy variable for mothers whose work experience is less than 20 percent (15.7 percent). Interviews were conducted in both English and Spanish. Respondents who were not native speakers were asked about their English language skills. Those who reported that they speak or read English "not well" or "not at all" were coded 1 and defined as having an English language obstacle (8.9 percent).

Characteristics of mothers' job that are associated with part-time work hours are feminized occupations and very low-wage jobs. We calculated the percent female for detailed occupations in the 2000 U.S. Census and then coded sample respondents with those percentages that matched their occupation. Then we dichotomized the variable and coded respondents whose occupation is 70 percent or more female as 1 (60 percent of our sample) and those with fewer than 70 percent as 0. Low-wage employment is defined as a job at which full-time work, year round still leaves the worker living below the poverty level. To measure low-wage work, we used the wage rate of $6.25 an hour, which is a poverty wage for a single mother and one child. This measure does not mean the family is necessarily living in poverty, only that the mother's wage rate is so low that she would not be able to support herself and one child solely on it. Mothers earning poverty level wages are coded as 1 (18.5 percent), while those earning more are coded as 0.

Family level work obstacles include child care problems, children's health or behavior problems, and transportation problems. Child care problems were measured by dichotomizing an index of five survey items. The items asked respondents: In the past 12 months did you have problems looking or applying for work because of child care issues? In the past 12 months have you had problems participating in school or a training program because of your child care situation? In the past 12 months, would you say that the quality of your work at your job suffered because you were concerned about your child's well-being with the care provider? In the past 12 months have you been offered a more desirable job that you were unable to take because of your child care situation? During the last 12 months, has an employer or prospective employer asked you what you will do with your children while you work? The "yes" responses were summed across the five items so that the index ranges from no problems with child care that interfered with work (0) through many child care problems that interfere with work (5). The internal reliability (Cronbach's alpha) for these items was .72. A crosstabular analysis between the child care problem index and the dependent variable, full-time work, showed a significant difference between 2 problems or less and 3 problems or more. We dichotomized the index at 3 or more problems and coded the child care problems obstacle as 1 (13.4 percent).

To measure the obstacle of a special needs child, respondents were asked "Do any of your children have a physical, learning, mental health, or behavior problem that limits their participation in the usual kinds of activities done by most kids their age, or limits their ability to do regular school work?" Those who responded yes were defined as having a special needs child with a health or behavior problem (20.3 percent). The third family level obstacle is transportation. Respondents who reported that they do not own a car were coded 1. The majority of respondents in the study do not own a car (57.7 percent).

We included one structural level obstacle in the analysis, whether the respondent lives in a high poverty neighborhood. This variable is one of the sampling strata of the survey; roughly equal numbers of respondents were sampled from both high and medium poverty neighborhoods. Recall that high poverty neighborhoods contain at least 40 percent of households in poverty, while medium poverty neighborhoods are only 20 percent to 40 percent poor, based on census tract level data analysis from the 2000 U.S. Census. We define high poverty neighborhoods as a work obstacle and coded them as 1 (48.1 percent).

Controls

Demographic control variables include dummy variables for married or cohabiting (32 percent), and race/ethnicity (non-Hispanic Black [42 percent], Hispanic/Latina [38.5 percent], White [19.5 percent]). Whites are the omitted category in the regression analysis. We also measured the age of the respondent in years (respondents are between 18 and 66 and the average respondent in the sample is 33), and the number of young children for whom the respondent is responsible. The variables measuring the number of young children are grouped into infants and toddlers aged 0 to 2, and preschool children aged 3 to 5. Both variables range from 0 through 2 children per household and have median of 0. The mean number of birth to 2-year-olds is .35 and the mean number of preschoolers is 0.4.

RESULTS

Table 1 analyzes the variables in the study by welfare status. We conducted an analysis of variance (ANOVA) to assess statistical significance for differences between the TANF and non-TANF samples. We find several large differences between the samples, as well as many factors that are indistinguishable for these families. Not surprisingly, welfare mothers are employed fewer hours on average than working poor mothers. However, it is important to note that contrary to popular perception, close to half (46 percent) of welfare mothers in the sample hold full-time jobs.

Among the work obstacles measured, we find significant differences between the samples for mothers' individual obstacles. TANF mothers in our data are much more likely to have poor physical health, low work experience, low educational attainment and very low wages. On the other hand, the two groups of women are also similar on several measures, including mental health, difficulty with English, and feminized occupational segregation. Regarding family level obstacles, we find that TANF mothers are 19 percent less likely to own a car and are more than twice as likely as non-welfare recipients to report many child care problems. We find no relevant difference for the special needs child obstacle that is faced by about one-fifth of families. Although welfare mothers are 9 percent more likely to face the structural obstacle of life in a high poverty neighborhood, the difference is not statistically significant.

Bivariate Analysis

Table 2 shows the results of a bivariate analysis of the effect of the independent measures of work obstacles on the dependent variable, full-time work hours. We compare the percentage of mothers working full time among those who face each obstacle to the percentage working full time among those who do not face the obstacle. Recall that about 70 percent of our sample reported full-time work. When we disaggregate and look at women facing obstacles, we find typically lower rates of full-time work from a low of 49 percent to a high of 74 percent. Most of the rates are in the 60s. The women who do not face obstacles have higher rates of full-time work in the low 70 percents. Chi-squared tests show that there are statistically significant differences between those facing obstacles and those who do not for most of the items. The biggest problem is caused by child care, which lowers the rate of full-time work

TABLE 2. Bivariate Analysis: Percent Working Full Time, by Type of Obstacle

Obstacles to Full-Time Work	Percent (n) Working Full Time *With* Obstacle	Percent (n) Working Full Time *Without* Obstacle	Difference
Individual			
Mother has low mental health score	54.4	72.5	18.1***
	(57)	(338)	
Mother has physical health problem	61.3	71.5	10.2†
	(62)	(333)	
Low educational attainment	64.3	72.1	7.8†
	(114)	(280)	
Low work experience	58.1	72.1	14.0**
	(62)	(333)	
English language difficulty	74.3	69.4	−4.9
	(35)	(360)	
Occupation			
Feminized occupation	66.7	74.7	8.0*
	(237)	(158)	
Poverty wage job	61.6	71.7	10.1*
	(73)	(322)	
Family			
Child care problems (severe)	49.1	73.1	24.0****
	(53)	(342)	
Child with health or behavioral problem	72.5	69.2	−3.3
	(80)	(315)	
Does not own a car	66.7	74.3	7.6†
	(228)	(167)	
Structural			
High poverty neighborhood	70.0	69.8	−0.2
	(190)	(205)	

Chi-Square, * p < .10, ** p < .05, *** p < .01, **** p < .001
† p < .10 in one-sided test

from 73 percent down to only 49 percent, a gap of 24 percent. Mothers with depression and anxiety are also much less likely to work full time, with a gap of 18 percent. For three items, the chance of full-time work is lower without the obstacle. For high poverty neighborhood, the gap is tiny and not significant. For English language difficulty, it is also not significant; the number of people with the obstacle is so small (only 26) that the percentage is very sensitive to the addition or subtraction of one or two observations. For special needs child, the difference is also not statistically significant. However, it may be that people with sick children do have to work more hours than others, perhaps because of health insurance or other issues. Nonetheless, until we use multivariate methods, we cannot accurately analyze these relationships. The next stage in the analysis uses logistic modeling to predict full-time work for all of the obstacles simultaneously, comparing models with individual, family, and structural obstacles.

Modeling Full-Time Work

Table 3 presents the outcome of the logistic regression model predicting full-time work for the whole sample of 395 low-income, working mothers. Results show that by far the biggest predictor of work hours is TANF recipiency; once we control for other factors, welfare mothers are about 28 percent less likely to work full time compared with similar mothers who are not on welfare (B = -1.3, p < .000).

Among the work obstacles measured for the analysis, we find one individual level obstacle and one family level obstacle that are statistically significant predictors of full-time work, although the magnitude of the effects is smaller than for welfare receipt. The individual level obstacle of mental health problems like depression or anxiety is associated with greatly reduced work hours (B = -0.91, p = .010). The family level obstacle of child care problems has a similar large and negative effect on the ability to work full time (B = -0.97, p = .009). None of the other individual level or family level factors has a large coefficient or is statistically significant in the model. Further, our hypothesis that living in a high poverty neighborhood would have a negative impact on work hours is not supported.

Among the demographic controls, Hispanics/Latinas are more likely than White women to work full time. Age, number of young children, and marital status are not found to be important predictors.

Modeling Full-Time Work by Welfare Status

Since welfare status was the single biggest predictor of full-time work, and also to test the hypothesis that TANF mothers are very different in their attachment to paid employment compared with similar poor women who are not on welfare, we ran separate models for the two pop-

TABLE 3. Logistic Regression Model Predicting Full-Time Work (35 Hours or More)

	B	Standard Error
Welfare (TANF) Recipient	−1.273***	0.312
Work Obstacles		
Individual-level obstacles		
Mother's general anxiety problem	−0.910**	0.355
Mother's physical health problem	0.0004	0.353
Low educational attainment	−0.052	0.294
Low work experience	−0.166	0.344
English language difficulty	0.556	0.535
Occupation-level obstacles		
Poverty-wage job	−0.234	0.332
Feminized occupation	−0.337	0.253
Family-level obstacles		
Child care problems (3 or more)	−0.967**	0.372
Sick/special needs child	0.469	0.333
No car	−0.225	0.263
Structural-level obstacles		
High poverty neighborhood	−0.164	0.259
Demographic Controls		
Married or cohabiting	−0.176	0.284
Black (White omitted)	0.486	0.333
Hispanic/Latina (White omitted)	0.785**	0.363
Age	0.0055	0.017
Number of children 0-2	0.259	0.249
Number of children 3-5	0.113	0.233
Constant	1.033	0.708
N	395	
R^2 (Nagelkerke)	0.172	
Model Chi-Square (significance of model)	51.2***	

* $p < .10$, ** $p < .05$, *** $p < .001$

ulations. The results of this analysis are presented in Table 4. When we study welfare and non-welfare mothers separately, we find little evidence to support the conclusion that the two groups are vastly different when it comes to their labor market behavior. That is, apart from welfare receipt, the two groups are quite similar.

TABLE 4. Logistic Regression Model Predicting Full-Time Work (35 Hours or More), by Welfare Status

	TANF/ Welfare		Non-Welfare Working Poor	
	B	Standard Error	B	Standard Error
Work Obstacles				
Individual-level obstacles				
Mother's general anxiety problem	−1.604[a]	0.990	−0.864**	0.404
Mother's physical health problem	−1.193	0.980	0.274	0.431
Low educational attainment	0.900	0.670	−0.250	0.343
Low work experience	−1.179	0.780	0.141	0.456
English language problem	−0.372	1.153	1.407*	0.844
Occupation-level obstacles				
Feminized occupation	−0.018	0.666	−0.359	0.291
Poverty-wage job	−0.594	0.677	−0.369	0.420
Family-level obstacles				
Child care problems (severe)	−1.328[b]	0.880	−0.867*	0.456
Sick/special needs child	1.377	0.882	0.294	0.371
No car	−1.112	0.841	−0.135	0.291
Structural-level obstacles				
High poverty neighborhood	−1.245[c]	0.771	−0.015	0.291
Demographic Controls				
Married or cohabiting	−0.015	0.828	−0.137	0.313
Black (White omitted)	−0.967	1.413	0.524	0.354
Hispanic/Latina (White omitted)	0.092	1.404	0.690*	0.389
Age	0.035	0.047	0.0029	0.019
Number of children 0-2	0.863	0.601	0.269	0.304
Number of children 3-5	−0.956	0.694	0.269	0.276
Constant	1.339	2.372	0.927	0.771
N	74		321	
R^2 (Nagelkerke)	34%		11%	
Model Chi-Square (neither is significant)	21.7		23.7	

* $p < .10$, ** $p < .05$, *** $p < .001$
[a] $p = .105$
[b] $p < .06$ in one-tailed test
[c] $p = .106$

We see that child care problems and mental health problems still have large, negative effects on full-time work hours. In fact, the coefficients for the welfare mothers are much larger than for the non-welfare working-poor mothers. The small number of welfare mothers in our sample, only 74 respondents, means that the statistical precision of the coefficients is not as high as in the full sample. However, the point estimate of child care problems is large and sociologically significant. Further using a one sided test (i.e., the alternative hypothesis is that the coefficient is negative), it is statistically significant at the 6 percent level. Child care problems and mental health problems pose serious obstacles to full-time work for low income working mothers in Philadelphia.

There is also a new obstacle whose effect was masked in the full model (Table 3), that emerges as important in Table 4 when we divide the samples: residence in a high poverty neighborhood.[3] Living in a high poverty neighborhood has a vastly different coefficient for welfare mothers (B = -1.2, p = .106) than it does for non-welfare mothers (B = -0.02, p = .96). All else held constant, a welfare mother living in a highly concentrated poverty neighborhood in Philadelphia (poverty greater than 40 percent within the census tract) is much less likely to find full-time work compared with a similar welfare mother living in a medium poverty neighborhood (20 percent to 40 percent of households in poverty).

Policy Predictions

Logistic regression models are nonlinear and therefore are difficult to interpret and understand intuitively. A more accessible way to understand the findings is to use the model to make predictions with the values from the dataset. To calculate the probability of full-time work, P, we used the logit equation, $P = 1/(1 + e^{-(a+BX)})$, where B is the set of coefficients we estimated in the model, X is the set of corresponding means for those variables and a is the constant. Holding all of the variables at their means, and setting only one dummy variable at a time to 0 or 1, we can simulate a policy experiment in which an obstacle is imagined to either exist or to disappear. In Table 5, we present the results of some of these simulated experiments. We present the results for the largest effects in the model that affect the probability of full-time work: TANF receipt, at least three child care problems, mental health problems and residence in a high poverty neighborhood.

TABLE 5. Policy Predictions for Full-Time Work

Obstacles	Predicted Rate of Full-Time Work*	
	With Obstacle	Without Obstacle
Full Model (Table 3)		
Welfare/TANF status	47.9%	76.6%
Multiple child care problems	52.8	74.6
Mental health problem	54.3	74.7
Highly concentrated poverty neighborhood	70.3	73.6
Welfare Model (Table 4)		
Severe child care problems	22.5	52.3
Mental health problem	17.3	50.9
Highly concentrated poverty neighborhood	30.5	60.4
Working-Poor Model (Table 4)		
Severe child care problems	61.0	78.8
Mental health problem	61.7	79.3
Highly concentrated poverty neighborhood	77.2	77.4

* All other variables held at their mean.

We find large gaps between the rates of predicted full-time work with and without each obstacle. The first panel in Table 5 uses the full sample to make predictions. First, we predict that all else held constant, about three-fourths of mothers sampled will work full time if they are not welfare-reliant, if they have only a few child care problems, if they do not suffer from anxiety or depression, or if they do not live in a high poverty neighborhood. Second, we find that if any of these obstacles (aside from neighborhood effects) is present, all else held constant, the rate of full-time work is substantially lower. That is, if a mother is welfare-reliant, she is less likely to work full time (48 percent) than if she is not welfare-reliant (76.6 percent). If a mother has severe child care problems, her predicted rate of full-time work is only 52.8 percent. If a mother has mental health problems, her predicted rate of full-time work is only 54.3 percent. For child care and mental health, there is a gap of about 21 percentage points in full-time hours between those who face the obstacle and those who do not. This is a substantively large gap for two factors that can be tackled by policy makers. The equation estimated for the full model did not show neighborhood poverty to be a statistically significant predictor of full-time work; this fact is clear in Table 5 where there is little change in the rate of full-time work between high poverty and medium poverty neighborhoods (70.3 percent versus 73.6 percent).

The remaining two panels of Table 5 use the coefficients from the models run separately by welfare status to make predictions about full-time work hours. Here we see two general patterns. First, the rate of full-time work is higher for the non-welfare group than for the welfare group regardless of the presence of particular work obstacles. Without the obstacles, welfare mothers are predicted to work full time at rates from 50 percent to 60 percent, and with obstacles such as severe child care problems or mental health problems, the range is 17 percent to 31 percent. For the non-TANF sample, more than three-fourths of mothers are expected to work full time if they are not encumbered with obstacles, while those with child care problems or mental health problems will work full time only 61 percent of the time. The second general pattern that emerges from this analysis is the large impact of neighborhood effects for the welfare population that disappears for the non-welfare group. We already saw this finding in the regression result, but it is much clearer in Table 5, where there is virtually no difference between the full-time employment rates by neighborhood poverty in the working-poor model, but there is a two-fold difference in the full-time rate for those on welfare.

We calculated one final prediction to look at the simultaneous effects of welfare and child care problems using the full model. The results are presented in Figure 1. We find that welfare-reliant mothers with severe child care problems have about a 28 percent chance of full-time work, while the other extreme–non-TANF mothers who have minor child care problems–have a much higher chance of full-time work (79 percent). Comparing the difference in the first two bars of Figure 1 is very informative, however. For the non-TANF working poor in the sample, there is still a fairly large effect from child care problems (20 percent). Thus, even though welfare further reduces mothers' access to employment, we can say based on Figure 1 that alleviating child care problems would be an important step for low-income families regardless of their welfare participation.

DISCUSSION AND CONCLUSIONS

In this study, we made two main extensions to the literature on barriers to work. We included a sample of low-income non-TANF families, and we expanded the set of obstacles to include family level and struc-

FIGURE 1

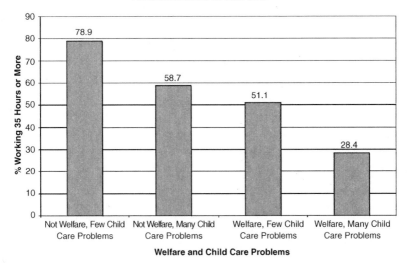

Predicted Rate of Full-Time Work

78.9

58.7

51.1

28.4

% Working 35 Hours or More

Not Welfare, Few Child Care Problems Not Welfare, Many Child Care Problems Welfare, Few Child Care Problems Welfare, Many Child Care Problems

Welfare and Child Care Problems

tural level factors that have not been fully analyzed in previous studies: child care problems and neighborhood poverty effects. We hypothesized that welfare and non-welfare low-income mothers would face many of the same employment obstacles, but we also speculated that there may be some noteworthy differences between them. Our results shed light on these issues.

We find that by focusing solely on individual obstacles researchers may overestimate their effects. Our results show that the largest factor that depresses full-time work is participation in the TANF program. We also find, however, that there is a substantively large and statistically significant relationship between a family level obstacle, child care problems, and full-time work that has not been fully explored in the literature. Only about half of families with severe child care problems are predicted to work full time, while removing those obstacles could potentially increase full-time employment to three-fourths of low-income families. An effect of similar size is also found between mothers' mental health problems and full-time work. Further, both of these obstacles affect mothers' work hours *regardless of welfare receipt*. While the rates of full-time employment are higher for the non-TANF sample than the TANF sample, our results clearly indicate that public policy to improve the child care situation for low-income families could have a very large impact for both groups.

Finally, our results show that despite similar studies suggesting that individual level factors matter the most to women's employment outcomes, the answer may not be so simple. Greater attention should be paid to the structural obstacles such as neighborhood effects. Among the welfare mothers in our sample, those living in highly concentrated poverty neighborhoods are half as likely (only 30 percent) to find full-time work hours according to our estimates.

Over the past few years, the U.S. Congress has been in the process of reauthorizing the TANF program (welfare). Under the new rules, TANF mothers will likely be required to spend 35 or 40 hours per week in paid work. Given this impending change, it is imperative that we understand the role of obstacles in the ability of very low-income families to manage their work and family lives.

AUTHOR NOTE

This study was supported by grants from the U.S. Department of Health and Human Services, Administration for Children and Families, Child Care Bureau, Grant #90YE0039/01-3, by the Ford Foundation, Grant #1005-2071, and by Temple University. The authors are grateful to Sandra Danziger and Simon Potter for many valuable suggestions. The authors are responsible for all of the content in this manuscript; their ideas do not necessarily reflect those of the funders.

Address correspondence to: Julie Press, Sociology Department, Temple University, Philadelphia, PA 19122.

NOTES

1. The word "barrier" connotes an insurmountable condition, while "obstacles" suggest a more temporary state, albeit to varying degrees. We conceptualize a barrier as a severe obstacle, the extreme end of the continuum of obstacles. Not all employment obstacles are actual barriers. Clearly, if a job requires a particular professional degree or license then lacking that credential is a real barrier, at least in the short run without going back to school. Lacking work experience, on the other hand, can be overcome over time by getting more experience in the labor market. Other obstacles, like family responsibilities, may be easier to overcome if outside help, like good child care, for example, were available. Some obstacles, such as race and gender, are hard to pin down and are harder to overcome. These are what Garfinkel (1967) calls omnirelevant, for they are deeply embedded in everyday social interaction, the cultural context of cities, labor markets, families, and other social institutions, and even in the very terms of the welfare state and public policies. We argue that obstacle is a better term to use for em-

ployment problems that do not necessarily rise to the level of such severe barriers, and we use this term throughout the rest of our analysis.

2. Interviews were collected from November 2001 through November 2003. Interviews were conducted on all days of the week and at different times of the day to obtain a sample of mothers who work several different types of schedules. Surveys were collected as early as 9:00 a.m. and as late as 10:00 p.m. The modal start time was 5:00 p.m. Interviewers did not necessarily conduct interviews at the same time they recruited participants. Often they screened respondents and made appointments to do the interview at a later date. In order to maintain rapport between respondents and interviewers, all of the survey interviewers were women and we were successful in matching the race of interviewers with the respondents for the vast majority of the respondents. Interviews were conducted in English and Spanish. Respondents were paid $15 in the form of a Kmart or Target gift card at the end of the interview.

3. The presence of a special needs child has a similar size effect as child care problems for the welfare population (B = 1.4). Having a special needs child is associated with an *increased* rate of full-time work. Note that rather than being an obstacle to full-time work, a sick child seems to create the need for more work hours, not fewer.

REFERENCES

Anderson, P.M. and P.B. Levine. 2000. "Child Care and Mothers' Employment Decisions." In *Finding Jobs: Work and Welfare Reform*, ed. David Card and Rebecca M. Blank. New York: Russell Sage Foundation.

Bane, M.J. and D.T. Ellwood. 1994. *Welfare Realities: From Rhetoric to Reform*. Cambridge, MA: Harvard University Press.

Brandon, P.D. and D.P. Hogan. 2001. "The Effects of Children with Disabilities on Mothers' Exit from Welfare." Paper presented at the Joint Center for Poverty Research Conference.

Brookings Institution Center on Urban and Metropolitan Policy. 2003. "Philadelphia in Focus: A Profile From Census 2000," from *Living Cities: The National Community Development Initiative*. Washington, DC: The Brookings Institution.

Browne, I., L. Tigges, and J.E. Press. 2001. "Inequality Through Labor Markets, Firms, and Families: The Intersection of Gender and Race/Ethnicity Across Three Cities." In *Urban Inequality: Evidence from Four Cities*, ed. Alice O'Connor, Chris Tilly, and Lawrence Bobo. New York: Russell Sage Foundation.

Bullard, R.D., G.S. Johnson, and A.O. Torres, eds. 2000. *Sprawl City: Race, Politics, & Planning in Atlanta*. Washington, DC: Island Press.

Danziger, S.K., M. Cocoran, S. Danziger, C. Heflin, A. Kalil, J. Levin, D. Rosen, K. Seefeldt, K. Siefert, and R. Tolman. 2000. "Barriers to the Employment of Welfare Recipients." In *Prosperity for All? The Economic Boom and African Americans*, eds. R. Cherry and W.M. Rodgers, III. New York: Russell Sage Foundation.

Edin, K. and L. Lein. 1997. *Making Ends Meet: How Single Mothers Survive Welfare and Low-Wage Work*. New York: Russell Sage Foundation.

Elliot, J.R. 1999. "Social Isolation and Labor Market Insulation: Network and Neighborhood Effects on Less-Educated Urban Workers." *The Sociological Quarterly* 40: 199-216.

Garfinkel, H. 1967. *Studies in Ethnomethodology.* Englewood Cliffs, NJ: Prentice-Hall.

Green, G.P., L.M. Tigges, and D. Diaz. 1999. "Racial and Ethnic Differences in Atlanta, Boston and Los Angeles." *Social Science Quarterly* 80(2): 263-278.

Harris, K. 1996. "Life After Welfare: Women, Work and Repeat Dependency." *American Sociological Review* 61(June): 407-26.

Hershey, A.M. and L. Pavetti. 1997. "Turning Job Finders into Job Keepers: The Challenge of Sustaining Employment." In *The Future of Children*, The David and Lucille Packard Foundation. Los Altos, CA: Center for the Future of Children. Spring: 74-86.

Jargowsky, Paul A. 1997. *Poverty and Place: Ghettos, Barrios, and the American City.* New York: Russell Sage Foundation.

Jayakody, R., S. Danziger, and H. Pollack. 2000. "Welfare Reform, Substance Use and Mental Health." *Journal of Health Politics, Policy, and Law* 24(4): 623-651.

Loprest, P. and G. Acs. 1995. "Profiles of Disability Among Families on AFDC." Working Paper. Washington, DC: Urban Institute, November.

Massey, D. and N. Denton. 1993. *American Apartheid: Segregation and the Making of the Underclass.* Cambridge, MA: Harvard University Press.

Meyers, M. 1993. "Child Care in Jobs Employment and Training Programs: What Difference Does Quality Make?" *Journal of Marriage and the Family* 55: 767-783.

Michalopoulos, C., K. Edin, B. Fink, M. Landriscina, D.F. Polit, J.C. Polyne, L. Richburg-Hayes, D. Seith, and N. Verma. 2003. "Welfare Reform in Philadelphia: Implementation, Effects, and Experiences of Poor Families and Neighborhoods." New York: MDRC.

Montgomery, J.D. 1992. "Job Search and Network Composition: Implications of the Strength of Weak Tie Hypothesis." *American Sociological Review* 57: 386-96.

Newman, K. 1999. *No Shame in My Game: The Working Poor in the Inner City.* New York: Knopf and the Russell Sage Foundation.

Olson, L. and L. Pavetti. 1996. "Personal and Family Challenges to the Successful Transition from Welfare to Work." Working Paper. Washington, DC: The Urban Institute.

O'Neill, J., L. Bassi, and D. Wolf. 1987. "The Duration of Welfare Spells." *Review of Economics and Statistics* 69: 241-49.

Parker, S., S. Greer, and B. Zuckerman. 1988. "Double Jeopardy: The Impact of Poverty on Early Childhood Development." *Pediatric Clinician, North America* 35: 1227-1240.

Pearce, D. 1978. "The Feminization of Poverty: Women, Work and Welfare." *Urban and Social Change Review* 11(1-2): 28-36.

Press, Julie E. 2000. "Child Care as Poverty Policy: The Effect of Child Care on Work and Family Poverty." In *Prismatic Metropolis: Inequality in Los Angeles*, ed. Lawrence Bobo, Melvin L. Oliver, James H. Johnson, and Abel Valenzuela. New York: Russell Sage Foundation.

Press, J.E. and F. Fagan. 2003. *The Philadelphia Survey of Child Care and Work.* Philadelphia, PA: Temple University.

Reskin, B.F. 1993. "Sex Segregation in the Workplace." *Annual Review of Sociology* 19: 241-270.

Ross, C.E. and S.J. Jang. 2000. "Neighborhood Disorder, Fear, and Mistrust: The Buffering Role of Social Ties with Neighbors." *American Journal of Community Psychology* 28: 401-420.

Shiono, P.H., V.A. Rauh, M. Park, S.A. Lederman, and D. Zuskar. 1997. "Ethnic Differences in Birthweight: The Role of Lifestyle and Other Factors." *American Journal of Public Health* 87(May): 787-793.

Stratton, L.S. 1996. "Are 'Involuntary' Part-Time Workers Indeed Involuntary?" *Industrial and Labor Relations Review* 49(3)(April): 522-536.

Tolman, R.M. and J. Raphael. 2000. "A Review of Research on Welfare and Domestic Violence." *Journal of Social Issues* 56(4): 655-681.

Turner, D. 1998. "Stated and Unstated Needs: Low Income Families and Child Care." Proceedings of the Twenty-Third Annual Women's Studies Conference University of Wisconsin System Women's Studies Consortium. *Speaking Out: Women, Poverty and Public Policy*, ed. Katherine A. Rhoades and Anne Statham. October 29-31.

U.S. Department of Health and Human Services. 1999. *Access to Child Care for Low-Income Working Families.* Washington, DC: Administration for Children and Families, U.S. Department of Health and Human Services. http://www.acf.hhs.gov/programs/ccb/research/ccreport/ccreport.htm (accessed 4/27/05).

Wilson, W.J. 1987. *The Truly Disadvantaged.* Chicago: University of Chicago Press.

Wolfe, B. and S. Hill. 1995. "The Effect of Health on the Work Effort of Single Mothers." *The Journal of Human Resources* 30: 42-62.

Challenges Faced by Women
with Disabilities Under TANF

Mary Kay Schleiter, University of Wisconsin-Parkside
Anne Statham, University of Wisconsin-Parkside
Teresa Reinders, University of Wisconsin-Parkside

SUMMARY. A number of studies report the multiple problems facing women during the welfare reform transition. Within this group is a large number of single mothers struggling with both poverty and chronic health problems or disabilities. Those with these additional challenges might be expected to experience less success in moving out of poverty than those without these health challenges. In this study, we examine the progress of 178 women around the state of Wisconsin who were interviewed repeatedly about their experiences with welfare reform and poverty between 1997 and 2000, when the Wisconsin Works (W-2) program was being implemented. The incidence of health problems is related to level of education, and the type of disability has major impacts on expected outcome. Those with less education are more likely to suffer from health problems, especially mental health issues, depression and post-traumatic stress, which seem to be the most debilitating. These women also had difficulty accessing non-work support, such as Supplement Security Income (SSI), a federal assistance program for disabled persons with little or no income, or assistance from the Department of Vocational Rehabilitation (DVR), a federal

---

[Haworth co-indexing entry note]: "Challenges Faced by Women with Disabilities Under TANF." Schleiter, Mary Kay, Anne Statham, and Teresa Reinders. Co-published simultaneously in *Journal of Women, Politics & Policy* (The Haworth Political Press, an imprint of The Haworth Press, Inc.) Vol. 27, No. 3/4, 2005, pp. 81-95; and: *Women, Work, and Poverty: Women Centered Research for Policy Change* (ed: Heidi Hartmann) The Haworth Political Press, an imprint of The Haworth Press, Inc., 2005, pp. 81-95. Single or multiple copies of this article are available for a fee from The Haworth Document Delivery Service [1-800-HAWORTH, 9:00 a.m. - 5:00 p.m. (EST). E-mail address: docdelivery@haworthpress.com].

doi:10.1300/J501v27n03_06

and state program of assistance to promote the employment abilities of adults with disabilities. *[Article copies available for a fee from The Haworth Document Delivery Service: 1-800-HAWORTH. E-mail address: <docdelivery@haworthpress.com> Website: <http://www.HaworthPress.com> © 2005 by The Haworth Press, Inc. All rights reserved.]*

KEYWORDS. Welfare reform, disability, health, mental health, single mothers, poverty, employment, Wisconsin, income assistance

INTRODUCTION

This study examines the impact the new work-focused welfare programs have had on women with health problems in the state of Wisconsin, which implemented a reform program (Wisconsin Works or W-2) before the Temporary Assistance for Needy Families (TANF) was enacted on the national level. In Wisconsin, the work requirement was applied to all parents receiving assistance virtually across the board, unless they had children younger than 12 weeks. Even those with disabilities, or children with disabilities, have had difficulty receiving exemptions to the rule. The change forced tens of thousands of people into the low-wage labor market, something thought to be nearly incomprehensible by major policy advisors only a few years before (Haveman 1995). The change may be partly responsible for the fall in Wisconsin's per capita income during this period of time (Ludeman 1999; Tornus 2001). Wisconsin can be considered a test case for the entire TANF experiment (Cohen 1997).

There is strong evidence that the incidence of health problems is high among welfare recipients (Danziger, Carlson, and Henly 2001; Siefert et al. 2001; Montoya et al. 2002), and that some of this risk is related to the stress of poverty (Schulz et al. 2000; Hahn et al. 1996). Health problems can become barriers to leaving poverty (Kneipp 2000; Danziger, Kalil, and Anderson 2000; Horwitz and Kerker 2001). Depression, especially, can become a barrier to economic self-sufficiency (Lehrer, Crittenden, and Norr 2002). Contrary to expectations, employment has not been shown to improve the health of single mothers (Baker and North 1999).

METHODS

We examine the importance of health issues in women's attempts to cope with the new welfare policies through repeated in-depth interviews between 1997 and 2000 with 178 women affected by welfare reform throughout Wisconsin. The interview schedules were developed in collaboration with a team of women in the population under study, who also conducted many of the interviews. The complete description of our methods is reported elsewhere (Schleiter, Rhodes, and Statham 2004; Statham, Schleiter, and Reinders 2004).

HEALTH PROBLEMS AND WORK
BY EDUCATIONAL LEVEL

Forty-five percent, or 80, of the 178 women we interviewed had serious disabilities or health problems that affected their daily lives and ability to work. One-fourth of those with a disability (20 of 80) had to leave a job at some time because of their disabilities. Only eighteen (23 percent) were receiving Social Security Disability or SSI. Some were in the process of applying for it at the time of the final interview, but others had been discouraged by bureaucratic road blocks. For most, it was a difficult gap between the end of AFDC and the start of SSI or Social Security Disability benefits.

Characteristics of the women with severe disabilities or chronic illnesses, compared to those who do not have these problems, are presented in Table 1. The geographic distribution of those with disabilities is similar to that of the rest of the sample: 17-18 percent are from Milwaukee and 83 percent are from other parts of the state. The racial/ethnic distributions of the two groups are somewhat different: those with disabilities and health problems are more likely than others to be African American, Latina/Hispanic, and Native American. At the beginning of the study, everyone in the sample was below the poverty level, but they differed by occupational status. As Table 1 reports, those with major disabilities and health problems are about twice as likely as other low income women to be unemployed, although the Wisconsin system of social services required virtually all who received public assistance to work.

In listening to the women's life histories and analyzing our data, we find that ability to meet the challenges of life often corresponds to level of education. To acknowledge this pattern, we report our results in three groups. Women in Group 1 did not have a high school degree when our study began, and they show a pattern of severe, continuing problems meeting their basic needs. Women in Group 2 had a high school degree (or equivalency diploma) and show a pattern of working at low-wage

TABLE 1. Women with and Without Major Health or Disability Problems

		Major health problems or disabilities 100% (80)	No major health problems or disabilities 100% (98)
Race/Ethnicity	White	59% (47)	66% (62)
	Black	30% (24)	21% (20)
	Latina/Hispanic	4% (3)	7% (7)
	Native American	8% (6)	4% (3)
	Asian	0% (0)	2% (2)
Occupational status	Unemployed	52% (42)	27% (26)
	Working part time	18% (14)	33% (32)
	Full time or more	30% (24)	40% (38)
Milwaukee vs. other	Milwaukee County	18% (14)	17% (17)
	Other location	83% (66)	83% (81)

Source: Authors' interviews.

jobs, often with some kind of public assistance that provides stability but the continued stress of poverty. Women in Group 3 had some post-secondary education or job training and show a pattern of skilled employment that provides the potential to leave poverty. These groups seem to be related to Corbett's (1995) typology of welfare use that also finds three groups of women–those with major dependency and little hope of independence; those who use the system intermittently depending on changes in economic conditions; and those who use the system once or twice in response to a major life change, such as divorce or abuse. Differences in health and disability problems among the three groups are presented in Table 2.

Group 1

The women in Group 1 face continuing problems. They may begin jobs, but problems with family and household, as well as difficulties meeting job demands can quickly overwhelm them. Without services to help them overcome these difficulties, they may not stay in a job for long. Homelessness, substandard housing, utility shut-offs, hunger, and lack of access to transportation are experiences they often report.

TABLE 2. Health and Disability by Group. Percentage of People in the Group (Frequency)[1]

	GROUP ONE	GROUP TWO	GROUP THREE
Mental illness[2]	29% (14)	19% (8)	21% (18)
Learning disability[3]	13% (6)	7% (3)	3% (3)
Current drug problem	6% (3)	0	0
Arthritis/fibromyalgia	6% (3)	12% (5)	7% (6)
Other physical illnesses or disabilities[4]	21% (10)	12% (5)	12% (10)
Seizure disorder	2% (1)	2% (1)	0
Blindness	0	0	1% (1)
Work-related injury	2% (1)	9% (4)	3% (3)
People in the group with health problems and/or disabilities	58% (28)	42% (18)	40% (34)
Those with two or more health problems and/or disabilities	19% (9)	14% (6)	12% (10)
Number without health insurance	25% (12)	42% (18)	24% (21)
Number of people in the group	48	43	86

Source: Authors' interviews.
Notes:
[1] Percentages add to more than the percentage of people with health/disability problems because 24 people have two disabilities or health problems.
[2] Depression, post-traumatic stress syndrome.
[3] Includes probable fetal alcohol syndrome as well as learning disabilities from other causes.
[4] Cancer, AIDS, migraines, lupus, multiple sclerosis, heart condition, diabetes, eczema.

Over half (58 percent or 28 of 48) of the women who did not finish high school have disabilities or serious health problems, a significantly greater incidence than for women in the other two groups. There are major differences in the types of illnesses these women experience (see Table 2). Mental health problems and learning disabilities are more common among women in Group 1, along with current drug problems. Depression and post-traumatic stress are the predominant mental health problems they report. Forty-two percent (23 of 55) of the women with depression, post-traumatic stress, severe learning disabilities, or current drug problems are in Group 1, compared to 30 percent (15 of 50) of those with physical illness or other disabilities (which include a wide range of problems), and 21 percent (20 of 97) of those who did not report major disabilities. Nearly one in five (9 of 48) of the women in Group 1 had more than one major disability, compared to 14 percent of Group 2, and 12 percent of Group 3.

The relationship between health or disability problems and the ability to work for women in Group 1 can be seen in the following quotes:

> I've been that way (depressed) for a long time . . . ever since I got kicked out of my mom's house . . . I'm 25 right now and I'm still in the same rut that I was when I was 17 . . . [had a child when 18 as the result of a rape . . . when I was 16 I ended up in treatment 'cause I tried killing myself. . . . The only reason I keep going is because of them [children] . . . I just figured I ain't gonna be happy. (162)[1]

> They . . . put me in the warehouse and I had to load trucks and I have a bad back problem . . . my back started bothering me real bad so I couldn't lift the crates . . . that they wanted on the truck. . . . They fired me because they said that I was not putting out enough products in the trucks . . . fast enough. (129)

> I got fired because in that supermarket . . . the cash register . . . the way they had everything marked . . . when they used to bring in personal checks . . . or WIC checks . . . or . . . a credit card, there was certain codes that you had to use . . . and I used to get confused with that. (183)

The women in Group 1 are more likely than those in Groups 2 and 3 to say early childhood traumas led to some of their problems. Here is one example:

> When my mom was pregnant with me she suffered a severe brain stroke and it affected my brain, so I have a severe problem . . . the slightest little thing agitates me . . . I have a problem dealing with people . . . I tried going back to school and with my medical problems, I could not comprehend or deal with the pressure . . . I could read something or have a telephone call and have a conversation and 5 minutes later I will forget it . . . I have grand mal seizures. I'm a slow learner. I got hyperactive disorder. I do not have a left hip . . . (129)

These disabilities most likely contributed to the problems these women had finishing high school.

Group 2

The women in Group 2 are focused on survival. Their struggles often require working more than one job while trying to squeeze in as much time with their children as possible. Their low salaries keep them in poverty, and their jobs offer few opportunities for advancement. Some in this category are receiving assistance, such as SSI or disability assistance. Forty-two percent of them (18 of 43) reported disabilities and/or other major health problems.

> Because of my medical condition, I'm working part time at Mrs. Fields in Cherryville Mall. . . . Everything I do is hard now. . . . It's only been a couple weeks ago when I finally accepted that I just can't do the things I used to. . . . At first I was . . . fighting it but . . . it's there, it's not going away . . . Everything that I do takes me twice or 3 times as long . . . I miss panning up cookies, putting 'em in the tray. Simple but not for me 'cause sometimes my wrists are swollen. . . . Even to wait on the customers, sometimes I'm just flying; some days I'm pushing buttons, my fingers are killing me. I just work through all the pain . . . (154)

Difficulties and limitations motivate some women to try self-employment, usually one of three types of small businesses–child care, sewing or hand crafts, or house cleaning.

> I started my crocheting at home, which is what I'm doing now. But that's so seasonal and . . . iffy. . . . The one place . . . I work with . . . the Easter Seal people, if I need to have . . . $10 . . . on something, they mark it up 100 percent so it's now a $20 item. Well, if I make an afghan and I need $50 out of it, who's gonna buy an afghan for $100? And I did voice my opinion on that and they says "Well, the cost to rent this place is just too expensive to lower prices." Have they ever thought of moving to a cheaper place? . . . On a good day I can crochet approximately 2 hours . . . I used to be able to crochet from 9 to 10 . . . 12 hours a day, and it wouldn't bother me at all. I could make an afghan in 3 days. . . . Now it takes me 3 weeks. (273)

Compared to those in Group 1, women in Groups 2 and 3 more often report suffering from temporary disorders.

> I was diagnosed with . . . rectal cancer, and my life changed completely. I had to go through surgery. I had to quit my job. I'm on medical disability right now, which is really hard to live on $110 a week . . . I'm still in recovery . . . I can't go back to work until the doctor okays it, and that won't be until May . . . (64)

The women in this group seemed able to cope somehow:

> I have MS . . . there's a problem, and yes, I'm losing my vision . . . I
> don't have my balance and they agreed . . . but it's not at a stage
> where I'm totally falling apart because I've learned to deal with it
> for so long. They only time I would be able to get financial help . . .
> would be . . . if I totally lost my vision. (32)

> I have difficulties comprehending because of a head injury when I
> was a child but I can read, I can write, I can spell, I . . . even went
> back and got my GED, finished that when I was pregnant with my
> daughter . . . I had been told . . . by the time I hit 40, I'll be in a
> wheelchair, so I need to find something I can do to support myself
> from a chair if need be . . . (132)

Group 3

Women in Group 3, our largest group of 86 women, are working in
skilled jobs or are attending post-secondary school. Most are still living
in poverty and those with health and disability problems are often limited in their ability to work. But they report major assistance from a support network that helps them overcome many of their issues. Only 28
percent, or 22, of the women in this group report major health problems
and/or disabilities. Their health problems are also often temporary:

> I have breast cancer; I'm furious that I cannot go to work. Even
> though I was only working 10 to 15 hours a week, I was doing
> what I was capable of . . . work's always been a mental stress re-
> liever for me . . . a mental way of staying strong and being out of
> the house . . . I had to miss a lot of work due to chemo . . . (218)

> I'm very happy with it [job] . . . I'm very unhappy with the head-
> ache situation . . . because when I first started my job . . . I depos-
> ited anywhere between $200 and $400 a week into my checking
> account. Now, I'm barely making a little over a $100, maybe $200.
> . . . That hurts. . . . Fortunately, my job . . . has been very flexible in
> giving me cases that I can do. But I'd like to get back to full time . . .
> I'm not making ends meet anymore. (3)

> After I had her I was very ill . . . I was on coumadin, blood thinners,
> and I was getting shots in the stomach because of blood clots. (27)

Some of these women report that they were being discriminated against in getting jobs because of their disabilities.

> They've asked a few employers . . . and they found that they're . . . shying away from it because they don't want somebody who has an injury who is seeking medical help . . . they're afraid that they're going to be sued if something happened. . . . There's a few computer manufacturers in Eau Claire and Chippewa that I've applied at and . . . they don't really want me because I'll cost them more because they'll have to have special chairs and all this other stuff . . . and they'd rather not. (19)

Like those in Group 1, women in Group 3 who suffer from depression and post-traumatic stress (21 percent of the group, or 18 of 86) report great difficulty holding jobs:

> I mentally cannot be around people . . . I can tolerate [it] for so long and then they put me back in . . . I take prozac . . . I have a sleeping disorder . . . sometimes get so depressed . . . I stay up. I can't sleep. I get my nights and days mixed up. (35)

This woman has managed to stay in college and may well be able to find a job situation that she can handle. The women in Group 3, along with those in Group 2, were less likely to suffer from these disorders compared with women in Group 1.

In the past, the welfare system allowed many women with disabilities or chronic health conditions to survive without working consistently; now many are being forced to work. While some of them would be eligible, the application process for either SSI or Social Security Disability is difficult and time consuming and many in our sample have been turned down, some more than once, after spending months, even years applying. Only 23 percent (18 of 80) of those with disabilities or chronic health problems have been successful in obtaining these benefits, and they often find that they are not receiving enough to support their families. For example, a woman in Group 2 quoted earlier (154) was receiving $236 per month from SSI, hardly enough to support herself and her children.

ACCESS TO HEALTH CARE

Access to health care is another major issue. About one-quarter of the women in our sample do not have any health insurance for themselves. Again, there were significant differences by group, as shown in Table 2.

Group 1

About a third of the women in Group 1 report problems with access to health care. Some had been denied Medical Assistance (MA, the state Medicaid program); only a few mentioned the option of getting insurance through their jobs or through their partner's employment. For example:

> He started out at $6.00 an hour and he's only up to $8.00. He's been there 3 years. . . . He's pushing pretty hard, especially when you don't have insurance and you have to come up with $6,000 every 2 months to keep the medical going . . . for the oldest one . . . an asthma child on top of it. (50)

Others describe problems getting Medical Assistance:

> I . . . applied last month to get medical cards and they denied me a card for my children . . . I have no insurance for my children. My daughter's fallen behind on her shots. . . . They slammed the door in my face. (167)

> . . . All of a sudden . . . my case ended . . . for the next 4 months I was trying to get a hold of him [caseworker]. He never responded . . . Matt has no glasses . . . he's squinting at the board . . . I started getting onto my caseworker. . . . "What's going on? Why can't you get this child some glasses?" (231)

Even when they have insurance or MA, access to care can be difficult:

> I'm 3 months pregnant and I'm bleeding and I had to call Dean Care and they said it wasn't important . . . I ended up calling my doctor and he told me to get my butt up there and get an ultrasound done. What gives them the right, they're not even a nurse, they're just people answering the phone . . . I never chose Dean Care, the welfare system did. (151)

Most of the women in Group 1 receive Medical Assistance, but 25 percent (12 of 48) have no health insurance at all.

Group 2

Women in Group 2 also report problems gaining access to health care. A few receive health insurance with their jobs. If they are eligible for Medical Assistance, they are more likely than those in Group 1 to manage the bureaucratic process and get it. The women in Group 2 are the most likely to be without health insurance: 42 percent or 18 of 43 have no coverage for themselves. They often work in jobs that do not offer benefits yet they no longer qualify for Medical Assistance. Women in Group 2 also report more problems dealing with the health care system than women in Group 3.

> There's a facility very close to me which I could get to very easily to do the therapy I need to get me to a state of wellness . . . but I have to travel all the way down to Mariner Hospital because my medical card does not belong at this facility. (277)

> I did request chiropractor through Workman's Comp and they denied it, just as they've denied all my meds now. . . . One was for depression and 3 were for pain. All they'll do is my right knee, they'll cover meds for that. . . . They asked the doctor, "What have you prescribed this for . . . isn't it helping her back and her legs?" . . . They're not covering it because it's not just going to my right knee. (273)

They also find that access to the health care they need is still a problem, even when they have Medical Assistance:

> You don't go to a really good psychiatrist if you're on MA . . . I can't do what I really need to do and that is . . . get to a psychiatrist who's going to listen to me . . . (17)

Group 3

Twenty-four percent of those in Group 3 also lack health insurance, but they often find creative ways to cope:

> We just don't get sick . . . I do herbal remedies . . . I did get sick one time. This is embarrassing. My dog had an infection and the vet gave her some penicillin and I saved it . . . I got bronchitis . . . and . . . I took the dog's stuff. How different could it be . . . ? It worked. (286)

These women more often express a fear of losing their coverage, since most of their available job opportunities also do not offer health insurance. As their earnings increase, they are no longer eligible for certain programs, and sudden loss of such supports . . . may feel like falling off a cliff.

> I worry . . . did I work too much extra to get MA? I need that medication and I'm afraid I'm going to get dropped. (31)

> . . . every time there's a change in your household that you have to report, you're scared because they may pull the rug out from under you and what are your alternatives? (24)

> I'm off of SSI. But I might . . . lose the medical too and I'm panicking about that. . . . If I do, I won't be able to afford to go to the doctor and continue to get the care that I'm getting now to keep myself going so that I can work. (35)

The women in Group 3 are much less likely than those in Group 2 to report problems gaining access to medical care, and those who do primarily speak about problems qualifying for SSI or DVR (the Department of Vocational Rehabilitation, a federal and state program of assistance to promote the employment abilities of adults with disabilities) services:

> I now have this medical problem that means I can only work for so long and then I am totally disabled again, which means I'm not disabled enough to qualify for Social Security or any other kind of disability . . . I . . . do not have the welfare system to fall back on anymore. (63)

> Like with DVR, I don't even qualify for that . . . because years ago I had . . . taken a couple of computer courses and I paid for it on my own, they consider me a self initiative so . . . it wouldn't matter how far my disability, I still would not qualify because I've had some training in the past . . . I went in and applied for the SSI. They gave me, at first it was a six month waiting period, and then they changed it to a year. A couple weeks before the year was up I had started working. I needed to support my kids and they said, "well now it's cancelled." (19)

Some women in Group 3 bring up even more complicated problems, such as misdiagnoses and errors in billing:

... The doctor blew me off ... I ... happened to connect up with a rheumatologist there who knows about fibro and ... had a pre-diagnosis within 15 minutes and then ... they went on to run the rest of the tests to rule out MS and all these other things that it could have been, which confirmed his ... early diagnosis of fibromyalgia ... (24)

I had some real mix-up with my healthcare billings ... I suddenly got a bill for something that took place while I was still on AFDC and had MA ... how many years later that they're wanting to make me responsible for because they didn't file it right ... (24)

POLICY IMPLICATIONS

The policy implications of our findings fall into two categories. First is the issue of access to health care. All three of our groups experienced problems with this in some way. For example, among women in Group 2, who have a high school degree or its equivalent, and considerable work experience, half of those with disabilities and severe health problems (9 of 18) do not have health insurance. Their jobs rarely offer sick pay or health insurance. They also face problems associated with under-funded Medical Assistance programs. Among women in Group 3, who have some post-secondary education training and experience in skilled jobs, stress in meeting job demands in spite of health problems is accompanied by their fear of losing benefits such as Medical Assistance. For women in Group 1, who did not have a high school degree at the start of the study and have continuing problems meeting their basic needs, disabilities and illness are long-standing, often resulting from instable or traumatic childhood experiences. While many of them receive Medical Assistance, they struggled to obtain treatment for mental illness or long-standing learning disorders. These problems suggest that policies that assure access to medical insurance in low-income jobs, access to SSI and Medical Assistance if disabled, and access to mental health care on parity with access to other health care would help these women a great deal. Findings from our larger study on the impact of poverty and welfare programs on self-esteem suggest that it is essential that this be done in such a way that the women feel they maintain control over their treatment. Perhaps a network of sensitized care providers, particularly in the area of mental illness and learning disabilities, could be developed that would assure this.

These problems are especially critical for the women in Group 1. About 35 percent of the women affected by welfare reform who have major health problems and disabilities are in Group 1, and their disabilities and health problems usually put them into an underserved category within the health care and social service systems, as they cope with learning disabilities, depression, or post-traumatic stress. Their problems are usually long-standing and have most likely prevented them from receiving key assets, such as a high school education, for the job market.

A second policy area related to our findings is that of the need for flexible work schedules. Many of these women report problems with supervisors arising from time off for their own or their children's illnesses or disabilities. Senator Kennedy's proposed Healthy Families Act, which would mandate that all jobs provide sick leave, would be beneficial for these women. Additional flexibility would allow some of these women to work, even with their disabilities. State TANF programs might also develop more reasonable work requirements that take these constraints into account. Also, developing an Earned Income Tax Credit for disabled single parents and/or larger disregards for people on SSI would help reduce the stress on these parents considerably.

NOTE

1. The numbers in parentheses following quotations refer to the ID number of the person interviewed.

REFERENCES

Baker, D. and K. North. 1999. "Does Employment Improve the Health of Lone Mothers?" *Social Science & Medicine* 49(1): 121-31.

Cohen, Adam. 1997. "The Great American Welfare Lab." *Time*, Vol. 149 Issue 16, April 21, 74-76.

Corbett, Thomas. 1995. "Welfare Reform in Wisconsin: The Rhetoric and the Reality." In *Politics of Welfare Reform*, ed. Donald Norris and Lyke Thompson. Thousand Oaks, CA: Sage Publications.

Danziger, S. K., M. J. Carlson, and J. R. Henly. 2001. "Post-Welfare Employment and Psychological Well-Being." *Women & Health* 32(1-2): 47-78.

Danziger, S. K., A. Kalil, and N. J. Anderson. 2000. "Human Capital, Physical Health, and Mental Health of Welfare Recipients: Co-Occurrence and Correlates." *Journal of Social Issues* 56(4): 635-54.

Hahn, R. A., E. D. Eaker, N. D. Barker, S. M. Teutsch, W. A. Sosniak, and N. Krieger. 1996. "Poverty and Death in the United States." *International Journal of Health Services* 26(4): 673-90.

Haveman, Robert. 1995. "The Clinton Alternative to 'Welfare as We Know It': Is It Feasible?" In *The Work Alternative: Welfare Reform and the Realities of the Job Market*, eds. Demetra Smith Nightingale and Robert Haveman. Washington, DC: The Urban Institute Press.

Horwitz, S. M. and B. D. Kerker. 2001. "Impediments to Employment Under Welfare Reform: The Importance of Physical Health and Psychosocial Characteristics." *Women & Health* 32(1-2): 101-17.

Kneipp, S. M. 2000. "The Health of Women in Transition from Welfare to Employment." *Western Journal of Nursing Research* 22(6): 656-74.

Lehrer, E., K. Crittenden, and K. F. Norr. 2002. "Depression and Economic Self-Sufficiency Among Inner-City Minority Mothers." *Social Science Research* 31(3): 285-309.

Ludeman, Terry. 1999. "Record Unemployment Creating 'Brain Drain.'" *Wisconsin State Journal* 28 (December).

Montoya, I. D., D. C. Bell, J. S. Atkinson, C. W. Nagy, and D. D. Whitsett. 2002. "Mental Health, Drug Use, and the Transition from Welfare to Work." *Journal of Behavioral Health Services & Research* 29(2): 144-56.

Schleiter, Mary Kay, Katherine Rhoades, and Anne Statham. 2004. "Women, Poverty, and Public Policy: A Community-Based Model for Collaborative Outreach Scholarship." *Journal of Higher Education Outreach and Engagement* 9(1): 11-24.

Schulz, A., B. Israel, D. Williams, E. Parker, A. Becker, and S. James. 2000. "Social Inequalities, Stressors and Self Reported Health Status Among African American and White Women in the Detroit Metropolitan Area." *Social Science & Medicine* 51(11): 1639-53.

Siefert, K., C. M. Heflin, M. E. Corcoran, and D. R. Williams. 2001. " Food Insufficiency and the Physical and Mental Health of Low-Income Women." *Women & Health* 32(1-2): 159-77.

Statham, Anne, Mary Kay Schleiter, and Teresa Reinders. 2004. "Dealing with Welfare Reform: Depth Interviews with Women in Wisconsin 1997-2000." Kenosha, Wisconsin: University of Wisconsin-Parkside.

Tornus, John. 2001. "Brain Drain Is Holding Back Wisconsin's Economic Growth." *Milwaukee Journal Sentinel* 8 (April).

The Work-Family Time Binds of Low-Income Mothers: Nurse Aides Struggle to Care

Peggy Kahn, University of Michigan-Flint

SUMMARY. Nurse aides at Convalescent Center, a for-profit nursing home in a low-income county in Michigan, struggle to accommodate routine care of children, using relative and informal care, and to deal with sudden, urgent demands related to parenting. The nursing home has relatively rigid workplace scheduling and attendance policies and practices, based upon state and corporate staffing rules and constraints on labor costs, with some limited elements of flexibility. Both rigid demands to work all scheduled hours, regardless of unpredictable child-related urgencies, and opportunities to select the preferred shift characterize the work environment. The dilemmas of the nurse aides who are mothers are the consequence of public policies that fail to protect families from workplace demands, compounded by public health reimbursement practices that constrict staffing options at the nursing home. *[Article copies available for a fee from The Haworth Document Delivery Service: 1-800-HAWORTH. E-mail address: <docdelivery@haworthpress.com> Website: <http://www.HaworthPress.com> © 2005 by The Haworth Press, Inc. All rights reserved.]*

KEYWORDS. Nurse aides, low-income parents, single mothers, women's employment, work and family, low-wage work

---

[Haworth co-indexing entry note]: "The Work-Family Time Binds of Low-Income Mothers: Nurse Aides Struggle to Care." Kahn, Peggy. Co-published simultaneously in *Journal of Women, Politics & Policy* (The Haworth Political Press, an imprint of The Haworth Press, Inc.) Vol. 27, No. 3/4, 2005, pp. 97-111; and: *Women, Work, and Poverty: Women Centered Research for Policy Change* (ed: Heidi Hartmann) The Haworth Political Press, an imprint of The Haworth Press, Inc., 2005, pp. 97-111. Single or multiple copies of this article are available for a fee from The Haworth Document Delivery Service [1-800-HAWORTH, 9:00 a.m. - 5:00 p.m. (EST). E-mail address: docdelivery@haworthpress.com].

Available online at http://www.haworthpress.com/web/JWPP
doi:10.1300/J501v27n03_07

Much research on work and family time dilemmas, emphasizing workers' strategies, corporate policies and workplace culture, and public policy, has focused upon professional and middle class, usually married, women (Blair-Loy 2003; Fried 1998; Gornick and Meyers 2003; Hochschild 1997; Jacobs and Madden 2004; Moen 2003; Perlow 1997). Studies of the dilemmas of parents working in a 24/7 service economy (Garey 1999; Kahn and Blum 1998; Presser 2003) and of low-income parents including single mothers (Crouter and Booth 2004; Dodson, Manuel, and Bravo 2002; Heymann 2000; Jacobs and Gerson 2004) have begun to emerge, especially in the wake of welfare changes in 1996.

While low-income, especially single, mothers have always struggled to work in order to try to meet basic household needs (Edin and Lein 1997; Spalter-Roth and Hartmann 1994), welfare changes since 1996 have increased the numbers of low-income mothers struggling to combine paid employment, often at non-standard hours, with caregiving to their children. New welfare policies have intensified work-family dilemmas through rigid work requirements for receipt of benefits, time limits on benefits, and inadequate child care provision for employed mothers. Welfare reform, in combination with the relatively strong economy of the later 1990s, increased employment rates of unmarried mothers. The employment of never-married mothers increased from 46 percent to 66 percent between 1994 and 2000. In the year 2000, low-income mother-only families were more dependent on earned income and less able to count upon benefits than at any other time in the past 40 years, with cash benefits (including food stamps) providing only 10 percent and earnings 73 percent of their household income (Bernstein 2004). Most of the jobs held by poor single mothers appear to be jobs with low pay and low control over many aspects of work, including schedules (Daly 2004).

Nurse aides, the majority of workers in nursing homes and the providers of 80-90 percent of the direct care residents receive, do physically and emotionally demanding work for low pay and with little job and scheduling autonomy. Full-time nurse aides–less-educated, low-paid workers, often single parents–appear to be part of the workforce suffering from a combination of money and time poverty; the impact of their low wages on their families is exacerbated by limited paid leave, scheduling rigidity, non-traditional working hours including second and third shifts, and little voice in their own scheduling (Heymann 2000; Presser and Cox 1997). Historically, nurse aides have cycled between welfare and work, or combined low-wage nursing assistant work with public benefits (Dawson and Surpin 2001; Riemer 2001; Spalter-Roth and Hartmann 1994). The demand for nurse aides is expected to grow as the very elderly population increases, yet nurse-aide turnover is alarmingly high.

In order to explore how workplace policies and practices create the time binds of nurse aides who are mothers, especially single mothers, I conducted a qualitative study of a 155-bed nursing home and its approximately 80 aides between January and June 2002. "Convalescent Center," part of a national for-profit chain, is in a suburban location in a high poverty county in Michigan. Its aides, organized by the Service Employees International Union (SEIU), are approximately 90 percent women, with a significant number of single mothers, 43 percent white and 57 percent African-American. Nurse aides are paid $9.30 per hour, about the average in the state. I conducted open-ended interviews with twelve nurse aides, all of whom were or had been single parents while working at the facility. In addition, I interviewed managers and supervisors; examined documentary material, including the union contract and written employment policies; attended a full-day nurse aide classroom orientation on policies and procedures; and observed aides working first shift. I supplemented the research at Convalescent Center with work at a second nursing home site, where I also interviewed aides and managers. The methodology was intended to give voice to nurse aide mothers and document their time dilemmas with regard to family caregiving in the context of workplace time policies and practices.

KEY MANAGEMENT TIME POLICIES
AND PRACTICES AT CONVALESCENT CENTER

Nursing managers at Convalescent Center are simultaneously responsible for meeting mandated minimum staffing levels in order to ensure quality of care and for containing labor costs within these constraints. The Director of Nursing sets basic staffing levels in accordance with public regulations, corporate staffing tools that use resident acuity information and time and motion studies, and the facility's budget. She must also guard against expensive overstaffing or excessive overtime pay.

Nursing managers operate a system of standard shifts, enforced by a disciplinary procedure. Full-time nurse aides work regular, repeating shifts (7:00 a.m.-3:30 p.m., 3 p.m.-11:30 p.m., 11:00 p.m.-7:30 a.m.) and every other weekend, for a total of 40 hours per week. The posted two-week schedule is sacrosanct, regarded as essential to the work of the nursing home and dominating the daily lives of nurse aides who have only small amounts of time not controlled by work schedules. The schedule is posted at least two weeks in advance, generally four weeks at a time, sometimes eight weeks in advance. This advanced scheduling is an attempt to help workers plan for, and ensure, their attendance.

A major, stressful preoccupation for managers is last-minute call-ins or no-shows, which can dangerously reduce coverage for residents and may in certain cases result in expensive overtime pay for full-time workers. All absences of four or more hours from scheduled work not arranged in advance count as absences for disciplinary procedure, even if they are due to child care difficulties, documented children's or workers' illnesses, or other unpredictable problems, and even if the aide still has paid days off available. Seven absences in a year result in a day-long suspension, and additional absences result in escalating penalties and eventual termination. The time clock, the conditions of the signing bonus, the emphasis of the orientation classes, and the general culture of the facility all underscore the importance of regular attendance and punctuality. Missed weekend duty results not only in an absence recorded for disciplinary purposes, but also a requirement to make up the missed hours on one of the three following weekends, in effect requiring work on consecutive weekends.

The bargaining agreement, while specifying that all absences from scheduled work contribute to the disciplinary record, also appears to allow workers to escape disciplinary absences by notification of supervisors at least two hours in advance of the scheduled shift of their inability to attend. The Director of Nursing generally interprets this provision to apply only when an emergency, a situation both extremely serious and totally unpredictable, presents itself. An additional clause appears to allow the employer to work with workers to make up recorded absences and ameliorate their record.

Full-time workers have up to seven personal paid leave days per year, accumulating at the rate of one day per month during the first seven months worked, at the onset of each year. However, use of these personal days must be notified in advance, before the schedule is posted. After one year of full-time work, an aide is also eligible for paid vacation of 40 hours (five days), though this time off must be arranged well in advance and approved; after three years a worker is eligible for 80 hours of paid vacation.

At the same time, in order to maintain staffing patterns while still accommodating the parenting and other needs of nurse aides, managers incorporate low-cost, flexible scheduling practices. The nursing scheduler, who knows the workforce well, encourages nurse aides to spec-ify–when they are hired and whenever they have a major change in their circumstances–preferred shifts and desired total hours. Managers work to accommodate requests for shift transfers, taking into account a com-bination of seniority and attendance records. In fact, because of high turnover, there is often space available on each of the three shifts. Thus, the problem of retention creates possibilities and incentives for manag-ers to schedule according to the needs of parents. The options of nurse aides at Convalescent Center contrast sharply with the restrictions on shift mobility of service staff at the low-turnover, high-seniority hospi-tal studied by Blum and Kahn (1996; Kahn and Blum 1998). At the hos-pital, overall turnover in housekeeping, laundry services, and food services was very low, hiring freezes and staff cuts limited the overall number of positions, and vacancies were therefore scarce. Movement into all positions, including the coveted day shift, was governed strictly by seniority rank, and mothers of young children had relatively low se-niority. This contrast underlines the fact that parenting-related schedul-ing is not a statutory employee right but contingent upon employer preferences, business needs, and negotiated contracts.

At Convalescent Center, the scheduler works with the Director of Nursing to alter shift start times to accommodate parenting and educa-tional schedules. One first-shift worker starts at 5 a.m. to pick up a child at 2 p.m., while two others start at 6:30 a.m. in order to pick up children close to 3:00 p.m. Other research has also found that even small amounts of flexibility are of considerable importance to lower-paid working par-ents (Blum and Kahn 1996; Kahn and Blum 1998; Swanberg 1997).

Finally, nurse aides are permitted to trade blocks of working time amongst themselves and then request approval for these schedule alter-ations. In theory, the advanced, posted schedule facilitates such working time exchanges. While this form of flexibility is very useful to some aides who want to attend pre-scheduled functions on their scheduled week-ends, it does not address sudden, urgent time demands well as aides face difficult burdens of quickly locating substitutes and getting approval, which is often withheld if the substitute would draw overtime pay.

MOTHERS' RESPONSES
TO WORKPLACE TIME DEMANDS

At Convalescent Center, nurse aides with young children make full use of shift flexibility options, in order to arrange routine care of their children. Two sisters at Convalescent Center work midnight and evening shifts, alternating care of the four children living in their two households; this strategy resembles the alternating shifts strategy of married couples who work non-standard hours (Presser 2003). Others work an evening shift due to availability of informal caregivers. Most mothers with school age children, however, work first shift by preference. Due to turnover, Convalescent Center generally has openings for first-shift workers. One aide recounts how she combined choice of shift with child care arrangements to accommodate the needs of her growing children and maintain her involvement in their education:

> Second shift was working good before she started at school and for the first two years . . . because she was going half days. I worked second. I would go to the school in the morning, volunteer and go on field trips. . . . And by her getting out at 12:30 I was able to be up most of the day, go home, get ready for work, then leave. Either her father or my mother looked after her. When she started first grade, by her being in school all day, I started thinking, well if she was gonna be at school all day I might as well switch my hours so I can be at work all day and then we can have more time together when she gets out of school and I get out of work. . . . So I started talking to (the scheduler) about it. When second shift was overstaffed and they needed somebody for first, they'd call me and say, "Hey, want to work first today and have second off?" or "You want to come in at 9 and be out by 5?" or something like that . . . I loved it, get up and going and do the job, get out and go home and see the kids all day. . . . They told me they would be posting it, and I should sign up, and they was almost positive I would get it, and I did.

Another aide with adolescent children explained her preference for first shift:

> I don't work second shift because I don't leave my kids at home by they self . . . I just don't. I don't. My . . . 14 year old, she's scared to stay at home by herself anyway. And my son, he ain't responsible enough to stay at home by himself. So I work first shift and I leave her . . . til I get off work. . . . And on the weekends I just pay somebody sometime, you know . . .

Responding to the options regarding total working hours, parents exercise some control over number of hours. These mothers tend to stick to scheduled work hours and avoid substantial overtime largely because their first priority is caring for their children; they do not use available work time as an opportunity to escape from family work or as an opportunity to earn extra money, contrary to the workers observed by Hochschild (1997). In addition, they honor the schedules and other commitments of their informal caregivers. Some aides are formally part-time workers hired to work 32 hours per week but do extra shifts at their convenience when they can get babysitters, in practice working almost full time.

Central to the selection of the shift and total number of hours is always the ability to make arrangements for routine child care. All mothers develop strategies for reconciling their shifts–none of which is encompassed wholly within standard school day or child care center hours, especially when transportation time is added to the working hours themselves–with routine care of children. According to their own reports and the observations of managers and supervisors, all the mothers who work as nurse aides at Convalescent Center use informal relative care, generally in place of licensed home or center care, but very occasionally in combination with them. The use of informal relative care is driven by taken-for-granted ideas that families provide care for children, desires to have children in home settings during the early and late working hours, fear of abusive practices in out-of-home neighborhood child care settings, lack of options for using licensed care during non-standard working hours, and lack of financial resources for paying for licensed care.

Even using relative caregivers, nearly all nurse aides with children make multiple arrangements, often involving complex schedules in which minutes matter and uncertainty is always present, arrangements that Foner's study of nurse aides describes as "complicated baby-sitting arrangements that [wear] them down" (1994: 107). Because of reliance on informal care, even routine arrangements cannot be completely routinized and create unpredictable problems–illness of the grandmother caretaker, aunts with cars that do not start, and so on. In several cases, nurse aides rely upon family members with disabilities or chronic illnesses, heart disease, kidney failure, arthritis, bipolar disorder, that render relatives unable to undertake regular employment and likely to have days on which they are not functioning well. Sometimes the caregivers themselves need to be cared for, and at the second nursing home in the study the nurse manager reports about four deaths per year of grandmother caregivers.

Aides who are mothers use several different types of informal child care, often in combination with each other: mothers of the adult mother share care with younger generation working mothers; adult sisters care for children; older children anchor care for younger siblings or undertake "self care"; fathers participate in care. Many nurse aides rely upon their mothers, especially if they live in shared households with them. The most important care arrangements are clearly those negotiated among female members of extended families. The nurse aides have limited or no expectations of the biological fathers of their children.

The story of the two sisters working on evenings and nights and alternating caregiving is somewhat unusual at this particular nursing home, but it illustrates the importance of relative care, the complexity and vulnerability of care arrangements, and the stress for children and parents produced by non-standard working hours. The first sister works evenings (second shift) while the second sister cares for the four children, 3, 5, 6, and 9, of both households. The sister who works evenings (3:00-11:30 p.m.) transports all the children to her house in the middle of the night, so that her sister can work third shift from 11:00 p.m. to 7:30 a.m. and sleeps from 1:00 or 2:00 a.m. until about 7:00 a.m. She then gets the children ready for school and takes them there, sometimes with the help of her mother. The second sister works the midnight shift from 11:00 p.m. to 7:30 a.m., while the first sister supervises the children as they sleep. The midnight shift worker needs to supervise her youngest child, not yet school age, when she returns from work around 8:00 a.m. (and should be sleeping). She also needs to be awake to pick up the older children around 3:00 p.m. and likes to be involved with school activities if possible. She says that she sometimes is able to sleep from 5:00 p.m. to 10:00 p.m. if she can find someone to look after all four children. All the children are transferred from one house to the other in the middle of the night, not an uncommon occurrence when single mothers work non-standard hours. However, the sisters must also improvise care arrangements between 11:00 p.m. and 12:00 midnight during the transition between shifts when neither can be with the children because they are both working and traveling to and from the workplace. The toddler's father, another adult sibling visiting from out of town, or the mothers' parents help out. Required work every other weekend creates additional child care problems, solved on a week-by-week and informal basis. Both sisters constantly battle exhaustion, ill health, and workplace attendance requirements. The midnight shift worker has asthma, exacerbated by chronic lack of sleep and stress, which results in illness-related call-ins up to three times per month, constant disciplinary warnings, and job insecurity.

Most of the working mothers have a strong sense of the limits of what they can ask relatives and the importance of reciprocity. They limit their working hours partly in order to limit demands on informal caregivers. The meager public child care subsidy available to the mothers is important not only to increase the income of the extended family but also to allow the working mother to provide some reciprocity for the hard work, inconvenience, and disruption created for relatives by regular caregiving. Several mothers reported difficulties and delays in accessing the relative care subsidy, a theme that surfaces in other research on welfare recipients transitioning to work (Chaudry 2004; Kahn and Polakow 2000).

While routine child care arrangements pose a great and stressful challenge to nurse aides, there are also sudden and unpredictable demands associated with parenting. While for managers, late notified absences represent a situation that compromises staffing levels and endangers resident care, for mothers they represent their own and their children's unpredictable illnesses, school problems, and child care crises. Nurse aides are especially unhappy about the difficulties they face when calling in just before the start of their shift due to their own or their children's sicknesses, even when they can document these illnesses. They regard these difficulties as cruelly ironic, since they are working to maintain the health of others and alongside health care professionals who recognize and treat illness; they see them as indications that they are valued only insofar as they do their paid work and not as people with their own failing bodies or important, intimate relationships that sometimes require direct care. "There's no excuse for being absent, except your death," one nurse aide says bitterly.

Nurse aides routinely have to call in when their children are sick. Even when using relative caregivers, they feel it is their job to attend to sick children, especially if the illness is physically severe or emotionally unsettling to the child. Several aides cite young children's bouts of severe gastrointestinal infection or severe asthma attacks, sometimes requiring doctor's visits or hospitalization, as reasons they have called in. Workers who are parents are inclined to report to work when they themselves are ill, sometimes with contagious illnesses, in order to conserve possible discipline-incurring absences for the occasions when they have sick children. Management permits or even indirectly encourages this, as they urge staff to follow universal precautions of masking and frequent hand-washing to prevent transmission of illness and disease.

Workers in turn sometimes report to work ill, hoping that management will send them home without the disciplinary consequences that a call-in might engender.

Strong incentives for mothers to report to work create complications in cases of children's emergent illnesses or health problems. Parents want to accompany their children to doctor or other health care appointments, but are forced to delegate this task. Sometimes, however, delegation to an informal caregiver results in failure to convey important information to professionals, distancing of parents from an expert for whom they likely have important questions, and last-minute summonses to the health or psychological clinic to make a decision, provide further information, or support the child. One aide reports:

> [My daughter] was crying about her gums hurting, [and I noticed a bump in her mouth] and I couldn't take the day off work, and I didn't want to call in and make everybody else be short. . . . So my sister took her to the dentist for me, and she had a cyst on her mouth. [The dentist's office] called me at work, and we can't have personal phone calls at work, so she wouldn't put the call through . . . I got the message to call the dentist because something was wrong with my daughter. [I called, and the office] said she had a cyst and told me I needed to come up there and sit down and talk with the doctor on how to take care of it . . . I was scared, so I wanted to go right away. And it was maybe 1:00, and she told me to make sure everyone was all right, and then I could leave. When I got up to the dentist, he was asking my sister questions that she couldn't answer, so that I felt like it was a problem, because she didn't know.

One story illustrates how a strict attendance policy framework forces parents and their children into negative situations by creating low parental expectations of what they can do without incurring formal or informal workplace penalties. A nurse aide recognized as an outstanding worker with a good attendance record over many years describes her reluctance to ask for flexibility when a crisis developed in her child's classroom. She was already under disciplinary warning because of an accumulation of unavoidable short-term absences–her young son had had two bouts of severe abdominal flu, she had had several debilitating migraines, and her car had been struck and immobilized by another vehicle one morning, and she wanted to avoid both disciplinary action and negative judgment in her attendance-conscious workplace. Her son's kindergarten teacher, who seemed to have an ongoing negative relation-

ship with the child, accused him in front of his class of deliberately uri-
nating on the bathroom floor and forced the child to clean it up. Unable
to resolve the situation directly with the teacher or through the principal,
both parents agreed they had to move the child to another school in the
district. This move required considerable paperwork and numerous
school visits. But because both parents had to wait for simultaneous
days off from scheduled work to do this together, the child was forced to
remain in the classroom with an antagonistic teacher who had humili-
ated him for another three or four weeks after the incident. The mother
was constantly worried about the child's well-being. While it seems
likely that management would have wanted to find some way to help the
mother respond to this distressing situation, it did not occur to the aide
to ask for flexibility because, she said, "It would have created trouble at
work."

NURSE AIDE TIME DILEMMAS AND PUBLIC POLICIES

At Convalescent Center, workplace time policies appear to both restrict and accommodate nurse aides' ability to care for children and
other family members. Compared to other nursing homes and low-wage
workplaces, the nurse aides regard Convalescent Center as good in relation to scheduling and other workplace conditions, yet they struggle
hard to find time to be with their children or to make safe, appropriate
child care arrangements for the hours they work.

These time dilemmas of nurse aides who are mothers are structured
through their specific workplace. However, the workplace's resources
and practices are structured by public policies, regulations and reimbursement through Medicaid and Medicare and public regulation of
working time. Workers in low-paid, low control jobs such as nurse aide
are particularly dependent upon public policy because compared with
many professional and managerial workers they are relatively power-
less to change, manage, control, or schedule their work (Daly 2004). In
addition, other public policies structure access to and availability of
child care and school programs, critical resources for aides trying to
respond to workplace time demands.

Restricted Medicaid and Medicare funding for skilled nursing facilities, with average Medicaid reimbursement less per day than the average cost of care, severely limits the ability of managers to improve nurse
aide-to-resident ratios. Reimbursement rates generally do not reflect
living wages, and current labor realities include very low mandated

staffing levels, minimal training, low pay and poor working conditions, average vacancy rates of 8.5 percent, and average turnover rates of 70 percent (American Health Care Association, 2005, 2004, 2003). Thus, one incremental workplace solution to inflexibilities surrounding the "predictably unpredictable" (Heymann 2000)–scheduling more nurse aides on shifts in order to create some flexibility without lowering care standards and allowing a certain number of discipline-exempt call-ins in the form of short-notice personal days or sick days–is unacceptable to management under current budgetary constraints. Managers, however, do operate low-cost flexibility practices that seem to contribute to re-cruitment and retention–shift selection and transfers, slightly early or delayed starts, limited paid time off with notice, and hours trading among employees.

In addition, weak public regulation of working time (Gornick and Meyers 2003) allows managers to design personnel rules that respond to financial constraints but not to parenting imperatives, leaving parents like nurse aides to choose being with sick children and dealing with school problems at the risk of being reprimanded and disciplined at work. According to Heymann (2000), 78 percent of low-income par-ents have no workplace flexibility to attend to children's (or their own) needs, 84 percent of parents in the bottom income quartile have two weeks or less of sick and vacation leave, and 53 percent of all working mothers cannot take days off for sick children. Such restrictions exist despite the fact that lower- and middle-income adults and children get sick more often and have more chronic conditions than upper-income adults and children and that there are demonstrably positive effects of parental involvement with sick children, their medical care, and educa-tion (Heymann 2000). Statutory sick leave provision and Family and Medical Leave extensions that cover small necessities, including medi-cal leaves not covered under FMLA and/or parental participation in children's educational activities, would alleviate some of the problems. The Massachusetts' 1998 Small Necessities Leave Act, for example, permits eligible employees to take up to a total of 24 hours of leave in a 12-month period to attend to a child's school activity or accompany a child or elderly relative to a doctor's appointment. It requires 7 days no-tice if the need for leave is foreseeable, or such notice as is practicable. While the normal working week defined in the Fair Labor Standards Act is long, reducing the standard work week cannot solve the problems of low-paid single-parent workers if their hourly pay and public benefits do not increase.

Finally, the experience of nurse aides shows that the availability of child care and school-based supervision at extended hours is critical to many mothers' ability to accommodate workplace time demands. Yet, early care and education in the United States is "a disorganized jumble of services of varying but mostly poor to mediocre quality that families have trouble finding, affording and evaluating . . . suffer(ing) from the trilemmas of affordability, availability and quality" (Helburn 1999). Low-income single mothers spend 18-20 percent of their earnings on child care, and the care that they find and use is most often informal and of poor quality (Chaudry 2004; Giannerelli and Barsimantov 2000; Helburn 1999). Welfare-to-work policy and the administration of the child care block grant–which include harshly enforced work require-ments that mandate employment on any schedule, child care subsidies that are low and slow, and the absence of interventions to substantially increase the supply of good quality care–restrict the options of and in-crease the stress faced by single mothers. They are driven into informal, relative care. Short school days, a short school year, and school holidays create additional problems for single mothers.

Nurse aides struggle to provide care for their own children, as they struggle also to provide care for the frail elderly and disabled in their workplace. They are caught not only between work and family time commitments, but also doubly, in their workplace and in their families, in a societal care deficit structured by public policies (Folbre 2001; Hochschild 1995).

REFERENCES

American Health Care Association (AHCA). 2003. "New National Study of Health Care Staffing Needs in American Nursing Homes." *http://www.ahca.org/news/nr030507.htm.*

American Health Care Association (AHCA). 2004. "Workforce Shortage: Who Will Answer the Call Button?" (Issue Brief) *http://www.ahca.org.*

American Health Care Association (AHCA). 2005. "Protect and Preserve Medicaid Long Term Care" (Issue Brief) *http://www.ahca.org.*

Bernstein, Jared. 2004. "The Low-Wage Labor Market: Trends and Policy Implica-tions." In *Work-Family Challenges for Low-Income Parents and Their Children,* ed. Ann Crouter and Alan Booth. Mahwah, NJ: Lawrence Erlbaum.

Blair-Loy, Mary. 2003. *Competing Devotions: Career and Family Among Women Ex-ecutives.* Cambridge, MA: Harvard University Press.

Blum, Linda and Peggy Kahn. 1996. "'We Didn't Hire You for Your Children': Gendered Practices and Non-standard Working Hours in the Service Sector." Presented at the Annual Meeting of the American Sociological Association, New York City.

Chaudry, Ajay. 2004. *Putting Children First: How Low-Wage Working Mothers Manage Child Care.* New York: Russell Sage Foundation.

Crouter, Ann C. and Alan Booth, eds. 2004. *Work-Family Challenges for Low-Income Parents and Their Children.* Mahwah, NJ: Lawrence Erlbaum Associates.

Daly, Kerry. 2004. "Exploring Process and Control in Families Working Nonstandard Schedules" In *Work-Family Challenges for Low-Income Parents and Their Children,* ed. by Ann C. Crouter and Alan Booth. Mahwah, NJ: Lawrence Erlbaum.

Dawson, Steven L. and Rick Surpin. 2001. "Direct Care Health Workers: The Unnecessary Crisis in Long-Term Care." Aspen Institute Domestic Strategy Group. *http://www.aspeninstitute.org/aspeninstitute/files/Img/pdf/lohng_term_care.pdf.*

Dodson, Lisa, Tiffany Manuel, and Ellen Bravo. 2002. *Keeping Jobs and Raising Families: It Just Doesn't Work.* A Report of the Across the Boundaries Project. Cambridge, MA: Radcliffe Public Policy Center.

Edin, Kathryn and Laura Lein. 1997. *Making Ends Meet: How Single Mothers Survive Welfare and Low-Wage Work.* New York: Russell Sage Foundation.

Folbre, Nancy. 2001. *The Invisible Heart: Economics and Family Values.* New York: New Press.

Foner, Nancy. 1994. *The Caregiving Dilemma; Work in an American Nursing Home.* Berkeley, CA: University of California Press.

Fried, Mindy. 1998. *Taking Time: Parental Leave Policy and Corporate Culture.* Philadelphia: Temple University Press.

Garey, Anita Ilta. 1999. *Weaving Work and Motherhood.* Philadelphia: Temple University Press.

Giannarelli, Linda, and James Barsimantov. 2000. "Child Care Expenses of America's Families." Assessing the New Federalism, Occasional Paper 40. Washington, DC: Urban Institute.

Gornick, Janet C. and Marcia K. Meyers. 2003. *Families That Work: Policies for Reconciling Parenthood and Employment.* New York: Russell Sage Foundation.

Helburn, Suzanne E., ed. 1999. "The Silent Crisis in U.S. Child Care." *Annals of the American Academy of Political and Social Science* 563(May). Thousand Oaks, CA: Sage Publications.

Heymann, Jody. 2000. *The Widening Gap: Why America's Working Families Are in Jeopardy and What Can Be Done About It.* New York: Basic Books.

Hochschild, Arlie Russell. 1997. *The Time Bind: When Work Becomes Home and Home Becomes Work.* New York: Metropolitan Books.

Hochschild, Arlie Russell. 1995. "The Culture of Politics: Traditional, Postmodern, Cold-modern, and Warm-modern Ideals of Care." *Social Politics: International Studies in Gender, State, and Society* 2: 331-346.

Jacobs, Jerry A. and Kathleen Gerson. 2004. *The Time Divide: Work, Family and Gender Inequality.* Cambridge, MA: Harvard University Press.

Jacobs, Jerry A. and Janice Fanning Madden, eds. 2004. "Mommies and Daddies on the Fast Track: Success of Parents in Demanding Professions." *Annals of the American Academy of Political and Social Science* 596(November). Thousand Oaks, CA: Sage Publications.

Kahn, Peggy and Linda Blum. 1998. "Not Just 9 to 5: The Problems of Nonstandard Working Hours." *Working USA* (November-December): 50-59.

Kahn, Peggy and Valerie Polakow. 2000. *Struggling to Stay in School: Obstacles to Post-Secondary Education Under the Welfare-to-Work Restrictions in Michigan*. Research Report. Center for the Education of Women, University of Michigan. *http://www.umich.edu/~cew*.

Moen, Phyllis, ed. 2003. *It's About Time: Couples and Careers*. New York: Cornell University Press.

Perlow, Leslie A. 1997. *Finding Time: How Corporations, Individuals, and Families Can Benefit from New Work Practices*. Ithaca: Cornell University Press.

Presser, Harriet and Amy Cox. 1997. "The Work Schedules of Low-Educated Women and Welfare Reform." *Monthly Labor Review* (April): 25-34.

Presser, Harriet. 2003. *Working in a 24/7 Economy: Challenges for American Families*. New York: Russell Sage Foundation.

Riemer, Frances J. 2001. *Working at the Margins: Moving Off Welfare in America*. Albany, New York: State University of New York Press.

Spalter-Roth, Roberta and Heidi I. Hartmann. 1994. "AFDC Recipients as Caregivers and Workers: A Feminist Approach to Income Security Policy for American Women." *Social Politics: International Studies in Gender, States and Society* 1: 190-210.

Swanberg, Jennifer. 1997. "Work and Family Issues Among Lower-Level Workers." PhD diss. Brandeis University.

When the Spirit Blooms:
Acquiring Higher Education
in the Context of Welfare Reform

Avis A. Jones-DeWeever, Institute for Women's Policy Research

SUMMARY. Established within a political context greatly influenced by stereotypical assumptions of impoverished women of color, welfare reform codified a work-first philosophy meant to attack perceived "dependency" and spur "self-sufficiency." This article describes the shortcomings of the work-first approach and highlights the importance of higher education for helping women, and especially women of color, achieve economic well-being. It then reports key findings from a study that examines the impact of higher education on the lives of welfare participants in California. Utilizing a mix of surveys, focus groups, and personal interviews, this study finds that despite the challenges associated with balancing parenthood, college-level coursework, and the bureaucratic demands of welfare reform, the stereotypical notions of the "welfare queen" do not apply. Instead, study participants exhibited a high

[Haworth co-indexing entry note]: "When the Spirit Blooms: Acquiring Higher Education in the Context of Welfare Reform." Jones-DeWeever, Avis A. Co-published simultaneously in *Journal of Women, Politics & Policy* (The Haworth Political Press, an imprint of The Haworth Press, Inc.) Vol. 27, No. 3/4, 2005, pp. 113-133; and: *Women, Work, and Poverty: Women Centered Research for Policy Change* (ed: Heidi Hartmann) The Haworth Political Press, an imprint of The Haworth Press, Inc., 2005, pp. 113-133. Single or multiple copies of this article are available for a fee from The Haworth Document Delivery Service [1-800-HAWORTH, 9:00 a.m. - 5:00 p.m. (EST). E-mail address: docdelivery@haworthpress.com].

Available online at http://www.haworthpress.com/web/JWPP
doi:10.1300/J501v27n03_08

level of ambition, persistence, determination, and hard work in pursuit of their educational ambitions; and in the process, improved their lives and the lives of their children. *[Article copies available for a fee from The Haworth Document Delivery Service: 1-800-HAWORTH. E-mail address: <docdelivery@haworthpress.com> Website: <http://www.HaworthPress.com> © 2005 by The Haworth Press, Inc. All rights reserved.]*

KEYWORDS. Welfare reform, work-first, higher education, women of color, California, quality of life, poverty, self-sufficiency, single parent, interviews

The question I like to ask every child I visit in the classroom is: 'Are you going to college?' In this great country, we expect every child, regardless of how he or she is raised, to go to college.

–President George W. Bush (2001)

Some people could spend their entire five years . . . on welfare going to college. Now, that's not my view of helping people become independent. And it's certainly not my view of understanding the importance of work . . .

–President George W. Bush (2002)

INTRODUCTION

At the heart of President Bush's seemingly contradictory statements lie the basic quandary policymakers across the country face when it comes to the issues of welfare and higher education. While the importance of obtaining a college degree is seemingly incontrovertible, when it comes to the welfare population–primarily poor women and disproportionately women of color–the pursuit of higher education is somehow called into question. For these women, work, any work, is deemed preferable to the act of pursuing a college degree. So much so that despite the well-established economic pay-offs associated with obtaining post-secondary credentials, the "work first" emphasis of welfare reform has resulted in the severe restriction of post-secondary educational opportunities. Faced with the pressure of balancing strict work requirements, increased bureaucratic hurdles, persistent parenting responsibilities and the demands of college coursework, thousands of welfare participating degree-seekers have abandoned their pursuit of higher education under the squeeze of welfare reform. By examining the struggles and pay-offs associated with pursuing higher education while receiving welfare in California, this article takes a look at some of those who refused to let go of their dream.

BACKGROUND

Seeking Self-Sufficiency

In the run-up to welfare reform, the looming politicized image of the lazy, unapologetic, welfare queen breathed life into stereotypical notions of impoverished black women content to live off the public dole. The "problem" was clearly defined as one of dependency (Murray 1984). And attacking that "dependency" through a policy meant to spur "self-sufficiency" and "personal responsibility" was ultimately a prevailing ideal surrounding the conception and passage of welfare reform. Yet, the strategy for obtaining self-sufficiency, like the stereotypical notions of welfare participants themselves, was largely detached from reality. Unfortunately, the work-first philosophy encapsulated in welfare reform falls short of providing a long-term solution to the poverty problem.

During the economic expansion of the mid-to-late 1990s, hundreds of thousands of welfare participants successfully transitioned from welfare to work, but landed squarely within the ranks of the working poor. Welfare leavers typically found themselves concentrated in low-wage occupations that were characterized by job instability, non-traditional work-hours, and few, if any, benefits such as health care and sick leave (Brooks-Gunn et al. 2002; Jones-DeWeever, Peterson, and Song 2003; Loprest 1999).

The most disadvantaged ironically sunk deeper into poverty under welfare reform. Despite a 50 percent increase in their work participation rate, the monthly income of dire poor families[1] declined significantly under TANF, by over 20 percent among families with young children and by 9 percent among families with school-aged children. Unable to earn enough wages to offset the loss in cash assistance, even in relatively good economic times, and unlikely to maintain access to health care and food stamps despite qualifying for such assistance, the dire poor found themselves significantly worse off under welfare reform (Lyter, Sills, Oh, and Jones-DeWeever 2004).

As the economy plummeted in early 2001, spiraling budget deficits led states across the nation to drastically cut back on services aimed at meeting the needs of the poor. Such vital programs as child care assistance, transportation assistance, welfare-to-work programs, and programs addressing other barriers to employment were all being rolled back in order to balance state coffers. In the meantime, the well-being of single-parent families, and African American women and their children in particular, took a significant downturn. Employment rates for black single mothers fell more steeply during this period than for any other demographic group (Lovell 2004; Sherman, Fremsted, and Parrott 2004). Simultaneously, those industries that employed the majority of women who had successfully transitioned from welfare to work in the mid-to-late 1990s were the hardest hit by job losses, accounting for some 51.6 percent of the jobs lost during the recession and weak recovery (Boushey and Rosnick 2004).

In an environment of job loss, rather than job growth, poverty increased. Between 2000 and 2004, more than 5 million people joined the ranks of the poor (U.S. Census Bureau 2005a). Not only were more people poor, but individuals found themselves in deeper poverty. In 2003, the average poor person's income was further below the poverty line than at any other time since 1975–the first year that statistic was collected (Center on Budget and Policy Priorities 2004).

Interestingly, while poverty went up, little change occurred in the welfare rolls. According to a report by the U.S. Department of Health and Human Services, despite an increase in the number of TANF eligible families during the recession, the proportion of families who actually received assistance dropped to only 48 percent, down from an assistance rate of 80 percent in the mid 1990s. This significant drop suggests a large gap between the level of need and the level of assistance available to the nation's poor (U.S. Department of Health and Human Services 2003).

Clearly, in order to achieve the goal of spurring economic well-being resulting in self-sufficiency, the work-first paradigm has fallen exceedingly short. Far more likely to make this goal a reality is the time-tested method of class ascension through the acquisition of higher education.

The Special Importance of Higher Education to Women of Color

Higher education–particularly in the post-industrial economy of the late 20th and early 21st centuries–has for many, proven to be the gateway to the middle class. Although the lasting economic benefits associated with post-secondary education are applicable to all, its benefits are especially key to the economic well-being of women and particularly crucial for women of color. Women with at least some college exposure increase their earnings by 57 percent over the average earnings of women who have not completed high school. The education premium then jumps to a 182 percent earnings increase over non-high school graduates for those who complete a Bachelor's degree (U.S. Census Bureau 2003).

When comparing earnings between high school graduates and those with just some exposure to post-secondary education, the importance of a four-year degree comes clearly into focus. Women who had only some exposure to college increased their earnings by only 5 percent over those with a high school diploma, but those who completed at least a Bachelor's degree enjoyed at least a 59 percent increase in earnings (U.S. Census Bureau 2003).

Interestingly, women of color received the largest college premiums. While a white woman with a four-year degree experiences an earnings increase of 77 percent over her high school graduate counterpart, Latinas experience an 88 percent increase in earnings with a college degree, while the earnings of African American women jump by 92 percent (U.S. Census Bureau 2003).

Education clearly matters. And it matters most for women seeking a pathway out of poverty. Women with low levels of education must often rely on traditional "women's work" which is characterized by low wages, job instability, and little access to even the most basic benefits such as health care and sick leave. As a result, women with low levels of education run a much greater risk of living in poverty than men at the same educational levels. Thus, for many women, acquiring a college degree can literally mean the difference between being relegated to a lifetime of poverty and having a real chance at acquiring true economic self-sufficiency.

According to recent Current Population Survey data, in 2003, among men and women who did not complete high school, women were 43 percent more likely to live in poverty than their male counterparts. Completing high school only slightly narrowed the gap as women with a high school degree were still 40 percent more likely to be poor then men with the same level of education. Among those who completed at least a Bachelor's degree, however, poverty rates for men and women were miniscule and virtually identical at only 3.8 percent and 3.9 percent respectively (U.S. Census Bureau 2004b).

For women of color, higher education is especially critical for in-creasing one's chances of escaping poverty. Just some exposure to higher education decreases the poverty rate for African American women tremendously—from 41 percent among those without a high school degree down to 17 percent for those with some post-secondary education; and among Latinas, poverty drops from 32 percent to 12 percent. Completing college reduces poverty rates even further as only 5.3 percent of African American women and 5.9 percent of Latinas with at least a Bachelor's degree live in poverty (U.S. Census Bureau 2004b).

All and all, exposure to higher education is key to a woman's ability to earn above poverty-level wages. Although incremental steps on the post-secondary ladder do not go unrewarded, by far the biggest payoffs are associated with obtaining at least a four-year degree. Therefore, ob-taining a Bachelor's degree is critically important for those seeking to escape poverty permanently and is particularly vital for single mothers who must raise a family on a single income.

Access to Higher Education Under Welfare Reform

Despite the high economic pay-offs associated with post-second-ary education, welfare reform severely restricted higher education opportunities for welfare participants. According to a study by the Center for Law and Social Policy, between 1996 and 1998, some two-thirds of AFDC/TANF families participating in post-secondary education or training discontinued their pursuit of higher education as the number enrolled in college plummeted from 172,176 to only 58,055 (Greenberg, Strawn, and Plimpton 1999). As a result, colleges across the country saw dramatic declines in the enrollment of students who uti-lized welfare. For example, enrollment among welfare participants at the City University of New York (CUNY) dropped from more than 27,000 students in 1996 to less than 10,000 in 2000 (Price, Steffy, and McFarlane 2003). Likewise, the enrollment of welfare participants in Massachusetts community colleges dropped significantly, from 8,000 to 4,000 following the enactment of welfare reform, as did community college enrollment in California (down from 136,000 in 1996 to 113,000 in 1999); and enrollment in the nation's largest technical col-lege, Milwaukee Area Technical College, went down from 1,600 to only 244 students following TANF enactment (Gruber 1998; Price, Steffy, and McFarlane 2003).

Perhaps upon acknowledging the limitations of the work first para-digm, states began exercising flexibility in their interpretation of "work requirements" as set forth in TANF. As a result, by 2002, 49 states[2] and the District of Columbia allowed at least some access to post-secondary education as an allowable work activity, although there remained wide variation in the level of access allowed from state to state (Center for Women Policy Studies 2002).

In spite of expanded access to post-secondary education on the books, in practice, students face a mountain of challenges in their quest to obtain a college degree under welfare reform. By 2002, half of welfare recipients were expected to work at least 30 hours per week. In addition, states were required to cap their education and training participants at no more than 30 percent of their caseload. And few provided sufficient supports, such as child care and transportation, to make college a realistic option (Schmidt 1998). Some research suggests that although many states allowed at least some post-secondary education to count towards work requirements, in practice, welfare administrators limited participation in higher education due to pressures to place as many as possible into "real jobs" (Kahn 1998). Faced with the pressure of balancing work, child care responsibilities, bureaucratic hurdles, and college classes, tens of thousands of welfare participants were forced to abandon their aspirations for higher education altogether and turn back to a cycle of low-wage work and perpetual poverty.

Welfare and Higher Education in California: An Overview

California represents a unique case for analysis of access to higher education for low-income populations. This state has in place one of the nation's most well-respected community college systems that routinely serves as a bridge to the state's four-year institutions for students across the social and economic spectrum. In addition, the state has historically demonstrated a special commitment to expanding access to higher education for low-income and welfare participating students. Even prior to the Federal JOBS legislation, which sought to expand access to post-secondary education and training under AFDC, California had already established a variety of key programs meant to expand access to higher education for disadvantaged populations. Through such programs as the Expanded Opportunity Program and Services (EOPS, founded in 1969), the Cooperative Agencies Resources for Education program (CARE, founded in 1982), and the Greater Avenues to Independence program (GAIN, founded in 1985), California distinguished itself as a leader in the provision of services to meet the special needs of low-income students working to improve their lives through higher education. Together, these programs granted access to post-secondary education for welfare participants for up to two years (GAIN), while also providing financial and academic assistance, counseling, and other support services for low-income students in general (EOPS), as well as low-income single parents (CARE) in particular (Price, Steffy, and McFarlane 2003).

In response to welfare reform, California adopted the California Work Opportunity and Responsibility for Kids Act (CalWORKs). Simultaneously, the state set aside $65 million in state Maintenance-of-Effort (MOE) dollars specifically for programs to support CalWORKs participants at community colleges across the state. Under the CalWORKs system, participants already enrolled in post-secondary education when entering the welfare system were allowed to count their educational activities towards the state's 32-hour work requirement as long as the student was enrolled in an approved field of study deemed likely to lead directly to employment. In addition, if the participant's classroom, laboratory, and/or internship activities did not meet the 32-hour minimum work requirement, the participant would be required to engage in a work activity for the amount of time necessary to fulfill the work-hour minimum codified in CalWORKs legislation (Center for Women Policy Studies 2003; Fein et al. 2000; Price, Steffy, and McFarlane 2003).

Although at the time of this study state law allowed CalWORKs students the opportunity to pursue up to 24 months of post-secondary education, counties could limit educational access to less than 24 months and some did, in practice, place greater emphasis on short-term (typically 18 month) certificate programs at the expense of allowing access to the full 24-month Associate's Degree programs (Price, Steffy, and McFarlane 2003).

California's unique history and contemporary policies make it an interesting case for analysis. While the state has historically been quite proactive in its approach to supporting the educational needs of low-income populations in general, and welfare participants in particular, in the wake of welfare reform, state policy has become significantly more restrictive. This circumstance allows us the opportunity to examine the outcomes of two very different policy approaches on the lives of individuals seeking to escape poverty through the acquisition of post-secondary education.

In order to examine these outcomes, we put forth the following set of research questions: How does access to higher education impact the lives of current and former welfare participants and their families? What challenges do students face? What impacts do their children experience? In sum, do current and former student-parents substantially benefit from the higher educational experience, and if so, how?

In order to answer these questions, this study examines the educational experiences of student-parents in California who either completed post-secondary education or are currently working towards degree completion under the state's welfare system.

DATA AND METHODOLOGY

To obtain a sample of current and former student-parents, the Institute for Women's Policy Research partnered with the Oakland non-profit group, LIFETIME: Low-Income Families Empowerment Through Education. LIFETIME provides support to welfare participants who seek to enroll in and complete college. Its current and former members include both current student-parents and college graduates who completed their education while receiving welfare. In support of this research, LIFETIME allowed IWPR access to its contact list of over 1,000 potential, current, and past members, each of whom sought to acquire higher education while participating in welfare.

The study employed a mixed-mode data collection strategy including mail and electronic mail surveys of current and former student-parents; three focus groups among current and former student-parents; and in-depth interviews with eight college administrators from various institutions across the state. The survey utilized here consisted of 56 primarily closed-ended questions. Open-ended responses, however, were gathered, grouped by like themes, and analyzed for frequency of similar response occurrence. Likewise, all focus group and interview transcripts were analyzed and grouped by thematic similarity. Particularly salient expressions were later extracted from open-ended responses as well as focus group and interview transcripts in order to highlight key points expressed by student-parents and college administrators throughout the study.

All data collection associated with this project took place during the Spring and Summer of 2004. The survey was distributed to a sample of 1,089 potential respondents, with 887 surveys distributed via postal mail and 202 surveys distributed via electronic mail. Of the 1,089 instruments originally distributed, a total of 132 were returned due to incorrect and/or outdated contact information. This left a total valid pool of 957 potential respondents. After two waves of survey distribution, a total of 92 responses were received resulting in a 9.6 percent response rate. While the response rate generated was lower than ideal, given the method of distribution,[3] and the population sampled,[4] the response was adequate to address the study's research questions in some depth.

Study Participants

Among the 92 survey respondents, just over two-thirds were current student-parents pursuing higher education under CalWORKs (69 percent) while nearly a third were previous AFDC or CalWORKs participants (30 percent). The overwhelming majority were women (97 percent), and three-quarters self-identified as women of color (75 percent). African Americans made up just over a third of respondents (36 percent), followed by whites (23 percent), Latino/as (17 percent), Asian Americans (5 percent), and Native Americans (1 percent). Roughly 15 percent of respondents self-identified as either Biracial or "other" and the remaining respondents failed to indicate their racial or ethnic hertiage. All of the respondents were parents, typically with two elementary school-aged children.

Most respondents (54 percent) had completed at least a high school degree when they made the initial decision to pursue higher education. Yet, significant numbers came to college after acquiring a GED (16 percent) or having failed to complete a GED or high school degree (16 percent). As a result, roughly a third of the sample came to college outside of the traditional transitional linkage of the high school diploma.

Focus group participants included both current and former student-parents. Participants exhibited a broad range of post-secondary experiences ranging from students just beginning their post-secondary work, to former students who had not only completed Bachelor's degrees, but either had completed or were currently completing graduate work. One former student, for example, was at the dissertation stage of the PhD process; another had completed a law degree and was currently working in the field. All of the focus group participants were affiliated with LIFETIME as either current or former members.

Lastly, the college administrators included in the study were selected from a list of eleven EOPS Regional Coordinators designated by the California Community Colleges Chancellor's Office. As campus-level EOPS Directors, each individual had personal experience working specifically with low-income and CalWORKs students at their respective campuses. While efforts were made to include perspectives from all eleven Regional Coordinators, after several scheduling attempts, only eight administrators were available for inclusion in the study. However, among those included, most had worked in the field long enough to have acquired experience working with welfare participants pursuing higher education both before and after welfare reform.

FINDINGS

Educational Expectations, Challenges, and Personal Sacrifices

Not unlike the general population, our findings indicate that student-parents clearly understand the link between education and the promise of economic/social upward mobility. When asked to indicate what factors most influenced the decision to attend college, the most often-cited reason was the desire to improve their financial situation (84 percent). While the promise of an economic payoff was perhaps the primary reason most chose to pursue higher education, the desire to set an example for their children proved to be a strong motivator as well and was indicated by 79 percent of our respondents. Also important was the desire to achieve a personal or career goal, with 71 percent and 67 percent of respondents selecting these choices respectively. Contrary to the sometimes implied notion that allowing the opportunity to acquire higher education would merely be used as an "out" for those who seek to prolong their detachment from employment, only 2 percent of respondents indicated the desire to delay employment was a motivator for pursuing higher education.

While most recognized the importance of a college degree, once on campus, respondents faced numerous challenges in making that dream a reality. For most (71 percent), merely finding time to study proved to be their biggest challenge, followed by the challenge of meeting financial obligations (70 percent), completing their educational pursuits within the allotted time limits (57 percent), spending adequate time with their children (55 percent), and finding child care during study time (53 percent). Although the vast majority of respondents (84 percent) indicated that they still struggle with these challenges, nearly two-thirds (63 percent) said that they relied on family and friends to help overcome this admittedly difficult situation.

According to one college administrator, familial support is critical to college success, particularly for this specific segment of the student population. She states:

> *My experience is people who do not have any family in the area struggle more . . . when it comes to child care concerns and being able to have someone watch the kids while they run to work or run to school or run to the store, families and extended families really take up a lot of the slack, so if a student doesn't have that . . . their chance of survival within the educational system becomes limited 'cause they can't make it to class.*

The reality of having to balance CalWORKs requirements along with the responsibilities of parenthood and college life is no easy task, even under the best of circumstances. Continuing to muddle through a life of poverty, and oftentimes having to overcome learning disabilities, or merely adjusting to the demands of student life when previous schooling may have occurred years ago, makes the pursuit of a college degree not only a challenge, but a pursuit replete with stories of personal sacrifice.

Roughly 95 percent of those surveyed indicated having made sacrifices to pursue higher education, most often citing time with children (73 percent), employment/income (65 percent), and leisure activities (61 percent). While sacrifices were indicated, more than 9 in 10 noted that education is worth the sacrifice. Many participants discussed anticipating the payoff of a better life for their children. As one study participant succinctly put it, "I know that my situation is only (temporary). I hate being on welfare and I will sacrifice anything for a degree and a great paying job with benefits."

Another described the choice she made between pursuing higher education or continuing the cycle of low-wage work when she stated:

> *I could have gotten a low-wage dead-end job with no problems. The reason why I did not want that life is because I knew if I had, I would most likely be there 10 years later. I didn't just want a job, I wanted a future, a career, a life for my daughter. Attending college will give me that. I attend USC and my whole life has changed for the better because of the doors my education has opened for me.*

These women clearly understood the link between higher education and improved earnings potential. Perhaps because of this understanding, most saw their educational journey as just beginning. Only 11 percent indicated that they wanted to stop with an Associate's Degree. Instead, the vast majority (82 percent) aspired to at least a four-year degree with a large proportion (53 percent) working towards the goal of graduate or professional education. But understanding the importance of education was just the beginning. Others experienced the change that educational acquisition provides and in the process, found out that post-secondary education ultimately results in much more than merely a bigger paycheck.

Changing Lives Through Education

While many participants had high hopes regarding the eventual pay-offs associated with higher education, nearly all (95 percent) indicated that the educational experience had already resulted in a positive change in their lives. The most often-cited changes were in the areas of self-esteem (80 percent), followed by the feeling of contributing to society (69 percent) and the opening up of better job opportunities (63 percent).

Several women described the financial benefits associated with completing higher education and how their lives have improved because of it:

> *Before taking the classes, my hourly wage (I worked at an elementary school) was $8.75/hr. I now make $18.00/hr in a position as an office manager.*

> *My sacrifice to attend school was extremely worthwhile. I have since graduated and have been gainfully employed for almost four years. My income has grown dramatically and my family is benefiting from the finances that we share.*

> *. . . Now I'm in a position to where I can spend more time with my kids, plan my financial future, take vacations, not having to live paycheck to paycheck . . .*

> *I started out with a toddler in a crappy tiny studio. Now I am working on an MA, rent a beautiful house with a yard, garage, have a dog, can pay for my son's sports activities, work, and go to school. It's tiring, but I have attainable goals.*

While improved financial well-being has afforded many a more enjoyable lifestyle, on a broader scale, for others, higher education opened up a whole new world simply by providing a new sense of self. As one participant put it, "You know, I really like the person that I've turned into being because of education. I'm not going to be nobody's punching bag no more. I'm not going to be nobody's floor anymore."

According to one college administrator, such inner-transformations were indeed the rule, rather than the exception. She states:

> *I have seen this in so many cases, where women with the biggest barriers—they have drug and alcohol problems or domestic violence—but once they get clear, something clicks in them and they have a tremendous source of strength that they tap from . . . they have a faith in themselves, in their . . . whatever their faith is in, they have that faith that they can do it, and that they can be successful. And they don't even entertain the idea of not making it. And I've noticed also that these are the students, they are—how can I say this?—it seems simple, but they are sweet, they are good. They are kind. And they seem to take this sense of kindness, not only . . . do they get along with their co-workers, but they get along with themselves. They can forgive themselves. They can forgive themselves as well as anyone else. And that takes a major blockage out of their way. They don't let people get in their way. They don't hold grudges. They just move right along. And then they do the same for themselves when they have a problem, or make a mistake, they don't beat themselves up over it. The say, 'Okay, I'm going to be better.' And they just don't entertain the idea that they are going to fail, or that they are not going to make it. And sometimes it's for their kids, but you know, it's usually that they have just made a decision that they are going to succeed. And . . . it's easier to help someone that you see this in, you think, 'Oh man, this person is wonderful and they are going to make it.' And everyone is different; this quality appears in all different kinds of people—older women with children, young women—'cause we have women of all ages. It's just a very interesting phenomenon and I think it has to do with spirit. I mean, what else can it be? A person's spirit, when it has been tested, sometimes it really—it just blooms."*

Impact on Children

The personal growth and sense of self-empowerment garnered through the educational process is clearly palpable in the lives of these women. However, their lives are not the only ones impacted by exposure to higher education. Roughly 8 in 10 indicated that their children's educational experience had been impacted since their enrollment in higher education as well. Nearly two-thirds (63 percent) indicated that their children are now more likely to express a desire to go to college, 42 percent said their children had improved study habits, and almost a third (30 percent) indicated that their children are making better grades.

The positive effects on children are perhaps not surprising, particularly given that 9 in 10 respondents indicated that they now feel better equipped to help their children achieve educational goals and many described how their successes have ultimately expanded their children's horizons. One participant provided a particularly poignant example of how personal educational success can serve as a source of inspiration for a child's educational future:

> *... when I was going through school here at the college, we became homeless for nine months and we really thought things were down and out for us, but I kept struggling in school to keep up my 4.0 GPA and I mean I was struggling hard with trying to find a home for us and so forth. When I started winning some scholarships my daughter saw that it actually paid to do good in school. She totally did a u-turn. By the time she was in sixth grade, she was one of the top students in her class, went on to junior [high] and just excelled. When she left junior high, that summer of graduating from junior high going into high school, she started taking college classes. She did high school and college together. When she graduated from high school she got her AA degree in engineering here at the city college. She got her degree in her hand before she actually received her high school diploma in her hand the following week. She's now at Long Beach State and she's just zooming right along in school ...*

While most indicated a positive impact on the lives of their children, a few mothers paid a high price for losing quality time. Some children experienced behavioral problems or got into trouble in an attempt to gain attention. Also, the pressures of trying to balance it all caused some parents to feel guilty about the lack of time with their children. Yet, despite the stress and reduced family time, the overwhelming majority of participants emphasized the expanded life chances now afforded them, as compared to the limited opportunities available before.

> *I remember looking in the mirror and thinking, I'm going to be pushing a shopping cart. What am I going to do? I couldn't pay for childcare. So as a result of going to school, I'm not pushing a shopping cart. And I, in terms of the overall impact, it's changed my son's future because nobody in my family had ever gone to college.*

Comparing the Experiences of Degree-Seekers and Degree Holders

While all study participants faced ups and downs in pursuit of their educational goals, certain differences emerged between the experiences of those currently seeking higher education under the CalWORKs system and those who were former CalWORKs and AFDC participants. Perhaps because some of these students pursued their education under the AFDC system, former participants were much more likely than current participants to indicate that their caseworker was helpful in supporting their college experience (57 percent vs. 38 percent); a key factor given that caseworker support can go a long way toward determining educational access and success.

Although both groups overwhelmingly indicated that the educational experience had changed their lives (98 percent of former participants agreed with this statement as compared to 93 percent of current participants), those who had completed a post-secondary degree experienced many more positive changes across several key aspects of life. For example, degree-holders were more likely to indicate that their personal relationships had improved since enrolling in higher education, both with their children (53 percent vs. 47 percent) and with other family members and friends (57 percent vs. 37 percent). Degree-holders were also more likely to indicate that they now felt like they were contributing to society (77 percent vs. 63 percent) and to report increased self-esteem (87 percent vs. 77 percent) and greater community involvement (81 percent vs. 54 percent).

Not surprisingly, degree-holders were much more likely to indicate that they now had better job opportunities (83 percent vs. 44 percent), and had more financial resources (68 percent vs. 35 percent) than those still working towards a degree. In fact, the earnings of degree-holders outpaced that of degree-seekers substantially. Degree-holders earned $13.14 per hour as compared to an hourly wage of only $7.50 for the typical respondent still working towards degree completion. Degree-holders, then, experienced a significant earnings premium associated with their educational attainment by earning roughly 75 percent more per hour than their degree-seeker counterpart.

Not only did degree-holders experience a variety of personal and financial benefits associated with their educational attainment, but the experience also equipped them with the necessary tools to ensure a variety of benefits to their children as well, particularly in the area of educational development. For example, degree-holders were more likely to indicate that they felt better equipped to help their children achieve educational goals (94 percent vs. 86 percent), and were much more likely to be involved in their children's educational experience by doing things like helping them with their homework (68 percent vs. 54 percent), taking them to the library (75 percent vs. 47 percent), and talking to them about the importance of education (85 percent vs. 72 percent). In addition, degree-holders were more likely to indicate their children's educational experience had been impacted by their exposure to higher education (87 percent vs. 67 percent). Perhaps as a result of these differences, degree-holders were much more likely to indicate that their children now expressed a desire to go to college (72 percent vs. 56 percent).

Interestingly, although the children of degree-holders have seemingly benefited most from their parents' exposure to higher education, the children of degree-seekers were just as likely to have had the benefit of parental involvement at school (65 percent vs. 64 percent). Yet, the demands of trying to balance it all are evident as degree-seekers were more likely than degree-holders to indicate that their lives are now more stressful (33 percent vs. 15 percent), and that they now have less time, overall, to spend with their children (33 percent vs. 26 percent). Despite these challenges, degree-seekers remain firm in their commitment to education and overwhelmingly assert that the educational experience is worthy of their current personal sacrifices (91 percent). The findings presented here seem to bolster that logic.

As evidenced by the experiences of those who have completed this journey, the payoffs associated with higher education are immense– better job opportunities, greater financial resources, better personal relationships, and improved educational outcomes/aspirations among their children. Payoffs though, are not limited to these specific families, but instead ultimately spill out to their larger communities. Nearly two-thirds (64 percent) of the degree-holders surveyed ultimately stayed in their communities after having completed their degrees, and four out of five (81 percent) indicated that they increased their level of community involvement after having been exposed to higher education. Given this finding it becomes clear that higher education benefits both individuals and communities while also serving as a potential force for intergenerational socio-economic change.

CONCLUSION

This study provides compelling evidence regarding the broad range of payoffs associated with higher education. Beyond the financial benefits, for many, a new level of self-assuredness produced an unwillingness to put up with abusive relationships or a future relegated to low-wage work. This new perspective on life expanded horizons, making what once seemed unobtainable, now well within reach. In order to further uncover this population's largely untapped human capital potential, policymakers must make a concerted effort to expand access to higher education for welfare participants. The following would make a good start:

- *Allow welfare participants access to post-secondary education for their full TANF-eligibility period.* Research shows that the greatest economic payoffs associated with education, particularly for women, are acquired through the acquisition of at least a four-year degree. Therefore, in order to maximize future earning power, participants should be allowed access to higher education for their full five years of cash-assistance eligibility. Such an investment provides the best opportunity for permanently escaping poverty and truly obtaining self-sufficiency.

- *Allow welfare participants to count classroom time and study time as work.* Requiring "work" outside of the classroom is counterproductive, unless that work is in the form of an internship or other experiential learning environment that will count toward degree acquisition goals. Given the importance of degree-attainment for future earning power, along with the importance of parental guidance and bonding for the children of those pursuing degrees, degree-seekers should not be burdened with work requirements that will neither support their long-term economic well-being nor their immediate parenting responsibilities.

- *Stop the clock for college-bound TANF participants.* Especially important for those participants not allowed the time required to complete a four-year degree, time spent receiving post-secondary education should not reduce the participant's TANF-eligibility period. Acquiring education should not mean forfeiting a financial safety net in case of future economic distress.

- *Increase the availability of need-based grant awards.* Allowing access to education is only part of the picture. Having the opportunity to acquire education is an empty promise if one cannot afford to take advantage of the opportunity that is availed to them. Increasing the availability of needs-based awards increases opportunities, especially for women of color, a population that has historically been less likely to consider utilizing loans to finance higher education.

For welfare participants in particular, the road to and through higher education is not an easy one. Having come this far, the women included in this study counter the stereotypical notions of the lazy, complacent "welfare queen" and, instead, exemplify an extraordinarily resilient, determined, and hopeful population struggling through challenging circumstances in search of a better future for themselves, their families, and their communities.

AUTHOR NOTE

The author would like to thank the members and staff of LIFETIME for their time and assistance with the data collection vital to the successful conclusion of this work. A special thank you is also reserved for the Ford Foundation for its generous support of this project.

NOTES

1. This study defines dire poor families as those whose incomes fall below 50 percent of the poverty threshold for their family size.

2. Oklahoma is the only state that does not allow post-secondary education as an allowable work activity.

3. While more economical, both postal mail and electronic survey distribution methods tend to garner significantly lower response rates than those associated with telephone and personally administered survey methodologies.

4. Low-income populations represent a special challenge in survey collection due to their greater tendency of mobility, their higher likelihood of living in multi-family households, and their lower level of motivation for survey participation (perhaps due to their overarching daily concerns of meeting survival needs) (Ploeg, Moffitt, and Citro 2002).

REFERENCES

Boushey, Heather and David Rosnick. 2004. *For Welfare Reform to Work, Jobs Must Be Available.* Washington, DC: Center for Economic and Policy Research.

Brooks-Gunn, J., P. Klebanow, J. Smith, and K. Lee. 2002. "Effects of Combining Public Assistance and Employment on Mothers and Their Young Children." In *Welfare, Work and Well-Being*, ed. M.C. Lennon. New York: The Haworth Press, Inc.

Bush, G.W. 2001. Remarks by the President at Griegos Elementary School, Albuquerque, NM. *http://www.whitehouse.gov/news/releases/2001/08/20010815-2.html*

Bush, G.W. 2002. "President Urges Senate to Pass Compassionate Welfare Reform Bill." *http://www.whitehouse.gov/news/releases/2002/07/20020729-6.html*

Center for Women Policy Studies. 2002. *From Poverty to Self-Sufficiency: The Role of Post-Secondary Education in Welfare Reform.* Washington, DC: Center for Women Policy Studies.

Center on Budget and Policy Priorities. 2005. *Economic Recovery Failed to Benefit Much of the Population in 2004.* Washington, DC: Center on Budget and Policy Priorities.

Fein, David, Eric Beecroft, David Long, and Andree Catalfamo. 2000. *College as a Job Advancement Strategy: An Early Report on the New Visions Self-Sufficiency and Lifelong Learning Project.* Bethesda, Maryland: Abt Associates.

Greenberg, Mark, Julie Strawn, and Lisa Plimpton. 2000. *State Opportunities to Provide Access to Postsecondary Education Under TANF.* Washington, DC: Center for Law and Social Policy.

Gruber, Andrew. 1998. "Promoting Long-Term Self-Sufficiency for Welfare Recipients; Post-Secondary Education and the Welfare Work Requirement." *Northwestern University Law Review* 93: 247, 280.

Jones-DeWeever, Avis, Janice Peterson, and Xue Song. 2003. *Before and After Welfare Reform: The Work and Well-Being of Low-Income Single Parent Families.* Washington, DC: Institute for Women's Policy Research.

Kahn, Karen. 1998. "Across the Country, Single Mothers Are Abandoning Their Hopes and Dreams of Higher Education as They Face Tougher Work Requirements and Benefit Time Limits." *Sojourner* 24(October): 31-32.

Loprest, Pamela. 1999. *Families Who Left Welfare: Who Are They and How Are They Doing?* Washington, DC: The Urban Institute.

Lovell, Vicky. 1994. "Black Women's Unemployment Rate Remains High." *Institute for Women's Policy Research Quarterly Newsletter* (Winter/Spring): 1.

Lyter, Deanna, Melissa Sills, Gi-Taik Oh, and Avis Jones-DeWeever. 2004. *The Children Left Behind: Deeper Poverty, Fewer Supports.* Washington, DC: Institute for Women's Policy Research.

Murray, Charles. 1984. *Losing Ground: American Social Policy 1950-1980.* New York: Basic Books.

Ploeg, Michele, Robert Moffitt, and Constance Citro. 2002. *Studies of Welfare Populations: Data Collection and Research Issues.* Washington, DC: National Research Council.

Price, Charles, Tracy Steffy, and Tracy McFarlane. 2003. *Continuing Commitment to the Higher Education Option: Model State Legislation, College Programs, and Advocacy Organizations that Support Access to Post-Secondary Education for Public Assistance Recipients.* New York: Howard Samuels State Management and Policy Center of the City University of New York.

Schmidt, Peter. 1998. "States Discourage Welfare Recipients from Pursuing a Higher Education." *The Chronicle of Higher Education*, January 23.

Sherman, Arloc, Shawn Fremstad, and Sharon Parrott. 2004. *Employment Rates for Single Mothers Fell Substantially During Period of Labor Market Weakness.* Washington, DC: Center on Budget and Policy Priorities.

U.S. Census Bureau. 2004a. *Income, Poverty, and Health Insurance Coverage in the United States: 2004.* Washington, DC: U.S. Government Printing Office.

U.S. Census Bureau. 2004b. Current Population Survey, 2004 Annual Social and Economic Supplement. *Years of School Completed by Poverty Status, Sex, Age, Nativity and Citizenship: 2003.* Table POV29. *http://ferret.bls.census.gov/macro/032004/pov/new29_100.htm*

U.S. Census Bureau. 2003. Current Population Survey. *Mean Earnings of Workers 18 Years and Over, by Educational Attainment, Race, Hispanic Origin, and Sex: 1975 to 2002.* Table A-3. *http://www.census.gov/population/socdemo/education/tabA-3.pdf*

U.S. Department of Health and Human Services. 2005. *Indicators of Welfare Dependence: Annual Report to Congress 2005.* Washington, DC: U.S. Government Printing Office.

Policy Implications
of Supporting Women of Color
in the Sciences

Angela Johnson, St. Mary's College of Maryland

SUMMARY. This research suggests that, contrary to popular perception, there exists a pool of women of color with avid interest in science,
and the academic skills to pursue that interest. It further suggests that
these women, if given the support necessary to persist in science, will
choose careers that address many other needs, domestic and international, including schooling and science education; rural and urban health
care, public health and medical research; the environment; and other
public service fields. Investing in the retention of high-achieving women
of color in science yields returns on multiple levels. This conclusion is
based on a study of high-achieving women of color interested in studying science, and an evaluation of a university enrichment program for
science students of color. *[Article copies available for a fee from The Haworth
Document Delivery Service: 1-800-HAWORTH. E-mail address: <docdelivery@
haworthpress.com> Website: <http://www.HaworthPress.com> © 2005 by The
Haworth Press, Inc. All rights reserved.]*

KEYWORDS. Higher education, science careers, African Americans,
Hispanics, American Indians, public service, enrichment, women of
color

[Haworth co-indexing entry note]: "Policy Implications of Supporting Women of Color in the Sciences."
Johnson, Angela. Co-published simultaneously in *Journal of Women, Politics & Policy* (The Haworth Political Press, an imprint of The Haworth Press, Inc.) Vol. 27, No. 3/4, 2005, pp. 135-150; and: *Women, Work, and
Poverty: Women Centered Research for Policy Change* (ed: Heidi Hartmann) The Haworth Political Press, an
imprint of The Haworth Press, Inc., 2005, pp. 135-150. Single or multiple copies of this article are available
for a fee from The Haworth Document Delivery Service [1-800-HAWORTH, 9:00 a.m. - 5:00 p.m. (EST).
E-mail address: docdelivery@haworthpress.com].

doi:10.1300/J501v27n03_09

INTRODUCTION

The image of the leaky pipeline is often used to explain the absence of women of color in the cadre of practicing scientists. This image suggests that girls and boys of all races begin school curious about the world around them–eager and ready to learn about science. Over time, however, interest wanes in several groups while persisting in others–particularly at important junctures, like the transition from middle school to high school and again from high school to college. In this article, I present evidence suggesting that in fact there is still a pool of academically able, science-oriented women of color at the transition from high school to college, that many of those women can be retained in science given appropriate support, and that this support goes on to yield double dividends, as these women are quite likely to pursue science-related careers in the public sector. I will argue that the leaky pipeline can be patched, and that investing in that patching not only retains women of color in the sciences but pumps valuable, well-educated individuals into jobs that serve others, primarily in health care and education.

I base this contention on eight years of research into the academic lives of women of color who chose to major in science. In 1997, I began an ongoing evaluation of the University of Colorado Minority Arts and Sciences Program (MASP). MASP was founded to promote the success of high-achieving students of color in the sciences. In 1999 and 2000, I undertook an extensive ethnographic study of the experiences of women science students of color; all but one of the women in that study were members of MASP. In this article, I present evidence about the dispositions, goals, and career trajectories of the women in the ethnographic study. Next I discuss the ways in which MASP supported many of those women through graduation in the sciences and on to science-related careers.

THEORETICAL FRAMEWORK

My research is based on the assumption that it is through the experiences of individuals and groups that useful directions for change are found. Through considering the personal interactions and institutional features (Davidson 1996) of the lives of individuals, their habitus and cultural capital or lack thereof (Bourdieu 1977), and the consequent development of grounded theory (Glaser and Strauss 1967), strategies that are concrete, effective, and accepted by all stakeholders can be developed.

The ideas I present here grow out of the finding by Seymour and Hewitt (1997) that all science students face roughly the same conditions, but not all students react to those conditions in similar fashion. They are founded in an understanding that race, ethnicity, and gender differences are socially constructed but, nonetheless, go on to construct individuals' experiences, constraints, and opportunities, including those different reactions Seymour and Hewitt documented. The dispositions that characterize the women I studied–enthusiasm for science coupled with a commitment to serving the public good–sometimes led them to interpret these similar conditions in discouraging ways. With support from MASP, that discouragement was contained and they went on to graduate and, in high numbers, become scientists or pursue careers (particularly in health and education) that make use of their science training.

DISPOSITIONS AND CAREER TRAJECTORIES OF UNDERGRADUATE WOMEN OF COLOR

Through ethnographic study, I explored the values, dispositions, and goals of twenty women of color who came to college intent on majoring in science. I knew some of the women through my work with MASP; MASP students suggested others to me. I invited women to participate based on two criteria: initial desire to major in science and adequate high school preparation to persist in science. The quality of curriculum offered by participants' high schools varied, but all of them had strong grades in high school. At the time of the study, all the women were juniors or seniors. All but three had persisted in science majors (thirteen in biology, two in kinesiology, one in biochemistry, and one in chemistry). The pool included six Black women (including one African immigrant), seven Latinas (predominantly Mexican Americans and southwestern Hispanas), three American Indian women (all raised on or near their home reservation), and four Asian American women of various ethnicities. In interviews, I asked them to reflect on their experiences studying science, including why they had originally been drawn to science majors, what they particularly enjoyed about their work in science, what they found difficult, how they thought their ethnicity had shaped their experiences, and whether they planned to pursue careers in science. I also spent a great deal of time with these students, accompanying them to upper-level science classes and labs (including organic chemistry, molecular biology, and human anatomy). To better understand their reports about their experiences in introductory science classes, I also accompanied freshmen and sophomore women of color to general physics, environmental biology, general chemistry, and honors chemistry classes and labs. I analyzed interviews and the field notes I made in classes and labs by searching for common patterns and themes, and elaborating on those themes until reaching theoretical saturation (Glaser and Strauss 1967). I read and re-read transcripts and notes, trying to understand not just the common experiences my informants reported, but the meanings they ascribed to those experiences (Spradley 1979, 1980). This analysis revealed two major themes that the women in this study held in common: enthusiasm for science that is maintained from childhood up through college, and a desire to pursue careers that are altruistic in nature.

Enthusiasm for Science

Twelve women in the study told me explicitly why they liked science. Nine told me they found it intrinsically interesting. Five mentioned they enjoyed the intellectual challenge. Eight had enjoyed it in high school. The following quotes from women in the study are typical, and indicate women with classic scientific traits, including a desire to know why things work they way they do, a skeptical mind, and an excitement about exploring the world through science. Nancy,[1] a Latina senior, told me: "I wanted to feel like I was learning something that nobody else knew, and discovering things. I want to find out why things are the way they are." Nancy is now pursuing a PhD in the biomedical sciences. Jaya, an Asian woman, told me ". . . I guess I'm more of a scientist. I like the whole intellectual aspect of it. I really like to think that way. Um . . . many things, like psychology, and like religious studies and things like that, you don't have physical evidence of some things, and I like to have the evidence in front of me. I guess that's what makes me a scientist." Jaya is also working on a biomedical PhD.

Kathy, an American Indian woman, also told me about the appeal of science over other majors:

I like biology, I like learning about cells, the body–the mechanisms of cells, and cell signaling–all that stuff. I thought it was the coolest thing. Because to me, everything comes down to a cell. Skin is made out of cells. In the end, a cell can kill you. Because when you get cancer, it's because you have a mutated cell, and it proliferates and proliferates, and it comes down to that one cell. And then, in the end, it might go back to your gene. So it's all on the littlest level that hurts you. Stuff that hurts you is on the littlest level. I thought that was *so* cool, that something so small has such a big effect.

I just like biology. I couldn't see myself doing anything but biology. And then some people were like "well, you can get an ethnic studies . . . ," and I didn't even–I didn't think twice about going into ethnic studies. I mean, that's a good major, and you can take a lot of interesting classes, but I like biology more than anything.

Kathy is working on an advanced degree in a health field; her goal is to return to her hometown and serve the elders in her community by using traditional concepts of illness to explain western medical diagnoses.

Kathy's career goals bring me to the second major finding of interest: That many of the women in this study held altruistic career goals, goals they saw as inextricably linked with their science studies. Twelve of the sixteen women who discussed their career goals with me told me about wanting to use their lives to help others, and many went on to talk about how they saw their pursuit of science degrees as a vehicle for this altruism.

Altruistic Career Goals

Chris, a Latina from a tiny, remote town, told me about her interest in helping people. As you can see, she repeatedly links helping with science, through her interest in the environment and in medicine and medical research:

I've always been interested in the environment, and helping the environment, but I don't know if that's something I'd want to do forever, because I'm *really* interested in medicine. I can't see myself working in a lab all the time, just because it's so–I don't like being by myself that much, I want to be able to interact with people, and I don't think that, if I just got a PhD and wanted to be a biologist, I would be able to be in that much contact with people. And so, with medicine, I could have patients, and I could do clinical research, and stuff like that. I think that would be really interesting. I think it's just the fact that anything that I can do to help people would really make me feel good.

Chris is currently engaged in medical research as she applies to medical school.

Jackie, an African American woman, told me:

> I don't really care for chemistry too much, don't care for physics, but biology, for some reason, I just really have always liked it. I've had a lot of people go through different aspects of needing medical help, and I think it's a way for me to make a place in the world where I feel like I'm making a difference for other people, which is important for me. I want to be able to–I guess I want to be able to look back and think I made a difference in someone else's life.

Jackie is finishing medical school now.

Beyond Graduation: Science in the Public Sector

In 2002, in the course of evaluating the MASP, I tracked 42 of the 61, 1997-2001 female graduates of the program; this included 13 of the 20 women in the ethnographic study. This allowed me to confirm that many of the women I studied, and women like them in MASP, persisted with their interest in public-service-oriented science. Among the MASP graduates, 24 (57 percent) are working or pursuing graduate work in health care. Seven alums (17 percent) are engaged in education, including classroom teachers, math and science educators both within traditional educational settings and in non-school settings, and college teachers and administrators.

Twenty-six female alums (62 percent) use science in their jobs in health care, science and math education, and biomedical research. Thirty of them (71 percent) work in the public sector in health care, education, biomedical research, the ministry, and as fire and rescue personnel.

RETAINING WOMEN OF COLOR IN SCIENCE MAJORS

The science-oriented, public-oriented early careers of these women are encouraging. Through my work with these women over the years, I believe that their participation in MASP was an essential element in that success. An analysis of graduation patterns of MASP students underscores this. Graduation rates of Black, Latina and American Indian women who participate in MASP not only surpass those of comparable students of color who don't participate, but those of White women, also.

Table 1 compares Black, Latino, and American Indian MASP students to several other groups of women students. As a group, Black, Latino, and American Indian women students had fewer financial resources than White and Asian women students. The women in MASP had predicted freshman grade point averages (based on a weighted average of standardized test scores and high school grade point average) comparable to White and Asian women. MASP students had higher college graduation rates than either White and Asian women or Black, Latina, and American Indian women not in MASP.

The argument can be made that MASP graduation rates are so high because of self-selection; the students who would seek out an academic enrichment program are the kind of students who would graduate no matter what. While this may be true, program participants consistently praised MASP as an important factor in staying in school. When asked on a survey "How much has your participation in MASP encouraged you to continue at this university?" with answers ranging from 1 (not at all) to 5 (very much), 82 percent of (male and female) respondents circled 3 or above, and 56 percent circled 4 or 5. When asked "Would you recommend MASP to a friend?" 96 percent indicated they would, and several students spontaneously wrote in comments, including "definitely," "for sure," and "I already have!"

These comparisons are based not on a random sample but on an entire population: all of the female students who enrolled as freshmen between 1993 and 1999 in the university where this research was conducted. Because of the uniqueness of MASP, it is difficult to generalize

TABLE 1. Female students admitted to the University of Colorado, Boulder, as freshmen, 1993-1999.

	Not in MASP: Black, Hispanic/Latino or American Indian N = 1,031	In MASP: Black, Hispanic/Latino or American Indian N = 82	White or Asian, not in MASP N = 10,856
Predicted first year GPA	2.58	2.82	2.85
Graduation GPA	2.96	3.16	3.18
Percent who received financial aid during first semester	54%	68%	27%
Graduated	50%	71%	65%

these findings to any larger population; however, I calculated an analysis of variance to measure how different the groups being compared are. The predicted GPA for Black, Latino, and American Indian students who were never members of MASP was significantly lower than for the other two groups ($p \leq 0.001$). The graduation GPA for Black, Latino, and American Indian students who were never in MASP differed significantly from those of ongoing MASP students and White and Asian students ($p \leq 0.05$). The percent of White and Asian students receiving need based aid was significantly different from that of all other groups ($p \leq 0.001$). Family resources of all three differed significantly ($p \leq 0.05$). Graduation rates and graduation GPAs of Black, Hispanic, and American Indian women never in MASP were significantly lower than those of all other groups of students ($p \leq 0.001$).

Twelve of the women included in Table 1 in the MASP participant group dropped out of MASP; the remaining 70 women continued to participate actively through graduation. When the 12 women who did not have ongoing MASP participation were removed from the sample, the graduation rate, formerly 71 percent, rose to 80 percent, which was significantly higher than that of White or Asian women (65 percent).

Table 2 shows graduation rates for women whose first declared major was in science. The university where this study took place collects data on the first major students officially declare, and then the major they hold on graduation. For the purposes of this analysis, science majors included applied mathematics, astronomy, atmospheric chemistry, biochemistry, chemistry, environmental biology, geology, kinesiology, mathematics, molecular biology, and physics. Mathematics and applied mathematics were included because several students who entered college interested in math majors participated in MASP, since there was no comparable program for mathematics students. Again, program participants were more likely to graduate than students in comparison groups, despite greater financial need.

Analysis of variance indicates that the predicted GPA and graduation GPA of Black, Latina, and American Indian students never in MASP was significantly lower than that of other groups ($p \leq 0.05$). The percent of White or Asian students receiving financial aid was significantly lower than that of both other groups ($p < .001$). The graduation rate in science and overall of Black, Latina, and American Indian students not in MASP was lower than that of the other two groups ($p < .05$).

When the nine women with initial science majors but without ongoing MASP participation were eliminated from the sample, the graduation rate in science rose to 64 percent. This rate was significantly higher

TABLE 2. Female students with first declared major in science admitted to the University of Colorado, Boulder, as freshmen, 1993-1999.

	Not in MASP: Black, Hispanic/Latino or American Indian N = 186	In MASP: Black, Hispanic/Latino or AmericanIndian N = 59	White or Asian, not in MASP N = 2675
Predicted first year GPA	2.66	2.87	2.94
Graduation GPA	2.97	3.15	3.18
Percent who received financial aid during first semester	52%	63%	29%
Graduated in science	29%	54%	43%
Graduated in any field	56%	73%	70%

than the two other groups ($p \leq 0.01$). The overall graduation rate (with any major) of continuing MASP women rose to 84 percent; this was significantly higher than the graduation rate of Black, Latina or American Indian women not in MASP ($p < .001$) and approaching significance when compared to the White and Asian women ($p < .10$).

A Latina senior offered an explanation of how MASP supported her interest in science through offering an enrichment workshop:

> For chemistry workshop, we did a lot more problems, more–it was like, we got what we got in class, and then you got what you got in the book, and all the problems they assigned in the book, which basically then went over in class; and then you came to workshop, and even if we hadn't done it in the class, we were still learning it, because it was part of chemistry, not just because we had to do it for the test.

This young woman is now pursuing a PhD in biomedical science.

POLICY IMPLICATIONS

Supporting women of color interested in science appears to yield double dividends, as many go on to reinvest that support by working in the public sector. So what does a successful support program look like?

The program in this study, the University of Colorado Minority Arts and Sciences Program, was founded in 1993 to increase science graduation rates of well-prepared students of color. In 1999, it was expanded to serve students majoring in the humanities. MASP is open to women and men, and to all interested students (the Asian MASP students, and the few White students who have been in the program over the years, were omitted from this analysis in order to keep the focus on women from under-represented groups). It is a matriculation-to-graduation program. Students attend an intensive summer program before their freshman year, and then participate in weekly academic enrichment seminars aligned with their coursework for their first two years in college. Juniors and seniors may still attend seminars, are required to undertake independent research, are assisted in applying to graduate and professional school, and are expected to take on mentoring roles. Students in good standing are eligible for annual $1,000 participation grants. The program is surprisingly inexpensive given its extent and its success. It costs about $2,500 per student per year, including the annual grants. Of that, $1,500 comes from University of Colorado funds; the remainder is made up through a combination of merit-based scholarship funds, private donations, and small grants.

Systematic study of the existence or effectiveness of similar programs is rather scattered. Gándara and Maxwell-Jolley (1999) conducted a comprehensive overview of support programs for high-achieving students of color, particularly in the sciences, mathematics, and engineering. They found that while many such programs exist, "few programs have formal evaluations" (p. 23). An exception is the Meyerhoff Scholars Program at the University of Maryland, Baltimore County, which has been shown to raise graduation rates in the sciences, mathematics and engineering (Maton, Hrabowski, and Schmitt 2000). The Meyerhoff program, however, costs about 3-5 times as much per student as MASP. Programs modeled on the Mathematics Workshop Program pioneered at the University of California, Berkeley, have also been evaluated rigorously and shown to significantly improve performance in calculus, even by students with mediocre mathematics preparation (Fullilove and Treisman 1990; Murphy, Stafford, and McCreary 1998).

Given the paucity of existing research on successful support programs, I worked with the director of MASP, Dr. Alphonse Keasley, to come up with some guidelines for identifying or developing successful support programs. Extensive analysis of MASP, coupled with other theoretical work on the retention of high-achieving students of color, suggests that successful programs need to consider ways of:

• Emphasizing academic enrichment, not remediation.

- Helping students hook into power structures on campus; enabling them to make connections in powerful places.
- Establishing an academic space for a diverse ethnic minority community.
- Fostering a sense of cohesion and community among high-achieving students of color, and helping students to form new ties in addition to their older family, friendship, and community ties, not in lieu of them.
- Providing financial support.

Enrichment, Not Remediation

The work of Steele (1997) and others shows that when individuals suspect that they are the objects of negative stereotypes, they exhibit an anxiety (rooted in the desire to disprove the stereotypes) that can actually diminish their performance (thus, ironically, serving to confirm the stereotypes). MASP students, and the director of MASP, have told me that when they begin to describe MASP, people often assume that, because it serves students of color, it must be a remediation program. Jackie, the African American woman now in medical school, speculated on why this might be:

> I think, from the outside, maybe just from the way that the minorities have like this minority support group, and this minority support group, and this minority support group. There's no real white support groups. There's not, you know, Caucasian Arts and Sciences Program. So maybe it's like, more of a feeling like . . . they don't need more extra support, or something like that. Because in a way, it's like "Ah, all the minorities need all this stuff to make it through. I don't need anything."

Other conditions also make students vulnerable to stereotype threat. For instance, MASP students told me about feeling overwhelmed by the whiteness of the university where this study took place. Chris, the medical researcher, told me how this experience affected her in science classes:

> In a class where there's me and then like one or two other people of color, it seems like there's—we all seem to stick together, and somehow we all end up being lab partners, or something like that. Some people may feel like they're being left out, or they can't in-

teract with the white people in the class, or something like that, because it seems like whenever I'm sitting there and it's time to pick your lab partner, whoever else is the minority in the classroom will come and find me. Most of my lab partners have been minorities.

In this context, students can easily feel that they must disprove negative assumptions being made about them. One way to counter this is to emphasize the enrichment components of a support program or a science class; MASP does this by, as the quote about the chemistry workshop indicates, specifying that students are learning science because it is intrinsically interesting: "because it was part of chemistry, not just because we had to do it for the test."

Networking Opportunities

Many students in the program discussed above reported that most of the university adults they saw who looked like them worked as janitors, gardeners, and cooks. A Latina junior put it this way:

We go to the dorms and see our people cooking and cleaning. And when something goes bad, like a bad test, or a bad experience with a person, we just have that as a reference point. And say, "is that where I belong?" As opposed to higher positions like striving for a PhD or something like that. And that is very real for us.

MASP makes systematic efforts–ranging from social events to facilitation of undergraduate research–to help students get to know professionals on campus, whether of their own race or not, and to nurture connections. A student told me "I think the most important thing that MASP did was it gives you connections. It gives you a lot of contacts and important connections that you will be using throughout your school here."

Space for a Diverse Minority Community

The next necessary component for retaining well-prepared students of color is to provide a setting, centered on scholarly excellence, in which those students can be with others like them. This gives students a shelter from an institutional culture that they may find unfamiliar; a place where they do not feel conspicuous, where they can be with other people who share some of their experiences in the world, and where they can get to know people who are *not* like them, but who are also not White. It provides them with a place where they are not, as one student put it, "in the minority." One African American biology major explained how this sense of being different affected her as she prepared a report for one of the classes in her major:

> I was doing my report on Grave's Disease a couple weeks ago. There's different genes related to Grave's Disease, for different ethnicities, and for a long time, they were like "OK, it's just this one gene," but it was only found with white people. And I thought that was really interesting. But then in my presentation, I was like "should I mention the part about African Americans having a different gene?" And women get affected a lot more. And I thought "damn, that's kind of messed up, that I should re-think presenting–it's as normal to the disease as its symptoms, know what I'm saying?" But still, I sort of felt "damn, should I not mention that?"

A number of women told me that the only time race was mentioned in their science classes was in the context of sickle cell anemia; for the student quoted above (who has just finished a master's in public health with an emphasis on Third World health), the fact that it was not mentioned led to a sense that it *should not be* mentioned. This is particularly ironic given the way that science has, for the past four or five decades, been a potent force in fighting racism, disproving any biological basis for the suppression of particular races. For race-conscious science students, MASP provides a place where considerations of race and science need not be muted.

Cohesion and Community in Addition to, Not in Lieu of, Older Ties

Hurtado and Carter (1997) found that "for academically talented Latino students who attend college full time, maintaining family relationships and support is among the most important aspects of transition that facilitates their adjustment to college." Tierney (1999) argued that many African American students have to commit "cultural suicide" in order to fit themselves into predominantly White institutions. One student, a Latina senior from a rural community, told us about how MASP reassured her parents:

> At first, [my parents] wanted me to stay and go to the junior college for a couple years, and then maybe go to [a local university]. But once they came up and visited, and once they–I think what re-

ally convinced them that it was going to be OK was the fact that I was in the MASP program, because I came up for summer bridge, and they got to meet with [the director], and all of the people who were helping, and they were like "oh, they're so nice, and you'll have such a good time!" And so after that, I think they were OK.

MASP was able to provide this student and her parents with a sense of security and home, and thus persuade her to attend her state's flagship research university rather than her local community college.

Financial Support

Since 1980, tuition costs have risen at several times the annual rate of inflation (Mortenson 2000). At the same time, federal financial aid has shifted, with students receiving more aid in the form of loans, and less as grants. "In 1979 a student from the top quartile of family income was about four times more likely than a student from the bottom quartile to earn a baccalaureate degree by age twenty-four. In 1993, the difference was 13 times greater" (Mortenson 2000). In their survey of programs for high-achieving minority university students, Gándara and Maxwell-Jolley (1999) found five components in common across the programs: "mentoring, financial support, academic support, psychosocial support, and professional opportunities." Furthermore, they found that "direct financial support was the least commonly employed of the five strategies, which we find interesting given the fact that inadequate financial resources is so often the reason cited for underrepresented students failing to continue their education." MASP helps students pay for college in three ways: the $1,000 participation grant, contingent on good grades and enthusiastic program participation; help finding work study jobs, especially in science labs; and, for upper level students, small stipends to cover their own scientific research. None of these sums is large; however, for students struggling to stay in college, they can be just enough both to keep them there and to keep them in science (which, because of its long times to graduation, can be a particularly expensive field). One young woman told me, "I kind of like how MASP has professors that deal with MASP, they help me. I got a research job with [one professor affiliated with MASP]. And [another professor], I went down to Puerto Rico [to do research] because of him. That's why I like having that connection through MASP." In this example, MASP's policy not only helped this young woman (now in a pre-professional health program) find work, but also helped her foster connections among science faculty.

CONCLUSION

These studies suggest that leaks in the science pipeline can be fixed. There is a pool of academically able, enthusiastic women entering college intent on the study of science. Policy to retain and develop this pool of talent needs to take into account that women in this study were drawn to science because they enjoy its intellectual rigor and feel up to the challenge, and they see science as a place where they can combine their altruism with their pleasure in science. Effective support must emerge from a framework of enrichment and challenge; it must bridge theory and application, and present science in the context of the lives of others. Effective support is possible. Programs exist that are highly effective at retaining students of color in the sciences, and those students go on to careers in the service of the public in record numbers. Programs like MASP that are successful in supporting these women must be identified and provided with greater resources to reach more students. Successful programs must also be studied in more detail to identify the elements responsible for their success and make that knowledge widely available. Universities without support for women science students of color must be provided with the financial support and with the expertise to develop such programs. Science-oriented Black, Latina, and American Indian women are a valuable resource. My findings suggest that investing in their science studies yields double dividends, not only increasing their graduation rates in science but producing well-educated, enthusiastic teachers, researchers, and health professionals dedicated to the service of others.

NOTE

1. All names used in this paper are pseudonyms.

REFERENCES

Bourdieu, P. 1977. *Outline of a Theory of Practice*. Great Britain: Cambridge University Press.

Davidson, A. 1996. *Making and Molding Identities in Schools: Student Narratives on Race, Gender and Academic Engagement*. Albany: State University of New York Press.

Fullilove, R., and U. Treisman. 1990. "Mathematics Achievement Among African American Undergraduates at the University of California, Berkeley: An Evaluation of the Mathematics Workshop Program." *The Journal of Negro Education* 59(3): 463-478.

Gándara, P. and J. Maxwell-Jolly. 1999. *Priming the Pump: Strategies for Increasing the Achievement of Underrepresented Minority Undergraduates.* New York: College Board.

Glaser, G. and A. Strauss. 1967. *The Discovery of Grounded Theory: Strategies for Qualitative Research.* New York: Aldine de Gruyter.

Hurtado, S. and D. Carter. 1997. "Effects of College Transition and Perceptions of the Campus Racial Climate on Latino College Students' Sense of Belonging." *Sociology of Education* 70(4).

Maton, K., F. Hrabowski, and C. Schmitt. 2000. "African American College Students Excelling in the Sciences: College and Postcollege Outcomes in the Meyerhoff Scholars Program." *Journal of Research in Science Teaching* 37(7): 629-654.

Mortenson, T. 2000. "Financing Opportunity for Postsecondary Education." In *Access Denied: Race, Ethnicity, and the Scientific Enterprise*, eds. G. Campbell, R. Denes, and C. Morrison. New York: Oxford University Press.

Murphy, T., K. Stafford, and P. McCreary. 1998. "Subsequent Course and Degree Paths of Students in a Treisman-Style Workshop Calculus Program." *Journal of Women and Minorities in Science and Engineering* 4: 381-396.

Seymour, E. and N. Hewitt. 1997. *Talking About Leaving.* Boulder, CO: Westview Press.

Spradley, J. 1979. *The Ethnographic Interview.* New York: Holt, Rinehart, and Winston.

Spradley, J. 1980. *Participant Observation.* New York: Holt, Rinehart, and Winston.

Steele, C. 1997. "A Threat in the Air: How Stereotypes Shape Intellectual Identity and Performance." *American Psychologist* 52(6): 613-629.

Tierney, W. 1999. "Models of Minority College-Going and Retention: Cultural Integrity versus Cultural Suicide." *Journal of Negro Education* 68(1): 80-91.

The Production
of the Female Entrepreneurial Subject:
A Space of Exclusion for Women of Color?

Mélanie Knight, Ontario Institute for Studies
in Education of the University of Toronto

SUMMARY. Using critical discourse analysis, this paper examines how the female entrepreneurial subject is constructed/produced within entrepreneurial discourses, how this subject is racialized, gendered and classed, and examines what practices contribute to the shaping of the female entrepreneurial subject. I specifically look at four areas/discourses central to entrepreneurship; that of independence, self-definition/self-monitoring, networking, and women's abilities as businesswomen. I contend that contemporary self-employment discourses mirror those of neo-liberalism/modernization where the notion of the independent liberal subject has the ability to self-determine and self-monitor, which is a sign of autonomy and mastery of the self. I also argue that the space of women's entrepreneurship legitimizes white middle-class women's experiences and excludes women of color from becoming active subjects in entrepreneurial discourses. *[Article copies available for a fee from The Haworth Document Delivery Service: 1-800-HAWORTH. E-mail address: <docdelivery@haworthpress.com> Website: <http://www.HaworthPress.com> © 2005 by The Haworth Press, Inc. All rights reserved.]*

[Haworth co-indexing entry note]: "The Production of the Female Entrepreneurial Subject: A Space of Exclusion for Women of Color?" Knight, Mélanie. Co-published simultaneously in *Journal of Women, Politics & Policy* (The Haworth Political Press, an imprint of The Haworth Press, Inc.) Vol. 27, No. 3/4, 2005, pp. 151-159; and: *Women, Work, and Poverty: Women Centered Research for Policy Change* (ed: Heidi Hartmann) The Haworth Political Press, an imprint of The Haworth Press, Inc., 2005, pp. 151-159. Single or multiple copies of this article are available for a fee from The Haworth Document Delivery Service [1-800-HAWORTH, 9:00 a.m. - 5:00 p.m. (EST). E-mail address: docdelivery@haworthpress.com].

151

KEYWORDS. Gender, race, class, entrepreneurs, businesswomen, self-employment, training, critical discourse analysis

INTRODUCTION

This paper examines how the female entrepreneurial subject is constructed/produced within entrepreneurial discourses; how this subject is racialized, gendered, and classed; and examines what practices contribute to the shaping of the female entrepreneurial subject, and where and how white women and women of color become positioned within these discourses. I argue that the production of the female entrepreneurial subject works through the legitimization of white middle-class women's experiences and exclusion of women of color from becoming active subjects in entrepreneurial discourses. I also contend that contemporary self-employment discourses mirror those of neo-liberalism where the notion of the independent, liberal subject has the ability to self-determine and self-monitor, which is a sign of autonomy and mastery of the self. These discourses serve to produce particular subjects as dominant with others as subordinate. I rely on Hall's (1997) definition of discourse largely based on Foucault's work as being "a group of statements which provide a language for talking about–a way of representing the knowledge about–a particular topic at a particular historical moment . . . discourse is about the production of knowledge through language" (p. 44). Using critical discourse analysis, I focus on examining "power, dominance, hegemony, inequality, and the discursive processes of their enactment, concealment, legitimation and reproduction" (van Dijk 1993a, 132), in women's enterprising discourse. Power, according to van Dijk (1993b), involves, "control, namely by (members of) one group over (those of) other groups" (p. 254), but is mostly "cognitive, and enacted by persuasion, dissimulation or manipulation" (p. 254). There is a "hierarchy of power where some members of dominant groups and organizations have a special role in planning, decision-making and control over the relations and processes of the enactment of power" (p. 255). The following sections will examine self-employment discourses which I contend have served to produce a particular racially gendered entrepreneurial subject.

GETTING "OUT THERE" AND BEING "INDEPENDENT"

As an entrepreneur, you're in the driver's seat; you're in control and shaping things everyday. (Champions Newsletter 2002)

The space of entrepreneurship for women is often posited as a space of liberation, where women can take control of their lives and make strides in their economic and social lives. A video, titled *Women Entre-preneurs: Making a Difference*, is another example of material which presents the entrepreneurial space as a freeing, liberating space for women. The main argument in the video, however, is that independence for women should be obtained because women do things differently than men and therefore need their own space to succeed in their own way. It begins by asserting that women have been very frustrated with the rigidity of corporate traditional spaces and, because they love to make a difference in the world, they feel they cannot do so under those conditions.

The discourse of what I call "getting out there" plays on a notion that women would be better off being self-employed than being in "traditional" work spaces. The language suggests that women in self-employment have more control and autonomy than they would working for an employer. This discourse mirrors that of the 19th century modernization project and the production of the liberal subject. In considering the politics of modernization, Popkewitz (1999) notes that,

> people were expected to "be seen" and "see" themselves as individuals who could act on their world. In one sense, the individual now became a citizen of a nation. As such, the citizen had certain obligations, responsibilities, and freedoms. The construction of a democratic self came out of a general and pervasive belief dating from the Enlightenment belief that reason and rationality could produce a better world . . . individuals were expected to exhibit self-discipline and self-motivation. (pp. 18-19)

Alarcon, as cited in Mohanty (1991), calls this subject "the most popular subject of Anglo-American feminism . . . an autonomous, self-making, self-determining subject who first proceeds according to the logic of identification with regard to the subject of consciousness" (pp. 37-8).

The politics of autonomy and independence for communities of color is complex, contradictory, and must be historically contextualized. For one, notions of self-sufficiency and independence have on the one hand never been discourses available to people of color (Glenn 2002). There has always been a need for the containment, control, and surveillance of women of color around their labor, reproductive rights, and family ties, which dates back centuries ago. Can women of color therefore be seen as autonomous workers? One must question who has the ability to claim notions of independence and autonomy. Also the notion that freedom and independence from corporate rule is what is desired by women assumes that most women have been in such positions in the first place and negates the labor histories of working-class women and women of color who have always been in the workforce, both formal and informal, in order to support their families (hooks 1984). This discourse, therefore, does a great deal to reinscribe and privilege the histories of white middle-class women while silencing and oppressing that of women of color.

SELF-DEFINITION/PERSONAL GROWTH

I now want to look at the industry of personal growth/self-definition, which is geared towards determining whether one is really "cut out" to be an entrepreneur. Online self-assessment questionnaires are available on most major bank Websites as well as on Canadian government business Websites. The following questionnaire is listed on the Human Resource Development Canada Website geared towards enabling aspiring entrepreneurs to better know themselves as individuals and to determine whether they are "made out" to be entrepreneurs. They call it a reality check for small business owners.

1. Do I have a burning desire to be "on my own"?
2. Am I confident that I can succeed?
3. Am I willing to take calculated and moderate risks?
4. Am I a self-starter?
5. Am I able to set long-term goals? Can I stick with them? Even if I'm faced with a difficult problem or situation?
6. Do I believe that money is the best measure of success?
7. Am I creative? Am I always looking for new approaches and ideas? Am I innovative?
8. Am I good at making decisions? Are my decisions generally sound?
9. Am I willing to market my product or service?
10. Am I a good organizer? Do I pay attention to details?
11. Am I flexible? Do I adapt to change? Can I handle surprises?

It goes on to ask, "do you have what it takes?" and notes that,

> by now you will be able to put together a good picture of the qualities and skills required to succeed in your own business. You are

likely to be happy and successful in your own business if you: possess an inner drive to be independent; are able to set and achieve goals; are flexible and adaptable; are willing to work hard; have confidence in your ability to succeed; possess self-discipline, leadership abilities, and organizational skills; and have the confidence to make decisions and take calculated risks. (http://www.hrdc_drhc.gc.ca/hrib/hrp_prh/pi_ip/career_carriere)

This is one example of a self-assessment questionnaire provided to aspiring entrepreneurs where they must subject themselves to self-scrutiny and self-examination before attempting to start a business. The language of introspection psychologizes and places the onus and responsibility of success on the individual. One must be able to manage, organize, function cautiously yet take risks, and must examine if one's character can survive in such a space. The ultimate test is to introspectively try and determine if one is serious and dedicated to this endeavor. These entrepreneurial discourses shape the space as one that is controllable from within. Through responsibility, the management of oneself, inner drive, and self-discipline, one can potentially have success. O'Malley, Weir, and Shearing (1997) note that 'technologies of self' have "played an important role in directing attention to the . . . broad political rationalities and such micro-technologies of everyday life in 'developing' self-esteem and personal regimes of 'wellness'" (p. 502).

I argue that discourses of self-management and self-discipline are exclusionary to women of color and have historically served to oppress them. Valverde (1991) examines how bourgeois ideals and a fear of a loss of "civilization" became important in defining the terms of the moral reform project in the early 20th century. Working-class and immigrant families were seen as the cause of this deterioration of "civilization" and were often suspected of inappropriate conduct. Reformers often attributed poverty, living arrangements in small quarters, and loose morals with the potential for inappropriate sexual and immoral activity. The National Council of Women declared that "the country is suffering because poor women lack domestic science" (p. 145). Domestic duties, such as cooking and sewing, were seen as having the ability of helping working-class and immigrant women to focus, to have self-control, and to concentrate.

Women of color have often been seen as being unable to manage their lives or their families and as having to constantly be monitored. Invoking these discourses of self-mastery and discipline again legitimizes white, middle-class women's histories and negates how such discourses affect women of color in a different way.

NETWORKING

The concept of networking also plays a large part in entrepreneurial discourses. I examined an online networking Canadian newsletter *Women Like Me*, which publishes upcoming information and provides resources to women entrepreneurs. Networking is described as "the art of connecting people and information for mutual benefit," and that it is "a relationship of increasing exchange based on skill, experience and respect." The author also describes the relationship of networking as a "positive force that flourishes in the right atmosphere," and recommends that one join a professional group because it is more comfortable to spend time with people who "all speak your language."

Similarly, authors of a best-selling book, *Raising Your Business: A Canadian Guide to Entrepreneurship*, discuss "the art of networking" for women entrepreneurs as having to "go out of the office and into the real world. Set aside one evening, one morning, or one lunch a week to be with new people either socially, professionally, or as a volunteer. Learn to golf." In describing a network they note, "call it a clan, call it a network, call it a tribe, call it a family: whatever you call it, whoever you are, you need one. All networking is really, is a means of building an infrastructure of mutually beneficial relationships with other people" (Yaccato and Jubinville 1998, 149).

What do networking discourses look like? Who makes up these networks? What types of social relationships are they? Where and in what conditions do they thrive? How do some subjects come to be positioned as valued "modes" of networks, while others are not? I argue that networking discourses are often framed as racially neutral and classless, in that there is the assumption that all women have the ability of acquiring or being a part of thriving networks. Michandani (2002) examines how the experiences of home-based self-employed women vary between white women and women of color. For instance, she notes that only a small proportion of immigrants and women of color had experience and contacts in the sector in which they formed their businesses through their past labor market work. She further notes, "many women of color experience networks as structures of nepotism and exclusion" (p. 30). The space of networking is racialized and classed, in that it assumes that all women have equal access to this space and does not consider the lives of women of color/immigrant women who may not have similar social/political networks/connections to get them started.

NURTURING THE ENTREPRENEUR

In this next section, I argue that the discourse of women as caregivers and nurturers within self-employment in one sense essentializes women's nurturing nature while simultaneously excluding women of color from this discourse. The video, *Women Entrepreneurs: Making a Difference*, asserts that women in business (at work) function very differently than men, in that men function in a structural/authoritarian manner whereas women prefer being in a web-like/hub-like space at the center of everything. Women will work with employees versus having them work for them. Also, they suggest that women define success not from results of balance sheets but whether they are of service and whether they are having fun. Also interesting, Yaccato and Jubinville's book *Raising Your Business: A Canadian Women's Guide to Entrepreneurship* is organized around the concept of mothering. This is accomplished through the organization of the chapters and the advice that is given to aspiring women entrepreneurs. For example, the first chapter, "becoming the woman I am," talks about a failed business experience and that women should learn from other women who have experience. The second chapter is titled, "conception," the third "giving birth," followed by the "first year," and the "toddler years," which are all playing on the notion of women as mothers. The discourse primarily essentializes the notion of what women are naturally supposed to do, which is to have children. They are using this discourse and applying it to the business world possibly in the hopes of feminizing business. The business is given the place of child rearing and places women as masters of that domain and therefore are given the sense that they could also be in the business realm.

This discourse essentializes women as being more nurturing and caring than their counterparts. It is also interesting to note the kinds of nurturing practices that women are deemed to have, such as working in a web, having fun, being more people centered, etc. Another essentializing fact is that in framing business as a discourse of mothering, they reinforce the stereotype of the social position of white women as being good, compassionate caregivers and simultaneously excluding women of color who have never been thought of in this way. A great deal has been written about the representation of Black women being seen as the matriarchal superwoman who is aggressive, loud, and dominant (Brand 1999). Calliste (1996), for instance, notes that the image/stereotypes of Black women as being aggressive, less disciplined within the nursing profession is the "antithesis of femininity and the opposite of the soft-spoken, compassionate, nurturing, rational and professional nurse. Thus, the black woman nurse becomes an 'undesirable' identity in this context" (p. 369). In this context, even though the representation/stereotype of the Mammy conjures up the image of a nurturing Black motherly figure, we must recognize that she has predominantly been represented as an authoritative, commanding, all knowing figure.

CONCLUSION

In this paper, I tried to show how various discourses that construct the category of the female entrepreneur legitimize the experiences of white middle-class women and exclude women of color from being active participants. It becomes important to question the assumptions around narratives that supposedly challenge dominant ideals such as women's entrepreneurial discourses, to see what is essentialized, naturalized, and reinscribed in these 'alternative' discourses. As shown in this paper, 'alternative' discourses of independence, networking, self-governance, and mothering, although liberating in one sense for a particular group of women, namely white middle-class women, is oppressive to women of color. In order to understand fully how self-employment trends are affecting all women, future research looking at women entrepreneurs should begin by challenging the racialized and gendered ways in which women are produced as dominant or subordinate subjects.

REFERENCES

Brand, D. 1999. "Black Women and Work: The Impact of Racially Constructed Gender Roles on the Sexual Division of Labour." In *Scratching the Surface: Canadian Anti-Racist Feminist Thought*, eds. E. Dua & A. Robertson. Toronto: Women's Press, 83-96.

Calliste, A. 1996. "Antifeminism Organizing Resistance in Nursing: African Canadian Women." *Canadian Review of Sociology and Anthropology* 33(3): 368-390.

Champions Newsletter. 2002. Volume 5, Issue 1 (Spring).

Glenn, E. N. 2002. *Unequal Freedom: How Race and Gender Shaped American Citizenship and Labor*. Cambridge, Massachusetts; London, England: Harvard University Press.

Hall, S. 1997. "The Work of Representation." *Representation: Cultural Representation and Signifying Practices*, ed. S. Hall. London: Sage Publications, 13-74.

hooks, b. 1984. *Feminist Theory: From Margin to Center.* Boston, MA: South End Press.

Michandani, K. 2002. "A Special Kind of Exclusion: Race, Gender and Self-employment." *Atlantis* 27(1): 25-38.

Mohanty, C. T. 1991. "Cartographies of Struggle, Third World Women and the Politics of Feminism." In *Third World Women and the Politics of Feminism*, eds. C. T. Mohanty, A. Russo, and L. Torres. Indianapolis: Indiana University Press, 1-47.

O'Malley, P., L. Weir, and C. Shearing. 1997. "Government, Criticism, Politics." *Economy and Society* 26(4): 501-517.

Popkewitz, T. S. 1999. "A Social Epistemology of Educational Research." In *Critical Theories in Education: Changing Terrains of Knowledge and Politics*, eds. T. Popkewitz and L. Feudler. New York: Routledge.

Valverde, M. 1991. *The Age of Light, Soap and Water: Moral Reform in English Canada, 1885-1925.* Toronto: The Canadian Publishers.

van Dijk, T. A. 1993a. Editor's foreword to critical discourse analysis. *Discourse & Society* 4(2): 131-132.

van Dijk, T. A. 1993b. "Principles of Critical Discourse Analysis." *Discourse & Society* 4(2): 249-283.

Women Entrepreneurs: Making a Difference. 1998. Bronze Apple, National Educational Film and Video.

Yaccato, J. T., and P. Jubinville. 1998. *Raising Your Business: A Canadian Guide to Entrepreneurship.* Scarborough: Prentice Hall Canada, Inc.

ONLINE SOURCES

Human Resource Development Canada Website, http://www.hrdc_drhc.gc.ca/hrib/hrp_prh/pi_ip/career_carriere

Women Like Me, http://www.womenlikeme.ca

INCOME AND INCOME SECURITY

The Ability of Women to Repay Debt After Divorce

Jonathan Fisher, U.S. Bureau of Labor Statistics
Angela Lyons, University of Illinois at Urbana-Champaign

SUMMARY. This study uses questions on household repayment problems from the *Panel Study of Income Dynamics* to examine how the transition from marriage to divorce affects default rates by gender. The results show that divorced women are more likely to have repayment problems than divorced men and married-couple households. Further analysis reveals that divorced women who are receiving welfare are significantly less likely to default. Because average welfare benefits decreased in the early 1990s, the results suggest that this decrease provides a partial explanation for why the default rate increased between 1991 and 1995 for divorced women. The effect of welfare on the default rates of divorced men and married couples is insignificant. And there is no evidence that receiving child support and alimony payments significantly affects the probability of default. *[Article copies available for a fee from The Haworth Document Delivery Service: 1-800-HAWORTH. E-mail address:*

[Haworth co-indexing entry note]: "The Ability of Women to Repay Debt After Divorce." Fisher, Jonathan, and Angela Lyons. Co-published simultaneously in *Journal of Women, Politics & Policy* (The Haworth Political Press, an imprint of The Haworth Press, Inc.) Vol. 27, No. 3/4, 2005, pp. 161-168; and: *Women, Work, and Poverty: Women Centered Research for Policy Change* (ed: Heidi Hartmann) The Haworth Political Press, an imprint of The Haworth Press, Inc., 2005, pp. 161-168. Single or multiple copies of this article are available for a fee from The Haworth Document Delivery Service [1-800-HAWORTH, 9:00 a.m. - 5:00 p.m. (EST). E-mail address: docdelivery@haworthpress.com].

KEYWORDS. Bankruptcy, default, welfare, consumer debt, repayment, divorce, child support, alimony

INTRODUCTION

In 2001, the United States experienced its first economic downturn in almost a decade. The recovery, which has been slower than usual, has been called a jobless recovery (Schreft and Singh 2003). Because of this downturn and slow recovery, many low-to-middle income families are having difficulty repaying the large amounts of debt they accumulated during the 1980s and 1990s. Between 1980 and 2000, outstanding consumer debt rose from $355 million to $1,560 million, and the debt-to-income ratio for U.S. households increased from 12.5 to 14.4 percent. Consequently, delinquency and charge-off rates have been on the rise, and there has been a four-fold increase in the number of personal bankruptcy filings.

Previous research indicates that the rise in household repayment problems has occurred at a significantly higher rate for non-married women (Sullivan and Warren 1999), and the rise in the divorce rate has been identified as a plausible contributor to this rise. The dramatic change in family structure coupled with the increase in the number of households filing for bankruptcy raises two important questions: First, to what extent are divorced women more likely than others to have difficulty paying their bills and/or repaying their debts? Second, what factors may help to mitigate the likelihood of delinquency and bankruptcy for divorced women?

This study uses data on household repayment problems from the *Panel Study on Income Dynamics (PSID)* to examine how the transition from marriage to divorce affects default rates for women and men and why these rates have changed over time. The extent to which income payments such as child support, alimony, and welfare help to mitigate repayment problems for divorced households is specifically examined. Differences in the sources of income held by households by gender and marital status, especially welfare payments, are likely to have varying impacts on household default rates.

THE DATA

Data for this study is taken from the 1991-1995 waves of the PSID. The information on default in the 1996 wave is matched with the 1991-1995 data to create a sample of 19,939 *household years*.

In the 1996 PSID, households were asked if they had difficulty repaying their bills and/or debts. If they indicated that they had difficulty, the household was then asked in which year. Households are classified as having *defaulted* if they reported having at least one of the following repayment problems: (1) unable to repay bills when they were due, (2) had a creditor call to demand payment, (3) had wages garnished by a creditor, (4) had a lien filed against property because the household could not repay bills, (5) had property repossessed, and/or (6) filed for personal bankruptcy. It is important to note that this definition of *default* includes households that have been delinquent as well as those that have filed for bankruptcy. Previous studies such as Fay, Hurst, and White (2002) that have used micro-level data from the PSID have focused solely on bankruptcy and have not utilized the information on default found in the PSID.

Table 1 presents the proportion of households that defaulted by category between 1991 and 1995. Not surprisingly, being unable to repay bills has the highest response rate. Table 1 shows that 9.6 percent of all households reported that they were unable to repay their bills. With respect to the other repayment problems, the frequency is considerably smaller. Approximately 4.6 percent reported receiving a call from a creditor to demand payment, while less than one percent of households reported wage garnishment, a lien, repossession, or bankruptcy.

Averaged over the five years of our data, divorced women have the highest default rate at 15.9 percent. Divorced women, on the other hand, do not have the highest rate in all categories of default, namely bankruptcy and garnishment. However, the percentages reported for these categories are very small. Divorced men have the highest percent filing for bankruptcy. Married households have the lowest rates in most categories and overall, 9.5 percent.

These cross-sectional differences in default rates increased over time. Figure 1 shows the proportion of households that defaulted for each year by marital status and gender. In 1991, the default rate was approximately 8.0 percent for married, divorced men, and divorced women. In 1995, the overall default rate increased to 17.8 percent, with considerable variation across marital status and gender. Fourteen per-

TABLE 1. Proportion of Households that Defaulted (1991-1995)

	All N = 19,939	Married N = 15,494	Divorced Men N = 1,878	Divorced Women N = 2,567
Unable to repay bills (%)	9.58	8.11	10.70	14.41
Creditors demanded payment (%)	4.58	4.16	5.06	6.78
Wages garnished by a creditor (%)	0.06	0.03	0.32	0.08
A lien filed against property (%)	0.13	0.12	0.37	0.19
Property repossessed (%)	0.14	0.08	0.43	0.35
Filed for bankruptcy (%)	0.50	0.52	0.75	0.35
% of households that defaulted	11.08	9.53	12.94	15.93

Note: All data come from the Panel Study of Income Dynamics, 1991-1996.

FIGURE 1. Default rate by marital status and gender (1991-1995).

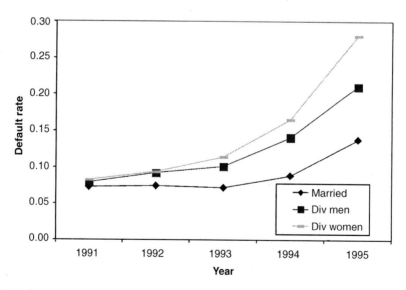

Note: Based on authors' calculations from the Panel Study of Income Dynamics.

cent of married households defaulted compared to 20.4 percent of divorced men and 27.5 percent of divorced women.

THE RESULTS

Separate equations are estimated for married households, divorced men, and divorced women using the probit method. The dependent variable equals one if the household defaulted in year t and zero otherwise. For each regression, the observations are pooled across all years. Year dummies are included to control for aggregate economic effects and any other effects that may be specific to that year. Robust standard errors are reported since multiple observations for each household are included in the sample.

Table 2 presents the marginal effects and standard errors for each group. The results indicate that increases in income per capita significantly decrease the probability of default for married households. Conversely, the effect of income per capita is statistically insignificant for divorced households. With respect to other income sources, the effects of receiving child support and alimony payments on the likelihood of default are statistically insignificant for all households, most likely because these payments are uncertain sources of income. Also, child support is designated for and used for child-related expenditures disproportionately and not for paying bills that are unrelated to child expenses (Del Boca 1994).

With respect to welfare, Table 2 shows that a $1,000 increase in AFDC benefits significantly decreases the probability of default by 1.2 percentage points for divorced women. The effect of AFDC is insignificant for married households and divorced men. In addition, the amount of AFDC benefits received by all divorced women in this sample decreased by 37 percent between 1991 and 1995 (Fisher and Lyons 2003). Divorced women are more likely than divorced men or married households to be AFDC recipients and more likely to be dependent on these payments for financial security. Thus, the results suggest that the decrease in AFDC provides a plausible explanation for why the default rate increased significantly between 1991 and 1995 for divorced women.

Increases in the number of weeks unemployed and being in poor health may have also contributed to the increase in the default rate for divorced women. As Table 2 indicates, these factors significantly affect the probability of default for all households regardless of marital status

TABLE 2. Probit Models for Households that Defaulted by Marital Status and Gender (1991-1995)

Variable	Married ME	Married SE	Divorced Men ME	Divorced Men SE	Divorced Women ME	Divorced Women SE
Household income ($10,000)/household size	-0.0165	(0.0004)**	-0.0059	(0.0097)	-0.0108	(0.0169)
Household income ($10,000)/household size)^2	0.0001	(0.0000)**	-0.0001	(0.0000)	-0.0001	(0.0002)
Lag of (Household income ($10,000)/household size)	-0.0146	(0.0042)**	-0.0069	(0.0093)	0.0235	(0.0182)
Lag of (Household income ($10,000)/household size)^2	0.0001	(0.0000)**	0.0001	(0.0000)	-0.0005	(0.0003)*
Child support/alimony income ($1,000)	-0.0007	(0.0017)	0.0033	(0.0041)	0.0007	(0.0012)
AFDC income ($1,000)	0.0032	(0.0034)	-0.0054	(0.0090)	-0.0118	(0.0046)**
Age	-0.0004	(0.0016)	0.0149	(0.0056)**	0.0091	(0.0041)**
Age^2	-0.0001	(0.0001)	-0.0002	(0.0001)**	-0.0001	(0.0001)**
Education (< 12 yrs)	0.0211	(0.0088)**	-0.0518	(0.0197)**	0.0746	(0.0321)**
Education (12 yrs)	0.0155	(0.0066)**	-0.0550	(0.0192)**	0.0167	(0.0272)
Education (13-15 yrs)	0.0077	(0.0071)	-0.0610	(0.0176)**	0.0309	(0.0289)
Black	0.0093	(0.0055)*	-0.0189	(0.0154)	0.0029	(0.0157)
Number of children	0.0042	(0.0022)**	0.0109	(0.0073)	0.0234	(0.0072)**
Weeks unemployed	0.0012	(0.0003)**	0.0026	(0.0008)**	0.0025	(0.0007)**
Poor health status	0.0618	(0.0099)**	0.0187	(0.0218)	0.0528	(0.0192)**
Homeowner	-0.0282	(0.0056)**	-0.0038	(0.0157)	0.0099	(0.0155)
State unemployment rate	0.0033	(0.0021)	-0.0068	(0.0075)	0.0013	(0.0079)
State per capita income ($10,000)	0.0019	(0.0159)	0.0738	(0.0052)	-0.0373	(0.0462)
Year 1992	-0.0005	(0.0070)	0.0098	(0.0275)	0.0234	(0.0303)
Year 1993	0.0029	(0.0071)	0.0049	(0.0263)	0.0320	(0.0296)
Year 1994	0.0211	(0.0080)**	0.0361	(0.0287)	0.0895	(0.0314)**
Year 1995	0.0670	(0.0098)**	0.0927	(0.0317)**	0.2067	(0.0345)**
Observations	15,494		1,878		2,567	
Households that defaulted	1,476		243		409	
R^2	0.0870		0.0891		0.1027	

Note: ME represents the marginal effects. Robust standard errors are in parentheses. (**) and (*) indicate statistical significance at the 5 and 10 percent levels, respectively. The specifications also include eight region dummy variables.

and gender. However, the combined effect of being unemployed and being in poor health has a larger impact on divorced women, suggesting that they are more likely than other households to be financially affected by unanticipated shocks. Further, being divorced means that they no longer have the benefit of a second earner to insure consumption against these shocks.

Table 2 also shows that the coefficients on the 1995 year dummy variables are positive and significant for all households, with the effect for divorced women being twice that for other households. The effect of the 1994 coefficient is also largest for divorced women. Figure 1 shows that the largest increase in the default rate occurred between 1994 and 1995. During the mid-to-late 1990s, a number of efforts were made by the financial industry to provide additional and more affordable borrowing opportunities to households traditionally credit constrained, with divorced women benefiting substantially (Lyons 2002). Increases in credit access over this time period, especially for divorced women, could help explain the large and significant coefficients on these two-year dummy variables.

CONCLUDING REMARKS

This study has examined how marriage and divorce affects default rates and why divorced women may be more likely than other households to experience repayment problems. The effects of various income payments such as child support, alimony, and AFDC on the decision to default were specifically examined. The results show that divorced women are significantly more likely to default than divorced men and married households. While the default rate has increased since 1991 for all divorced households, it has more than doubled for women. The findings indicate that an increase in AFDC benefits decreases the probability of default for divorced women, suggesting that these benefits among other things help smooth the transition from marriage to divorce for women. The effect of AFDC benefits on the default rates of divorced men and married couples is insignificant. Regardless of gender and marital status, there is no evidence that receiving child support and alimony payments significantly affects the probability of default.

The largest increase in repayment problems for divorced women occurred between 1994 and 1995, a period of economic expansion. Over this same time period, divorced women experienced declining AFDC benefits. Given these trends and limited financial resources, divorced women may have borrowed more to help smooth the transition from marriage to divorce. In the end, they may have overextended themselves, and given their precarious financial situation, were more likely to default, in part because of the decrease in the social safety net from AFDC.

AUTHOR NOTE

All views expressed in this paper are those of the authors and do not reflect the views or policies of the U.S. Bureau of Labor Statistics (BLS) or the views of other BLS staff members.

REFERENCES

Del Boca, D. 1994. "Post-Divorce Transfers and the Welfare of Mothers and Children in the United States," *Labour* 8: 259-77.

· Fay, Scott, Erik Hurst, and Michelle White. 2002. "The Household Bankruptcy Decision," *American Economic Review* 92(3): 706-718.

Fisher, Jonathan and Angela Lyons. 2003. "Gender Differences in the Likelihood of Default After Divorce: Does the Source of Income Matter?" *Manuscript.*

Lyons, Angela. 2002. "How Credit Access Has Changed for Divorced Men and Women," University of Illinois at Urbana-Champaign.

Schreft, Stacey L. and Aarti Singh. 2003. "A Closer Look at Jobless Recoveries," *Federal Reserve Bank of Kansas City Economic Review* 0: 45-73.

Sullivan, Teresa and Elizabeth Warren. 1999. "More Women in Bankruptcy," *American Bankruptcy Law Review.* July 30. <http://www.abiworld.org/Content/ NavigationMenu/News_Room/Research_Center/Bankruptcy_Reports_Research_ and_Testimony/General1/More_Women_in_Bankruptcy_-_Sullivan_and_Warren. htm#N_1_> (May 5, 2005).

Women's Job Loss and Material Hardship

Vicky Lovell, Institute for Women's Policy Research
Gi-Taik Oh, Institute for Women's Policy Research

SUMMARY. This research uses data from the Survey of Income and Program Participation to explore the relationship between unemployment and material hardship for women who were employed at the beginning of the 1996 survey panel. Using two-stage logistic regression analysis, we find that, controlling for demographics and initial poverty status, having been or currently being unemployed increases the relative odds of experiencing one or more of six hardship measures by half and doubles the relative likelihood of lacking telephone service or failing to receive needed medical care. Experiences of food insufficiency, inadequate dental care, and loss of or inability to pay for housing increase more than sixty percent with unemployment. Those previously or currently unemployed are also substantially more likely to have difficulty maintaining utility service than the continuously employed. The article concludes with a discussion of policies that would enhance employment tenure and help avoid hardship during unemployment. *[Article copies available for a fee from The Haworth Document Delivery Service: 1-800-HAWORTH. E-mail address: <docdelivery@haworthpress.com> Website: <http://www.HaworthPress.com> © 2005 by The Haworth Press, Inc. All rights reserved.]*

KEYWORDS. Unemployment, unemployment insurance, safety net, poverty, hardship, women

[Haworth co-indexing entry note]: "Women's Job Loss and Material Hardship." Lovell, Vicky, and Gi-Taik Oh. Co-published simultaneously in *Journal of Women, Politics & Policy* (The Haworth Political Press, an imprint of The Haworth Press, Inc.) Vol. 27, No. 3/4, 2005, pp. 169-183; and: *Women, Work, and Poverty: Women Centered Research for Policy Change* (ed: Heidi Hartmann) The Haworth Political Press, an imprint of The Haworth Press, Inc., 2005, pp. 169-183. Single or multiple copies of this article are available for a fee from The Haworth Document Delivery Service [1-800-HAWORTH, 9:00 a.m. - 5:00 p.m. (EST). E-mail address: docdelivery@haworthpress.com].

Available online at http://www.haworthpress.com/web/JWPP
doi:10.1300/J501v27n03_12

INTRODUCTION

The federal/state U.S. unemployment insurance system (UI) offers short-term partial wage replacement for previously employed workers seeking a new job. Its goals are to reduce economic hardship during spells without work; to maintain unemployed workers' attachment to the labor force; and to allow sufficient work search that individuals' skills are well-matched with their new jobs. Federal law provides for the overall structure of the system, with individual states setting their own eligibility criteria and benefit and tax levels. Typically, a worker's employment history must mirror a male breadwinner model in order to qualify for benefits–a substantial period of steady employment is required, and low-wage workers may be unable to reach earnings eligibility thresholds. In many states, part-time workers are excluded and job terminations related to caregiving work–e.g., having to quit because care for young children cannot be found–disqualify workers from receiving benefits.

While it provides benefits to many unemployed workers, the adequacy of the U.S. unemployment program is increasingly called into question. Even ignoring the fact that only those whose unemployment is immediately preceded by paid work are ever eligible for UI–i.e., workers entering or re-entering the workforce are not–critics argue that benefit recipiency has fallen substantially and that many groups of workers are systematically excluded from participating in the UI program (Blank and Card 1989; McMurrer and Chasanov 1995; Vroman 1998). The national rate of UI recipiency–the percent of the unemployed that claims UI benefits–fell from a high of over 75 percent in 1974-5 to less than 35 percent in 1993 (Emsellem and Lovell 2000). Women workers, whose employment patterns are uniquely affected by cultural expectations of caregiving effort and who are vulnerable to harassment and violence on the basis of sex, face an array of obstacles in trying to receive UI following a job loss (Pearce 1985; Bassi and Chasanov 1995; Lovell and Emsellem 2004).

Other policy changes make the issue of women's unemployment increasingly salient for individual, family, and societal well-being. The dramatic shift in emphasis in U.S. safety-net programs from entitlement to work "incentives"–that is, the withholding of benefits and services from low-income individuals, primarily mothers, who do not meet stringent requirements regarding employment–has magnified the importance of women's continued paid work effort for their own, and their families', ability to achieve and sustain economic well-being.

In this study, we explore the impact that job loss has on women's material hardship, controlling for demographic differences between women who do and do not become unemployed and for initial poverty status. (We do not specifically analyze women's access to, or the effects of, UI benefits, but an increase in hardship following unemployment indicates that whatever participation women have in income support programs is not adequate to prevent economic distress.) If women are able to struggle through temporary periods of unemployment with relative ease, the need for policy changes to enhance women's employment tenure, support unemployed women while they are between jobs, and improve the adequacy of our UI programs is less critical. If, on the other hand, losing a job creates financial disaster for women, advocates for better public policy have a more urgent mission.

DATA AND METHODOLOGY

Dataset. The U.S. Census Bureau's Survey of Income and Program Participation (SIPP) is a nationally representative panel survey in which respondents are interviewed every four months over a period of two or more years. Each four-month survey period is a "wave." Interviews conducted in the fourth month of each wave solicit information regarding each of the four months in the wave. We use data from the four-year 1996 panel, whose interviews, conducted between March 1996 and February 2000, cover activity from December 1995 to February 2000.

Only women who were 18 or older and employed in their first month in the SIPP panel are included in our dataset. We define respondents as unemployed in any month for which they report they had no job but were on layoff or seeking employment at least one week. Individuals who leave the labor force, retire, or enter school or another activity outside the labor market are not identified as unemployed in this analysis. Individuals who miss any waves of the panel are dropped from the dataset.

Measuring hardship in the SIPP. In the 8th wave (32nd month) of the 1996 SIPP, respondents are asked a special series of questions about their experiences of well-being and hardship related to their housing, neighborhood safety and desirability, and access to basic medical and food resources. We truncate our full dataset to include only data describing the 32 months of each respondent's SIPP participation leading up to the well-being module. Women with more than one spell of unemployment are characterized as currently employed or currently unemployed according to their employment status in the 32nd month. Our final dataset contains 11,595 cases that have full data for the 48 months of the panel (and thus are assigned a longitudinal weight value by the Census Bureau) and non-missing values for all the explanatory variables. Seven thousand eight hundred sixty-six women were continuously employed over the entire 32 months, 2,457 experienced at least one job loss but were employed in the 32nd month, and 1,272 women were unemployed at the 32nd month.[1]

Defining hardship. We select nine questions from the topical module to construct six hardship measures–either descriptions of material deprivation (including lack of needed health care) or paired responses that indicate either an inability to pay bills or the loss of housing or essential utility services. Our hardship measures are:

1. The individual's household has no telephone, or telephone service was terminated due to non-payment of bills.
2. A member of the individual's household was evicted and/or failed to make a rent or a mortgage payment.
3. Gas, oil, or electric utility service was terminated and/or a utility bill was not paid.
4. Needed medical services were not accessed.
5. Needed dental services were not accessed.
6. Members of the individual's household sometimes or often had too little to eat.

(These data reflect hardship experiences in the 12 months preceding the interview date except for food insufficiency, for which the survey captures experiences in the four months before the interview.) The general hardship dummy has a value of 1 for respondents experiencing any one (or more) of these measures.[2]

These are imperfect but valuable measures of a concept that is hard to identify with precision or objectivity. Individuals make different choices in allocating scarce budgetary resources in light of similar baskets of material needs, leading to different interpretations and descriptions of the same circumstances (Long 2003). As household-level indicators, the measures of inadequate medical service may misrepresent the survey respondents' own material hardship, if resources are not distributed evenly among household members (Beverly 2001) and because individuals differ in their evaluations of when medical or dental attention is required. We omit SIPP queries about respondents' satisfaction with various attributes of their housing and communities as being overly subjective, as well as questions about housing quality that are too broad to shed light on true material deprivation (Beverly 2000). On the other hand, unlike some other measures (see, e.g., Kalil, Seefeldt, and Wang 2002), ours are retrospective assessments of experiences of deprivation rather than prospective evaluations of the likelihood of future hardship, and empirical evidence supports the validity of survey questions measuring food insufficiency as accurately distinguishing between levels of nutritional resources (Beverly 2001).

Methodology. We first present descriptive statistics on the incidence of hardship in our sample, by demographic characteristics and poverty status, for three groups: women who were employed continuously over the first 32 months of the 1996 SIPP; women who were initially employed, had been unemployed at least once, and were re-employed in the 32nd month; and previously employed women who were unemployed at the end of our panel. We next use regression analysis to separate the effects of women's job loss from other characteristics and circumstances, such as education and poverty status that also affect the likelihood of experiencing both material hardship and unemployment.

Since poverty status is endogenous to hardship, we use a two-stage model in which we first estimate poverty status and then use predicted values of the poverty variable, along with unemployment experience, to estimate hardship. The model comprises the equations:

$$PS_i = \alpha_0 + \alpha_1 X_i + \varepsilon_i \tag{1}$$

$$HS_i = \beta_0 + \beta_1 PPS_i + b_2 UE_i + v_i \tag{2}$$

where PS_i in equation (1) is the poverty status of woman i's family in Month 1 of the 1996 SIPP panel, α_0 is a constant, α_1 is a vector of parameters to be estimated, X_i is a vector of demographic characteristics (household relationship, marital status, age, race/ethnicity, parent status, and presence of other earners) and human capital measures (education) that affect hardship experience for woman i, and ε_i is woman i's disturbance term; in equation (2), HS_i is the hardship measure being estimated for woman i, β_0 is a constant, β_1 and β_2 are parameters to be estimated, PPS_i is the predicted poverty status of woman i derived from equation (1), UE_i indicates the past and current unemployment experience for woman i as of Month 32 of the panel, and v_i is the error term.

FINDINGS

Demographic differences between women with different experiences of unemployment. Women who were employed in Month 1 of the 1996 SIPP panel and had experienced and/or were experiencing unemployment in Month 32 of the panel are different in many ways from women who were employed continuously over that period (Table 1). They are more likely to be a child rather than a household head. Previously unemployed but now employed women are less likely to be married than always-married women, but those currently unemployed have a higher marriage rate. The currently unemployed are much more likely to have children under 18 at home than either the always-working or the previously unemployed. Women with unemployment experience are younger than the always-employed and disproportionately Hispanic, while currently working but previously unemployed women are disproportionately Black compared to both the always-working and the currently unemployed. The educational achievement of the group with unemployment experience is much lower, perhaps because on average these women are younger than the always-working. Of the three groups, the currently unemployed have the highest rate of living with another earner, while the always-working and currently working have nearly identical levels of cohabitation with other earners.

Hardship experience. One-fifth of all women in our dataset experienced at least one type of hardship (Table 2). Problems with utilities is the most commonly experienced hardship (10 percent), followed by not seeing a dentist (8 percent) or doctor (6 percent) when needed, lacking a telephone (6 percent), and loss or threat of loss of housing (6 percent). Food insufficiency is the least common hardship, affecting 2 percent of women in the study.

Within households, individuals who are not part of the primary family unit are more likely than the household head, spouse, and children to experience hardship, for most types of hardship. Married women have much lower hardship incidence rates than unmarried women, with sixteen percent of married women experiencing at least one type of hardship, compared to 27 percent of unmarried women. Hardship incidence rates are at least 1.5 times higher for unmarried than married women for all hardship types and are more than twice as high for lack of a telephone and insufficient food.

Having at least one child increases the likelihood of inadequate telephone access, non-payment of utility bills or termination of utility service, and food insufficiency by about as much as being unmarried.

TABLE 1. Means of variables used in regression analysis (standard deviation in parentheses).

	All		Always employed		With unemployment– working		With unemployment– unemployed	
					By employment status:			
Status in household								
Household head or spouse	.80	(.40)	85	(.36)	.72	(.45)	.75	(.43)
Child of household head	.11	(.32)	.08	(.27)	.19	(.39)	.16	(.37)
Other	.08	(.28)	.08	(.27)	.10	(.30)	.09	(.28)
Married [a]	.56	(.50)	.58	(.49)	.48	(.50)	.61	(.49)
One or more own children	.46	(.50)	.43	(.50)	.46	(.50)	.56	(.50)
Age								
18-24	.16	(.37)	.10	(.30)	.28	(.45)	.29	(.45)
25 to 34	.26	(.44)	.25	(.43)	.25	(.43)	.32	(.47)
35 and older	.58	(.49)	.65	(.48)	.46	(.50)	.39	(.49)
Race and ethnicity								
NH White	.75	(.43)	.77	(.42)	.71	(.45)	.73	(.44)
NH Black	.13	(.33)	.12	(.32)	.15	(.36)	.12	(.32)
Hispanic	.08	(.28)	.07	(.26)	.10	(.30)	.12	(.32)
Other	.04	(.19)	.04	(.20)	.04	(.19)	.04	(.19)
Educational achievement								
No high school degree	.10	(.30)	.07	(.26)	.14	(.34)	.18	(.39)
High school only	.31	(.46)	.30	(.46)	.32	(.47)	.31	(.46)
Some college	.36	(.48)	.35	(.48)	.38	(.49)	.36	(.48)
College degree	.23	(.42)	.27	(.45)	.16	(.37)	.15	(.36)
Poverty status [b]								
Non-poor	.72	(.45)	.79	(.41)	.59	(.49)	.59	(.49)
Near-poor	.18	(.38)	.16	(.36)	.21	(.41)	.22	(.41)
Poor	.10	(.30)	.06	(.23)	.19	(.39)	.19	(.39)
One or more other earners	.63	(.48)	.62	(.49)	.63	(.48)	.71	(.45)
Unemployment experience [c]								
Always employed	.66	(.47)						
With unemployment–working	.22	(.42)						
With unemployment– unemployed	.12	(.32)						
Hardship experience								
Telephone	.06	(.23)	.04	(.19)	.09	(.28)	.11	(.31)
Housing	.06	(.23)	.04	(.19)	.09	(.29)	.08	(.27)
Utilities	.10	(.30)	.01	(.10)	.14	(.35)	.14	(.34)
Doctor	.06	(.24)	.04	(.21)	.09	(.28)	.10	(.30)
Dentist	.08	(.27)	.07	(.25)	.11	(.32)	.11	(.32)
Food	.02	(.14)	.01	(.11)	.03	(.17)	.03	(.17)
Any hardship	.21	(.41)	.17	(.37)	.28	(.45)	.29	(.45)
Sample size	11,595		7,866		2,457		1,272	
Weighted N (population)	62,117,146		40,832,149		13,974,331		7,310,666	

[a] Married spouse present.
[b] "Non-poor" have family income of 200 percent of the poverty line or greater; "near-poor" have family income of 100 percent to 199 percent of the poverty line; and "poor" have family income under the poverty line.
[c] "Always employed" reported employment for at least one week of every month and no weeks seeking employment in the first 32 months of the 1996 SIPP panel; "with unemployment–working" had at least one completed spell of unemployment by the 32nd month of the panel; and "with unemployment–unemployed" were unemployed at least once between the 2nd and 32nd months of the panel and were unemployed in the 32nd month.
Note: Except for unemployment experience and hardship experience, all data are as of Month 1 of the 1996 SIPP panel. Means are longitudinally weighted.
Source: Institute for Women's Policy Research analysis of the 1996 panel of the Survey of Income and Program Participation.

TABLE 2. Incidence rate of hardship (percentage experiencing hardship) at 32nd month of 1996 SIPP panel, by demographic characteristics, poverty status, and unemployment experience, women aged 18 and older in 1996 who were employed in Month 1 of the panel.

	No phone, or phone disconnected	Couldn't pay mortgage or rent, or evicted	Couldn't pay utility, or service cut off	Didn't see doctor when needed	Didn't see dentist when needed	Not enough to eat sometimes or often	Any hardship
All	5.57	5.55	10.37	6.08	8.18	1.87	20.78
Status in household							
Household head or spouse	5.43	5.49	10.42	5.83	7.97	1.88	20.23
Child of household head	5.46	5.69	10.08	5.63	7.97	1.52	20.76
Other	7.06	5.95	10.33	9.21	10.49	2.17	26.16
Marital status							
Married [a]	3.57	4.13	7.72	4.33	6.73	1.18	15.82
Not married	8.11	7.36	13.74	8.32	10.01	2.74	27.08
Number own children in HH							
No children	3.97	3.62	7.39	5.63	7.03	1.27	16.95
One or more children	7.48	7.86	13.94	6.63	9.55	2.58	25.36
Age							
18-24	8.39	7.69	13.91	8.07	10.57	2.15	27.03
25 to 34	7.15	7.55	12.86	6.36	9.20	2.18	24.44
35 and older	4.05	4.04	8.24	5.39	7.03	1.64	17.34
Race and ethnicity							
NH White	3.92	4.41	8.67	5.75	7.84	1.45	17.91
NH Black	12.73	10.84	20.49	7.22	8.60	3.06	33.21
Hispanic	9.69	8.86	11.75	7.27	11.13	3.05	29.89
Other	5.40	3.49	7.44	6.36	6.94	3.47	16.62
Educational achievement							
No high school degree	14.50	9.71	17.17	12.29	12.46	4.77	36.18
High school only	6.33	6.28	12.42	6.08	9.05	2.01	23.56
Some college	4.83	5.97	10.82	6.57	8.58	1.95	21.07
College degree	1.84	2.17	4.06	2.67	4.55	0.30	10.05
Poverty status [b]							
Non-poor	2.71	3.39	6.74	3.77	5.60	0.81	13.83
Near-poor	10.49	9.44	15.90	10.53	14.12	3.69	33.28
Poor	17.06	13.92	26.21	14.56	15.91	6.13	47.78
Number of other earners							
None	8.46	7.68	14.66	8.58	10.73	3.06	27.98
One or more	3.90	4.32	7.89	4.64	6.70	1.18	16.62
Unemployment experience [c]							
Always employed	3.59	3.85	8.40	4.47	6.55	1.25	16.85
With unemployment–working	8.76	9.42	14.43	8.87	11.24	3.06	28.03
With unemployment–unemployed	10.52	7.67	13.65	9.79	11.38	3.06	28.88
All with unemployment (those currently working and those currently unemployed)	9.36	8.82	14.16	9.19	11.29	3.06	28.32
Sample size	618	614	1,183	690	939	187	2,355

[a, b, c] See corresponding footnotes to Table 1.
Note: Except for unemployment experience and hardship experience, all data are as of Month 1 of the 1996 SIPP panel. Incidence rates are derived using SIPP96 longitudinal weight.
Source: Institute for Women's Policy Research analysis of the 1996 panel of the Survey of Income and Program Participation.

Women who have children are much more likely than other women to experience housing hardship; being a parent is more detrimental in relation to this hardship type than any other. Mothers are more likely to postpone medical and dental care than are non-mothers.

Problems maintaining utility service are particularly severe for both unmarried women and mothers, with 14 percent of each group experiencing this hardship. One in thirteen either missed paying for housing or were evicted for not paying rent or a mortgage. Hardship incidence decreases with age for all hardship types.

Blacks experience hardships at nearly twice the rate that whites do overall, with the greatest differences in hardship experience relating to access to telephones and stable housing: Eleven percent of Black women experience housing-related hardship, and twenty percent have difficulty paying for or maintaining utility service. Blacks, Hispanics, and other women of color all experience relatively high levels of food hardship, with over three percent of each group going without sufficient food. The lowest rates of hardship incidence for housing, utilities, and dental care are for workers who do not self-identify as white, Black, or Hispanic. Hispanics have high levels of hardship compared to whites, the highest rates of failing to obtain needed dental care of all groups, and equivalent incidence rates of lack of access to medical care and food insufficiency to Blacks.

Lack of educational attainment creates enormous vulnerability to material hardship: Over one-third of women without a high school degree experience at least one type of hardship, with five percent lacking sufficient food and ten percent facing eviction. Completing high school reduces the overall incidence of hardship by one-third. With a college degree, one in ten women experiences at least one hardship.

Almost half of women living in families with income below the federal poverty line experience at least one kind of hardship. Six percent lack adequate food; more than one in four struggles to maintain utility service. Roughly 15 percent experience hardships related to telephone access, housing, and inadequate medical and dental care. Having another earner in the family helps to inoculate against material hardship, but is not a preventive. Twenty-eight percent of women who are the sole earners in their families experience at least one type of material hardship, as do 17 percent of women who live with at least one other earner. With another earner, hardship incidence rates are lower than the average rates for all women, for all hardship types.

Compared with women who are continuously employed, those experiencing unemployment are over half again as likely to experience a material hardship. Housing hardship occurs at twice the rate for currently unemployed as for continuously employed women, while currently employed women with unemployment experience have an even higher incidence of this hardship (9 percent). Women with unemployment experience who are currently unemployed experience telephone-related hardships three times as often as the continuously employed; for those with completed unemployment spells, the incidence of lack of access to a telephone is nearly two and a half times as high as that of continuously employed women. For other hardships, incidence rates are similar for both groups with unemployment experience, at about twice the rates of women with no unemployment.

Regression analysis. The first stage of the two-stage regression analysis, in which we estimate an equation for having family income below the poverty threshold, indicates that being a household head or spouse lowers the relative likelihood of being poor compared to being a non-family member of the household, although the result is not statistically significant (Table 3). Being a child of a householder has a larger and statistically significant effect in lowering the relative odds of being poor. Marriage has a small effect on the relative likelihood of being poor, but the relationship is not statistically significant.

Living with one or more of one's own children increases the relative odds of being poor by close to three times, while the relative likelihood of being poor decreases with age. Blacks are nearly twice as likely as whites to experience poverty; the odds of Hispanics being poor are two and a half times as great as for whites; and members of other racial and ethnic groups have double the odds of being poor as whites.

Lack of fundamental educational credentials increases the relative odds of being poor by nearly two and a half times as compared with obtaining a high school degree. Accessing some post-secondary education decreases the relative odds of poverty by one-third, and completing a college degree brings a further reduction of one-third.

Of all the factors included in our model, having at least one other earner in the household offers the best protection against poverty, reducing the relative odds of being poor to only ten percent of the odds for those not living with another earner.

In the second part of the two-stage analysis, we isolate the impact of unemployment on the experience of material hardship, holding demographic characteristics and initial poverty status constant. We estimate second-stage models for each of the six hardship indicators and for the experience of any one or more hardships, separately for those unemployed who are currently working and those still unemployed in the

TABLE 3. Results of first stage of logistic regression analysis: Odds ratios for predicting poverty status.

	Odds ratio (robust std. error)	
Head of household or spouse	.84	(.11)
Child of household head	.67**	(.13)
Married	.95	(.09)
Living with own child	2.75***	(.22)
Age 25 to 34	.39***	(.05)
Age 35 or older	.21***	(.02)
Non-Hispanic Black	1.96***	(.18)
Hispanic	2.46***	(.28)
Other	2.13***	(.40)
No high school degree	2.40***	(.24)
Some post-secondary education	.62***	(.05)
College degree	.29***	(.04)
Other earner in household	.10***	(.01)
Log-likelihood	-2703.8669	
Wald chi^2	1339.13	
Prob. $>$ chi^2	0.0000	
Pseudo R^2	0.2674	
Number in sample	11,595	

* $p < .10$
** $p < .05$
*** $p < .01$

32nd month of the SIPP panel. The results establish the impact of unemployment in increasing the relative likelihood of experiencing each of the six individual hardships, as well as general hardship indicator, for both those with completed unemployment spells and those currently unemployed, as compared to women who are employed continuously (Table 4).

The first row of Table 4 shows the impact of being poor on the six hardships. Overall, poor women are 34 times as likely to experience at least one material hardship as non-poor women. Disruption of telephone service is the most likely outcome of poverty, followed by food and utility problems, difficulty maintaining utilities, and inadequate access to medical care.

Unemployment increases the relative odds of hardship by more than 60 percent, both for those now back at work and for those currently unemployed. The relative likelihood of not having a telephone is twice as high for those with unemployment experience as for the continuously

TABLE 4. Results of second stage of regression analysis: Odds ratios for predicted hardship, for different experiences of unemployment.

	Phone	Housing	Utility	Doctor	Dentist	Food	Any hardship
			Odds ratio (robust std. error)				
			Type of hardship				
Predicted poverty status	42.32*** (8.02)	17.99*** (3.42)	24.44*** (4.06)	7.82*** (1.50)	6.46*** (1.16)	25.49*** (7.04)	34.10*** (5.38)
With unemployment experience, currently working	2.00*** (.20)	2.07*** (.21)	1.53*** (.11)	1.84*** (.17)	1.67*** (.13)	1.93*** (.31)	1.63*** (.10)
With unemployment experience, currently unemployed	2.15*** (.26)	1.61*** (.21)	1.37*** (.14)	1.98*** (.22)	1.63*** (.17)	1.64** (.35)	1.65*** (.12)
Log-likelihood	−2182.253	−2263.3043	−3606.9296	−2527.4991	−3178.109	−992.32931	−5472.1672
Wald chi^2	559.98	363.33	480.01	228.10	201.26	210.81	656.90
Prob > chi^2	0.0000	0.0000	0.0000	0.0000	0.0000	0.0000	0.0000
Psuedo R^2	0.0957	0.0576	0.0560	0.0338	0.0251	0.0624	0.0649
Number in sample	11,595	11,595	11,595	11,595	11,595	11,595	11,595

n = 11,595
* p < .10
** p < .05
*** p < .01

employed. For those now at work, the experience of housing-related hardship doubles with unemployment experience; those currently unemployed have 1.6 times the relative chance of not being able to pay for, or losing, housing as do those without unemployment. The risk of not being able to access needed health care is twice as high for the currently unemployed and nearly that for those with unemployment experience. Food hardship is twice as high among those with unemployment experience who are now working, and those currently unemployed have a 64 percent higher chance of not having enough to eat. For both women with completed unemployment and those now out of work, the risk of not being able to afford dental care increases by two-thirds. The relative odds of having difficulty paying for utility services, or of having those services terminated, are half again as high for women now back at work and one-third higher for those still unemployed.

DISCUSSION AND POLICY IMPLICATIONS

Our analysis establishes that women's job loss has a substantial impact on their families' economic well-being. Even holding demographic characteristics and initial poverty status constant, women's job loss increases their experience of material hardship by two-thirds. The relative odds of households being evicted or failing to pay housing costs more than double when a female wage-earner becomes unemployed; experience of inadequate nutritional resources is 93 (64) percent higher for women re-employed following a job loss (for still-unemployed women). The relative risk of not having a telephone is twice as high for women with an unemployment spell. Housing and telephone hardships are particularly salient for women seeking employment, who need to be able to provide potential employers with residential and telephone contact information.

Individuals' and families' reliance on women's earnings has increased substantially in the last 50 years (Danziger and Gottschalk 2003). When women lose their jobs, the resultant drop in earnings poses serious risks for economic sufficiency and stability.

While our study did not analyze the effect of UI benefits in alleviating hardship, clearly broader coverage and more generous benefits would help unemployed women and their dependents. Many states have recently enacted or considered policy changes such as inclusion of part-time workers and victims of domestic violence in the UI system, modernized earnings calculations that account for workers' most recent wages, and more adequate benefit levels, to ensure that UI provides the support it was intended to.

Better UI policies to help the unemployed avoid material hardship will ameliorate the deleterious effect of job loss, but a more pro-active policy approach is to enhance workers' prospects of maintaining employment. At the macroeconomic level, this could be implemented through a full employment policy that uses both monetary and fiscal policy to create the kind of jobs that are likely to endure (Goldberg 2000). For workers who have jobs, supports such as paid leave and work-hours flexibility help fit non-employment responsibilities and workers' own health needs into job structures in a planful and efficacious way. Workers need access to affordable, reliable child care to minimize work disruptions related to failed care arrangements. All the other employment supports that many middle- and upper-class workers take for granted–reliable transportation to and from job sites, stable housing in safe neighborhoods, a living wage–should be made available to low-wage workers as a means of increasing employment tenure. Appropriate education and training opportunities that prepare individuals with skills that can lead to high-quality jobs are also essential.

If we as a society demand that anyone not supported by their family or accumulated wealth participate in employment–which is the way U.S. welfare policy is evolving–we have to recognize a societal obligation to ensure that good jobs are available to all who want them. This requires that we manage job growth and regulate the quality of employment much more intensively than we currently do and ensure the adequacy of safety net programs for workers temporarily between jobs. If we fail to accept this responsibility, we are acquiescing in an economic system that denies opportunities for self-sufficiency to millions of workers and then ignores the hardships that arise from their employment instability.

NOTES

1. We distinguish between currently unemployed women and women with historical experience of job loss, under the assumption that re-employed women are likely to be in significantly different economic circumstances than women with no job at the time of the hardship interview. However, as will be seen, the currently-unemployed and re-employed-unemployed are quite similar in hardship experience, perhaps as an artifact of the survey timeframe (i.e., the time between re-employment and the hardship survey was insufficient to allow financial recovery) or because the financial impact of unemployment lingers substantially beyond re-employment. In the estimation analysis, combining all women with unemployment experience (past and current) into one group did not affect our results.

2. Few respondents in our sample had utilities cut off or were evicted from their housing. Thus, we are unable to follow Beverly's (2000) advice and only assess the combination of a failure to pay bills and the resultant loss of the associated service as a hardship, not one of these events on its own. This approach would better identify the concrete material hardship of losing housing or utility services due to inadequate income.

REFERENCES

Bassi, Laurie J. and Amy B. Chasanov. 1995. "Women and the Unemployment Insurance System." Unpublished paper.

Beverly, Sondra G. 2000. "Using Measures of Material Hardship to Assess Well-being." *Focus* 21(Fall): 65-69.

_____. 2001. "Material hardship in the United States: Evidence from the Survey of Income and Program Participation." *Social Work Research* 25(September): 143-151.

Blank, Rebecca and David Card. 1989. *Recent Trends in Insured and Uninsured Unemployment: Is There an Explanation?* National Bureau of Economic Research Working Paper No. 2871. Cambridge, MA: National Bureau of Economic Research.

Danziger, Sheldon and Peter Gottschalk. 2003. "America Unequal: Women, Government Hold Economy at Bay." In *Smart Library on Urban Poverty.* http://www.poverty.smartlibrary.org/NewInterface/segment.cfm?segment=<1728 (June 21, 2003).

Emsellem, Maurice and Vicky Lovell. 2000. *The Georgia Unemployment Insurance System: Overcoming Barriers for Low-Wage, Part-Time and Women Workers.* New York: National Employment Law Project.

Goldberg, Gertrude Schaffner. 2000. "How Good Is Four Percent Unemployment?" *Social Policy* 30(Spring): 28-30.

Kalil, Ariel, Kristin S. Seefeldt, and Hui-chen Wang. 2002. "Sanctions and Material Hardship Under TANF." *Social Service Review* 76(December): 642-662.

Long, Sharon K. 2003. *Hardship Among the Uninsured: Choosing Among Food, Housing, and Health Insurance.* Urban Institute New Federalism Series B, No. B-54. http://www.urban.org/urlprint.cfm?ID=8407 (June 17, 2003).

Lovell, Vicky and Maurice Emsellem. 2004. *Florida's Unemployment Insurance System: Overcoming Barriers for Women, Low-Wage, and Part-Time Workers.* Washington, DC: Institute for Women's Policy Research.

McMurrer, Daniel and Amy Chasanov. 1995. "Trends in Unemployment Insurance Benefits." *Monthly Labor Review* 118(September): 30-39.

Pearce, Diana. 1985. "Toil and Trouble: Women and Unemployment Compensation." *Signs: The Journal of Women in Culture & Society* 10(Spring): 439-459.

Vroman, Wayne. 1998. *Labor Market Changes and Unemployment Insurance Benefit Availability.* U.S. Department of Labor Unemployment Insurance Occasional Paper 98-3. Washington, DC: U.S. Department of Labor.

Who Gets What?
Gender Differences in "Spendable" Income

Tamara Ohler, University of Massachusetts, Amherst
Nancy Folbre, University of Massachusetts, Amherst

SUMMARY. Feminist policy makers need accurate measures of inequality in the economic well-being of men and women. In this paper, we explain why the wage gap by gender gives a misleading measure of women's relative economic well-being in the United States, emphasizing the effects of income pooling within households. We construct a household-level index of women's "spendable" income relative to men's that builds on Randy Albelda's (1988) "PAR index." We improve on the PAR index in three ways. First, we account for economies of scale associated with additional household members. Second, we utilize the Current Population Survey to capture the impact of government taxes and transfers, providing an indicator of "spendable," rather than "money," income. Finally, as a step toward redefining the concept of "spendable" income, we deduct a lower-bound estimate of child care costs. *[Article copies available for a fee from The Haworth Document Delivery Service: 1-800-HAWORTH. E-mail address: <docdelivery@haworthpress. com> Website: <http://www.HaworthPress.com> © 2005 by The Haworth Press, Inc. All rights reserved.]*

KEYWORDS. Income pooling, income measures, PAR index, households, child care, government transfers, economies of scale

[Haworth co-indexing entry note]: "Who Gets What? Gender Differences in "Spendable" Income." Ohler, Tamara, and Nancy Folbre. Co-published simultaneously in *Journal of Women, Politics & Policy* (The Haworth Political Press, an imprint of The Haworth Press, Inc.) Vol. 27, No. 3/4, 2005, pp. 185-194; and: *Women, Work, and Poverty: Women Centered Research for Policy Change* (ed: Heidi Hartmann) The Haworth Political Press, an imprint of The Haworth Press, Inc., 2005, pp. 185-194. Single or multiple copies of this article are available for a fee from The Haworth Document Delivery Service [1-800-HAWORTH, 9:00 a.m. - 5:00 p.m. (EST). E-mail address: docdelivery@haworthpress.com].

Feminist policy makers need accurate measures of inequality in the economic well-being of men and women. Constructing such measures is a more complex exercise than it may seem. The most widely cited indicator of gender inequality is relative labor market earnings. Relative wealth is also sometimes studied. Both these indicators are valuable. We believe they should be supplemented by better measures of women's "spendable" income relative to men's.

FIGHTING FIRE WITH FIRE: WHY PROGRESSIVE POLICY ADVOCATES MUST BE FLUENT IN ALTERNATIVE INCOME DEFINITIONS

Conservatives often construct alternative income measures in order to argue against downward redistribution. In particular, they undermine progressive public policy proposals that aim to benefit low-income households such as increases in minimum wages or the earnings disregard (i.e., reductions in the tax rate on earnings) of the earned income tax credit. Such policies, they argue, will only generate more "spendable" income and may thereby discourage paid work.[1] Their household income measures reflect net gains (in terms of poverty reduction) from additional work hours, neglecting expenditures incurred by parents, for example, such as child care costs. Carried to its logical conclusion, their staunchly pro-work agenda discourages family members from caring for their own kin.

Determining relative income is difficult for three reasons. First, income is typically measured on the family or household, rather than individual, level. As a result, measures of household income hinge on assumptions regarding economies of scale and income pooling. Second, income has a number of different components, and can be defined in a variety of ways, depending on sources (such as government transfers), types (such as in-kind benefits), and treatment of taxes. Third, conventional definitions of disposable (or "spendable") income are somewhat misleading because they fail to account for employment-related expenditures particularly relevant to women, such as child care costs.

In this study, we explore these three issues and construct an index of women's "spendable" income relative to men's. We build on an estimate of average per capita income of women relative to men, an approach first suggested by Randy Albelda (1988). We utilize data from the Current Population Survey to capture the impact of government taxes and transfers and explore the impact of pooling and economies of scale. We also subtract an estimate of child care costs from "spendable" income.

POOLING AND ECONOMIES OF SCALE

The advantage of focusing on earnings is that they are unambigu-ously linked to individuals. But while earnings are the most important component of income for working-age adults, many individuals receive income from other sources, including interest, capital gains, and gov-ernment transfers. Measures of family and household income are based on the assumption that income is pooled, an assumption that is probably more plausible for families than for households, but whose empirical validity remains unclear.[2]

The relationship between family and household as units of analysis complicates an analysis of pooling. For the Census Bureau, a family is defined as "a group of two people or more (one of whom is the house-holder) related by birth, marriage, or adoption and residing together." In 2000, nearly 12 percent of all households contained more than one fam-ily (U.S. Department of Commerce, Census Bureau 2001). The exclu-sion of unrelated family members from the Census' definition of family ignores both the contributions (such as money and time) and the extra costs associated with unrelated individuals, such as cohabiting partners or foster children. For this reason, the household is the preferable unit of analysis.

Income pooling has countervailing implications for women's well-being. On the one hand, pooling with other adults, including adult men, often increases the resources available to an individual household mem-ber. On the other hand, pooling with dependents, including children, generally decreases the resources available to adults. If all men and women lived in the same households, their per capita household income would, by definition, be equal. However, since many women live in households with children, but without male partners, and these house-holds have significantly lower income than married couple households, women's per capita household income is lower than men's.

Albelda's index of women's access to income is based on an estimate of their per capita household income relative to that of men. Assuming that that income is shared equally among all household members, she measures the gap between gender equality and the actual ratio, dubbing this the "PAR" index. She shows that this index rose over the period be-tween 1967 and 1985 as a result of increases in the share of households maintained by women alone. In other words, women's relative per capita household income declined relative to that of men.

While this is a promising approach, it suffers from several limitations. First, as aforementioned, it assumes that income is shared equally within households, which seems unlikely. Even if income is shared equally within married couple families (an assumption that has been widely challenged) there is little reason to believe that it is shared equally among household members who may be cohabiting for only a brief period, or who have chosen not to marry precisely because they do not want to pool their income.

Second, this assumption ignores the effect of economies of scale. For a variety of reasons, including the prominent role of rent, utilities, and consumer durables, households with larger numbers of individuals generally enjoy lower per capita costs. One way of taking economies of scale into account, widely used in analysis of the Luxembourg Income Survey, is to divide household income by the square root of the number of household members (Jäntti and Danziger 2000).

We do not, at this point in time, have any way to improve upon the assumption of equal pooling. However, we can show the impact of adjusting Albelda's PAR index by adjusting for economies of scale. Chart 1 compares the PAR index for 2000 (following Albelda's method) with an adjusted index. Apparently women benefit slightly more than men from living in larger households; the adjustment results in a small increase in the measure, from about 80 percent to about 84 percent.

THE EFFECT OF GOVERNMENT TRANSFERS

Albelda's PAR index relies on the most common measure of family income, what the Current Population Survey terms "money income." It is widely recognized that this measure is incomplete, because it does not include the value of in-kind benefits (such as health insurance) or in-kind transfers (such as Food Stamps or Medicaid). Conservatives at the Heritage Foundation (Rector and Hederman 2004) argue that the exclusion of such transfers leads to the underestimation of women's "spendable" income.

Expanded measures of income can be defined in a way that reveals the impact of government transfers and taxes. Using data collected from the U.S. Census Bureau's March 2001 Current Population Survey, we construct a broad measure of income that encompasses both public and private benefits and subtracts major federal and state taxes. The Census

CHART 1

**Per Capita Household Income of Women Relative to Men:
Albelda's "PAR" Index vs. "PAR" Adjusted for Household Size**

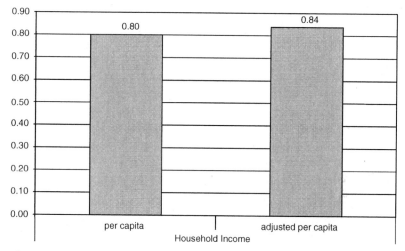

Source: Authors' calculations, Census Bureau, Current Population Survey, March 2001

calls this household income measure "Definition 15." A comparison of the two measures of household income follows.

Money Income (CPS Definition 1)	Income Plus Benefits After Taxes (CPS Definition 15)
Personal Earnings Public Assistance Social Security Supplemental Security Income Disability Income (public/private) Survivor's Benefits (public/private) Educational Assistance Retirement (public/private) Unemployment Compensation Workers' Compensation Veteran's Administration Benefits Assets (Interest, Dividends, Rent) Child Support/Alimony Financial Assistance (private)	**Money Income** Food Stamps Housing Subsidy Medicare (fungible value) Medicaid (fungible value) Earned Income Tax Credit (EITC) School Lunch Employer Contribution to Hlth Ins. Net Return to Home Equity Capital Gains Tax Liability (Federal, State, FICA)

Median levels of money income and Definition 15 income vary little in the aggregate (in 2000, the ratio of the former to the latter was .98). As can be seen in Chart 2, median disposable Definition 15 income of

CHART 2

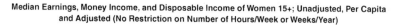

Median Earnings, Money Income, and Disposable Income of Women 15+; Unadjusted, Per Capita
and Adjusted (No Restriction on Number of Hours/Week or Weeks/Year)

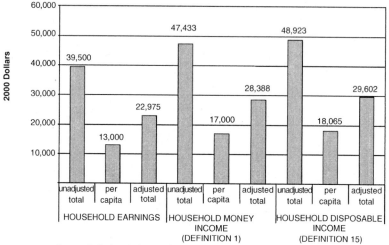

Source: Author's calculations, Census Bureau, Current Population Survey, March 2001

women is only slightly greater than their money income ($48,923 for Definition 15 versus $47,433 for unadjusted total money income; adjusted and per capita amounts also show small differences).

Significant differences between money income and Definition 15 income are apparent, however, in comparisons of households with children and elderly members. Furthermore, the measure of income has significant implications for comparisons between married and single mothers living with children. In 2000, the ratio of money income to Definition 15 income for married mothers living with children under 18 was 106.4, but for single mothers the ratio was .88.

The comparison between money income and Definition 15 income offers insights into the effects of government transfer and tax policies on different groups of women, and is therefore particularly useful to disaggregated comparisons.

In the aggregate, women gain more Definition 15 income relative to money income than men do. As a result, the index of "spendable" earnings based on Definition 15 is higher than Albelda's index of relative income. (Compare the third set of bars in Chart 2 to the second set–this comparison is only about women and shows women's incomes do increase under Definition 15.) Still, this measure of women's economic well-being is misleading; the "improvement" for women using Definition 15, reflected in the height of the last set of bars, is based on a measure that omits the most gender-relevant component of household budgets: child care costs.

CHILD CARE AND "SPENDABLE" INCOME

The adjustments that we have made so far improve the accuracy of the index of relative income, and also promise important insights into differences among groups of women, a reflection of tax and spending policies. However, they all have the effect of increasing women's apparent economic well-being. We now incorporate a third gender-sensitive factor that may reduce measures of women's relative economic well-being.

Measures of women's income that do not take the costs of child care into account almost inevitably show that increased earnings lead to increased well-being. For instance, in her analysis of women's poverty rates based on the Current Population Survey from the 1970s to the 1990s, Karen Christopher (2001) finds that any trend towards "pauperization of motherhood" abated in the late 1990s. But this finding reflects the fact that the official poverty threshold matrix fails to deduct the extra costs associated with child care from household earnings.

Furthermore, over the lifecycle, women's responsibility for children tends to lower their earnings. In their paper titled "The Wage Penalty for Motherhood," Michelle Budig and Paula England (2001) find penalties of 7 percent per child. And even after controlling for less job experience due to time spent caring for children, a 5 percent per child penalty remains. The penalties only increase when a woman is married. This is especially problematic since most women (18+) living with children are married (69 percent in 2000).

Some scholars have made efforts to estimate the size of work-related child care costs and deduct these from measures of household income. Since the Current Population Survey does not contain direct survey data on out-of-pocket child care expenses, Isabel Sawhill and Adam Thomas (1999) estimate these expenses using logistic regression analysis with independent variables such as number of children in the household and dummies by race and region. They impute child care expenses only if all parents in the household work and there is at least one child under the age of twelve in the family. They find that "when income is adjusted for child care expenses, 1.9 additional people–of whom more than 1 million are children–are thrown into poverty." That is, the overall poverty rate jumps from 11.5 percent to 12.2 percent when child care expenses are subtracted from family income.

We use a simpler method, also based on the Current Population Survey, to construct "D15Careadj," a variable that captures the differential impact of child care costs on men and women's post tax and transfer income. We base our construction of care costs on Mark Lino's finding: of all households paying for child care, the average amount spent is roughly 10 percent of their annual income in 2000 (Lino 2001).

Chart 3 compares three median income measures by gender; all have been adjusted for household size in order to reflect economies of scale. The three household income measures are (1) money income (D1adj), (2) post tax and transfer income, i.e., "spendable" income (D15adj) and (3) "spendable" income with child care expenses deducted at the rate mentioned above (D15Careadj). The difference in heights of D15Careadj by gender is driven by the higher proportion of women residing in households with children relative to men. Fifty percent of all women 18-64 live in households with children compared with 45 percent of all men in the same age range. The difference would be larger if we relaxed the assumption of equal pooling. That is, if we incorporate a deduction in women's income for their higher expenditure on children, the wedge by gender of D15Careadj would increase.

CONCLUSIONS AND FURTHER RESEARCH

Money income offers a misleading picture of low-income households; economic well-being is understated as cash and cash-like public and private benefits are excluded from this household income measure.

Money income also offers a misleading picture of middle and high-income households, who receive private benefits such as employer contributions to health insurance and pensions, which are exempt from taxation. Relatively affluent families also derive greater advantages than others from tax breaks such as the deduction of mortgage interest from taxable income.

Even with a broader measure of income, which better reflects disposable income, a serious shortcoming persists; expenditures on children remain invisible. We need a measure such as D15Careadj, which reflects this expense. These alternative measures generate different ratios of women's to men's household income than Albelda's index. By her measure, women's per capita income represented about 80.3 percent of

CHART 3

Median Income Definitions by Gender in 2000

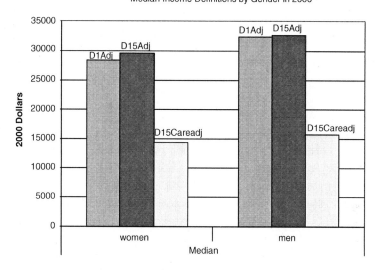

Source: Authors' calculations, Census Bureau, Current Population Survey, March 2001

men's in 2000. Since more women live in households with several members, an adjustment for economies of scale yields a higher estimate of about 83.9 percent. Adding in cash and cash-like benefits measured by the CPS raises the estimate further to about 89.4 percent. Our conservative estimate of child care costs has virtually no effect, lowering women's overall access to income relative to men to about 89.2 percent.

We hope to develop a better picture of changes in women's relative economic well-being over time by imputing more accurate estimates of child care expenses. We expect this change to further reduce D15Careadj relative to D15adj. We also plan to explore the effect of imputing the value of the non-market work that is reduced as hours of paid employment increase.

NOTES

1. Dennis Ventry (1999) provides an historical overview of the factors that have influenced Republicans' waxing and waning support of the EITC.
2. A growing international literature points to evidence of higher expenditures on children when mothers control the household purse. In their study of PROGRESA,

Mexico's largest anti-poverty program (which directs benefits only to mothers), Luis Rubalcava, Graciela Teruel, and Duncan Thomas (2003) find that as the share of household resources from PROGRESA increases, the share of the budget spent on child clothing, education, and higher quality diet increase.

REFERENCES

Albelda, Randy, Elaine McCrate, Edwin Melendez, June Lapidus, and the Center for Popular Economics. 1988. *Mink Coats Don't Trickle Down: The Economic Attack on Women and People of Color.* Boston, MA: South End Press.

Budig, Michelle and Paula England. 2001. "The Wage Penalty for Motherhood," *American Sociological Review* 66(April): 204-225.

Christopher, Karen. 2001. "Mother's Poverty in the U.S. Over Time: The Effects of Single Parenthood and Employment," Presented at the 2003 Institute for Women's Policy Research Conference, Washington, DC.

Jäntti, Markus and Sheldon Danziger. 2000. "Income Poverty in Advanced Countries." In *Handbook of Income Distribution*, eds. Anthony B. Atkinson and François Bourguignon. Amsterdam: North-Holland, 309-378.

Lino, Mark. 2001. "USDA's Expenditures by Families on Children Project: Uses and Changes Over Time." *http://www.usda.gov/cnpp/FENR/FENRv13n1/fenrv13n1p81.pdf*

Rector, Robert and Rea Hederman, Jr. 2004. "Two Americas: One Rich, One Poor? Understanding Income Inequality in the United States." Washington, DC: Heritage Foundation.

Rubalcava, Luis, Graciela Teruel, and Duncan Thomas. 2003. "Welfare Design, Women's Empowerment and Income Pooling," Presented at the 2003 Population Association of America Meetings, Minneapolis, MN.

Sawhill, Isabel and Adam Thomas. 2001. "A Hand Up for the Bottom Third: Toward a New Agenda for Low-Income Working Families." Washington, DC: The Brookings Institute.

U.S. Department of Commerce, Census Bureau. 2001. *Money Income in the United States: 2000.* Current Population Reports, P-60 Series, No. 213. *http://www.census.gov/prod/2001pubs/p60-213.pdf*

Ventry, Dennis. 1999. "The Collision of Tax and Welfare Politics: The Political History of the Earned Income Tax Credit, 1969-1999." Washington, DC: The Brookings Institute.

About the Contributors

Jay Fagan, DSW, MSW, is Associate Professor in the School of Social Administration at Temple University. His research has focused on fathers and fathering and on the relationship between childcare and paid work. His books include a recent textbook, *Fathers and Early Childhood Programs*, with Glen Palm, and *Clinical and Educational Interventions with Fathers*, with Alan J. Hawkins. He has published more than 25 journal articles on fathers and is also editor of the journal, *Fathering: A Journal of Theory, Research, and Practice About Men as Fathers*. Dr. Fagan is principal investigator of the Adolescent Father Involvement Intervention Project, funded by the U.S. Department of Health and Human Services, Public Health Service. He is also the co-principal investigator of the study, *The Philadelphia Survey of Child Care and Work*, funded by the Child Care Bureau of the U.S. Department of Health and Human Services and by the Ford Foundation.

Jonathan Fisher, PhD, Economics, University of Kentucky, is a public and labor economist. He works as a Research Economist at the U.S. Bureau of Labor Statistics in the Division of Price and Index Number Research, and he is an adjunct professor in the Georgetown University Public Policy Institute. Dr. Fisher's research focuses on issues surrounding personal bankruptcy, inequality, poverty, and consumption. His current research includes the effect of government transfer programs on the likelihood of defaulting on debt and the likelihood of bankruptcy. Recent work also focuses on measuring poverty using income and consumption and how the perception of well-being differs when using consumption as opposed to income.

Nancy Folbre, PhD, is Professor of Economics at the University of Massachusetts at Amherst. Her research focuses on the interface between feminist theory and political economy, with a particular interest in caring labor and other forms of non-market work. She has received a five-year fellowship from the MacArthur Foundation and also served as co-chair of the MacArthur Research Network on the Family and the Economy. She is a staff economist with the Center for Popular Econom-

Available online at http://www.haworthpress.com/web/JWPP
doi:10.1300/J501v27n03_14

ics and is an Associate Editor of the journal, *Feminist Economics*. Her recent books include *Family Time: The Social Organization of Care*, co-edited with Michael Bittman (Routledge, 2004), and *The Invisible Heart: Economics and Family Values* (New Press, 2001).

Avis A. Jones-Deweever is the Study Director for Poverty and Welfare Programs at the Institute for Women's Policy Research. Her work both examines the impact of welfare reform on the lives of women and families and searches for effective programmatic strategies aimed at poverty reduction. Dr. Jones-DeWeever received her doctoral degree in Government and Politics from the University of Maryland, College Park where she specialized in public policy and the politics of race. Her areas of expertise include poverty in urban communities, inequality of educational opportunity, and the impact of welfare reform on women and communities of color. Prior to working at IWPR, Dr. Jones-DeWeever served on the faculty of the University of Richmond where her teaching and research interests focused on issues of race and gender inequality in the United States.

Angela Johnson is Assistant Professor of educational studies at St. Mary's College of Maryland. She received the PhD in Social Foundations of Education from the University of Colorado at Boulder. Her focus is on the social foundations of education and on preparing pre-service teachers to be effective in diverse classrooms. Before becoming a professor, Dr. Johnson worked at the University of Colorado Minority Arts and Sciences Program as a retention specialist and physics instructor. She has also taught high school physics in a diverse urban school in the Washington, DC, area.

Janice Johnson-Dias received the PhD in Sociology from Temple University in Fall 2004. Her dissertation focused on the contribution of welfare job-training programs to recipients' employment outcomes. Dr. Johnson-Dias is currently a postdoctoral fellow at the National Poverty Center, University of Michigan, Gerald Ford School of Public Policy. Her publications include: "The Violent Matrix: The Relationship Between Structural Violence, Interpersonal and Intrapersonal Violence" in *American Journal of Community Psychology Special Edition on Structural Violence* (with Susan James, Chitra Raghavan, Tessa Lemos, and Diana Woolis) and "Contextualizing Violence: A Social Network

Study" in *Violence Against Women* (with Susan James and Chitra Raghavan).

Peggy Kahn teaches in the Political Science Department and Women's and Gender Studies Program at the University of Michigan-Flint. She is a co-editor of and contributor to *Shut Out: Low-Income Mothers and Higher Education in Post-Welfare America* (SUNY Press 2004). Her recent research, publications, and advocacy have focused upon access of low-income mothers to post-secondary education; single parent families and the 1996 welfare changes; and low-income mothers' work and family time dilemmas. She is also co-author with Deborah Figart of *Contesting the Market: Pay Equity and the Politics of Economic Restructuring* (1997) and co-editor with Elizabeth Meehan of *Equal Pay/Comparable Worth in the United Kingdom and United States of America* (1992). She has been the recipient of the UM-Flint David M. French Distinguished Professor Award and the University of Michigan Academic Women's Caucus Sarah Goddard Power Award.

Mélanie Knight is a doctoral candidate in the Department of Sociology and Equity Studies and collaborative program in Women's Studies and Gender Studies at the Ontario Institute for Studies in Education of the University of Toronto. Her areas of interest include the formal and informal economy, transnationalism, the racially gendered division of labor, and the black diaspora. Her published work includes, "Black Canadian Self-Employed Women in the Twenty-First Century: A Critical Approach" in *Canadian Woman Studies/les cahiers de la femme, Vol. 2 (2004)*. Ms. Knight has also appeared on Ondes Africaines, televised world wide, to talk about the politics of black women's labor.

Arielle Kuperberg is a doctoral student and Benjamin Franklin Fellow in the Sociology Department at the University of Pennsylvania. Her research focuses on work and gender, the family, and policy. She is currently examining family-friendly policies for graduate students and faculty in academia.

Hilarie Lieb is a lecturer in the Department of Economics at Northwestern University. She received the PhD from the Department of Economics at Northwestern University in 2001. Her research integrates labor market theory with public policy to analyze outcomes that differ across race, gender, and/or ethnicity. Her recent publications include analysis of the historical impact of national policy on gender segregation in college and a historical analysis of the changing role of marriage, work, and children on women's poverty.

Vicky Lovell holds the PhD in public policy and has been the Study Director for Employment and Earnings at the Institute for Women's Policy Research for six years. Her work focuses on issues related to women's employment and economic security, including job quality, family and medical leave policies, pay equity, work supports, and unemployment insurance. She has provided extensive technical assistance to national and state policy makers on paid time off programs. Dr. Lovell's research has been published in *Feminist Economics*, the *Journal of Global Awareness*, and *Strengthening Community: Social Insurance in a Diverse America*. Her most recent IWPR publications are *Valuing Good Health*; *No Time to Be Sick: Why Everyone Suffers When Workers Don't Have Adequate Paid Sick Leave*; and *Staying Employed: Trends in Medicaid, Child Care, and Head Start in Ohio* (co-authored with Dr. Jon Honeck of Policy Matters Ohio).

Angela Lyons is Assistant Professor in the Department of Agricultural and Consumer Economics at the University of Illinois at Urbana-Champaign. She received the PhD in Economics from the University of Texas at Austin. Dr. Lyons' research focuses on issues related to family finance and household economics. Her current research examines issues related to household liquidity and credit access, health and financial strain, delinquency and bankruptcy, and gender and marital differences in household investment decisions. She was recently invited to participate in the U.S. Comptroller General's forum on "Improving Financial Literacy: The Role of the Federal Government." In 2003, she presented testimony on the importance of financial literacy for young adults before the Subcommittee on Education and the Workforce for the U.S. House of Representatives. In 2002, Dr. Lyons was a delegate to the National Summit on Retirement Savings in Washington, DC.

Gi-Taik Oh served as a Senior Research Analyst at the Institute for Women's Policy Research where he conducted statistical programming and data analysis for numerous studies on issues related to welfare, child care, paid sick leave, poverty, and unemployment. Prior to working at IWPR, Mr. Oh spent nine years working at the World Bank as a Research Analyst/ST Consultant. His work focused on data management, research analysis, and field operations. Mr. Oh has an ABD and a Master's in Business Information Systems from Virginia Commonwealth University, as well as a Masters in Economics from Sogang University in Seoul, Korea.

Tamara Ohler is a graduate student in the Department of Economics at the University of Massachusetts, Amherst, and is currently writing her dissertation on gender, children, and standards of living in the United States. Her interests include how federal tax and spending policies promote an unequal division of financial responsibility for the care of children and the elderly. She has worked as a research assistant for the Joint Economic Committee of the United States Congress and the Congressional Budget Office in Washington, DC.

Julie Press, PhD, is Assistant Professor of Sociology and Women's Studies at Temple University. Her research interests include the sociology of gender, work and family, and race, urban poverty, and social inequality. Her work is published in *The Journal of Marriage and Family*, *Gender & Society*, the *Journal of Family Issues*, the *Journal of Family and Economic Issues*, and the Russell Sage Foundation volumes *Prismatic Metropolis* and *Urban Inequality*. She is currently writing a book, *Working to Succeed: How Child Care Impacts Mothers' Work and What We Can Do About It* using data from the Philadelphia Survey of Child Care and Work. Dr. Press is principal investigator of this project funded by the Child Care Bureau of the U.S. Department of Health and Human Services and by the Ford Foundation.

Teresa Reinders is a Lecturer in Sociology and Director of the Center for Women's Studies at the University of Wisconsin-Parkside, and a student in the PhD program in Urban Studies at the University of Wisconsin-Milwaukee. She has been a consultant in nonprofit organization and an advocate for equitable access to food.

Mary Kay Schleiter is Associate Professor of Sociology at the University of Wisconsin-Parkside. Her research focuses on the intersections of occupation, race-ethnicity, health, and inequality. She has published in journals and books in the areas of Sociology, Women's Studies, Health Care Policy, and Teaching Pedagogy. She is currently developing a teaching program in evaluation research and program assessment. Dr. Schleiter holds the PhD in Sociology from the University of Chicago.

Jo Anne Schneider is an urban anthropologist focusing on dynamics among organizations and communities in social welfare policy, opportunity structures for marginalized populations, and inter-group relations. She is an Associate Research Professor at the George Washington University Institute for Public Policy and the Anthropology Department. She was lead editor for the *American Anthropologist* special issue forum on welfare reform (2001). Ms. Schneider has also developed and overseen innovative welfare to work programs. This paper draws on her forthcoming book, *Social Capital and Welfare Reform: Government, Non-profits, Churches and Community in Pennsylvania and Wisconsin* (Columbia University Press, 2006).

Anne Statham is Professor of Sociology and Women's Studies and Director of the Institute for Community Based Learning at the University of Wisconsin-Parkside, where she has taught for the last 23 years. She has published numerous articles, chapters, and books on the topics of women, work, and equity, with a recent emphasis on poverty issues. Books she has authored, co-authored, and edited include *Women and Work: A Qualitative Synthesis, Gender and University Teaching: A Negotiated Difference, The Rise of Marginal Voices: Gender Balance in the Workplace,* and *Speaking Out: Women, Poverty, and Public Policy.* She has received the Women Educator's Research on Women Award from the Association of Researchers in Education, the William Sewell Outstanding Scholarship Award, the UW-Parkside Distinguished Faculty Service Award, and has been entered into the Kenosha Labor and Education Partnership Hall of Fame.

Pamela Stone is Associate Professor of Sociology at Hunter College and The Graduate Center of the City University of New York. Her research focuses on gender inequality in employment, including such topics as job segregation, pay equity, and work and family issues. She is currently completing a book (forthcoming, University of California Press) based on her study of career interruption among women professionals.

Susan Thistle holds the PhD from University of California-Berkeley in Sociology, and a Masters in International Studies from the University of Washington-Seattle. She is currently Assistant Chair and Senior Lecturer in Sociology at Northwestern University, and is also a Faculty Associate at the Institute for Policy Research at Northwestern. She is the author of *From Marriage to the Market: The Transformation of Women's Lives and Work,* University of California Press, forthcoming (Spring 2006). She has also published articles on feminist theory and on gender and welfare state formation, including "The Trouble with Modernity: Gender and the Remaking of Social Theory," *Sociological Theory,* 2000.

Index

BOOK ORDER FORM!

Order a copy of this book with this form or online at:
http://www.haworthpress.com/store/product.asp?sku= 5817

Women, Work, and Poverty
Women Centered Research for Policy Change

___ in softbound at $24.95 ISBN-13: 978-0-7890-3246-1 / ISBN-10: 0-7890-3246-5.
___ in hardbound at $49.95 ISBN-13: 978-0-7890-3245-4 / ISBN-10: 0-7890-3245-7.

COST OF BOOKS ___

POSTAGE & HANDLING ___
US: $4.00 for first book & $1.50
for each additional book
Outside US: $5.00 for first book
& $2.00 for each additional book.

SUBTOTAL ___

In Canada: add 7% GST. ___

STATE TAX ___
CA, IL, IN, MN, NJ, NY, OH, PA & SD residents
please add appropriate local sales tax.

FINAL TOTAL ___
If paying in Canadian funds, convert
using the current exchange rate,
UNESCO coupons welcome.

❑ **BILL ME LATER:**
Bill-me option is good on US/Canada/
Mexico orders only; not good to jobbers,
wholesalers, or subscription agencies.

❑ **Signature** ___

❑ **Payment Enclosed: $** ___

❑ **Please charge to my credit card:**

❑ Visa ❑ MasterCard ❑ AmEx ❑ Discover
❑ Diner's Club ❑ Eurocard ❑ JCB

Account # ___

Exp Date ___

Signature ___
(Prices in US dollars and subject to change without notice.)

PLEASE PRINT ALL INFORMATION OR ATTACH YOUR BUSINESS CARD
Name
Address
City   State/Province   Zip/Postal Code
Country
Tel   Fax

May we use your e-mail address for confirmations and other types of information? ❑ Yes ❑ No We appreciate receiving
your e-mail address. Haworth would like to e-mail special discount offers to you, as a preferred customer.
We will never share, rent, or exchange your e-mail address. We regard such actions as an invasion of your privacy.

Order from your **local bookstore** or directly from
The Haworth Press, Inc. 10 Alice Street, Binghamton, New York 13904-1580 • USA
Call our toll-free number (1-800-429-6784) / Outside US/Canada: (607) 722-5857
Fax: 1-800-895-0582 / Outside US/Canada: (607) 771-0012
E-mail your order to us: orders@haworthpress.com

For orders outside US and Canada, you may wish to order through your local
sales representative, distributor, or bookseller.
For information, see http://haworthpress.com/distributors

(Discounts are available for individual orders in US and Canada only, not booksellers/distributors.)

Please photocopy this form for your personal use.
www.HaworthPress.com

BOF06